CHINA AND SOUTH ASIA

Strategy in 21st Century

CHINA AND SOUTH ASIA

Strategy in 21st Century

Brig. J. N. Mehta (Retd.)

NEHA PUBLISHERS & DISTRIBUTORS

DELHI

Publisher
NEHA PUBLISHERS & DISTRIBUTORS
4832/24,Prahlad Lane,S-207 Ansari
Road, Daryaganj, Delhi-110002
Ph.: 43570976, 23278261
Email: nehapubdistributors@gmail.com

Edition: 2016

ISBN: 978-93-80318-82-0

Laser Typesetting
JEE-VEE Graphics, Delhi

Price: 1295/-

Printed
Vikas Computers, Delhi

Preface

China's increasing strategic presence in South Asia has to be viewed in this global environment. China's moves would undoubtedly contribute to optimize the rapid growth of the vast underserviced South Asian markets while increasing the import of Chinese products. However, these developments would progressively reduce India's dominant influence in the sub continent and Indian Ocean Region (IOR) with the progressive increase in China's strategic reach to the Indian Ocean littorals.

China's South Asia connectivity projects underway also have a broader context to the ambitious China Western Development (CWD) plan started in 2000. It involves six provinces (including Yunnan) and five autonomous regions including Tibet and Xinjiang bordering India. As per 2002 estimate this backward region forms 71% of China's area but contains only 28.8% of its population contributed only 19% of China's economic output as of 2009.

That China is one of the most powerful states in the world is no longer a contested claim, but cataloguing China's increasing material resources does not in itself demonstrate that China is powerful. Southeast Asia presents an apparently 'easy' case for investigating China's rising power. Given the significant asymmetry of power, if China's power has grown we would expect to see altered preferences and behaviour among these weaker neighbours in response to coercion, persuasion or inducement. Results so far are mixed. While China has been able to harness much of the region's economic energy in a favourable direction, it does not always get its way in territorial and resource conflicts.

As the book addresses this crucial issue quite deftly, it is hoped that it would prove to be a source of great information for the reader.

—Editor

Contents

1

Introduction

CHINA'S STRATEGIC PERSPECTIVE

China's interests in Afghanistan and Pakistan are complex and multi-dimensional, and are primarily driven by internal considerations. Currently, China's leaders are concerned that a significant drop in economic growth – a result of the global economic crisis – will lead to increased levels of unemployment and destabilizing levels of popular unrest. China's need to maintain economic growth and domestic stability significantly inform its approach to Afghanistan and Pakistan. China certainly does not want to see nuclear-armed Pakistan be overrun by Islamic extremists. Nor does it want to see a degree of instability in either country that could complicate China's access to their resources and transit routes. Additionally, of particular concern to Chinese authorities is the possibly that extremists could migrate from Afghanistan or Pakistan into China, or that their activities could catalyze extremists groups in its interior provinces.

Regionally, China sees Afghanistan and Pakistan as components of a broader struggle for dominance over South and Central Asia. China's close relationship with Pakistan is largely a check against India's rise as a dominant power in South Asia. From this point of view, a stable and friendly Afghanistan gives Pakistan an important degree of "strategic depth" against India's nuclear capabilities and conventional military superiority. According to this logic, China benefits from an Afghanistan that is stable and friendly to Pakistan, because it allows Islamabad to focus on India.

Thus, India's forays into Afghanistan are seen by some in China as "designed to achieve four objectives: contain Pakistan, enhance energy security, combat terrorism, and pin down China's development."

Another key dimension of China's approach to Afghanistan and Pakistan is Beijing's perception of the United States. Since 2001, the United States has been profoundly focused on the "Arc of Instability" from the Middle East to South Asia, and the ongoing shift of military resources from Iraq to Afghanistan. In addition to requiring significant amounts of policymaker attention, this focus directly impacts the ability of U.S. leaders to engage in the Asia-Pacific region. This focus, combined with a difficult economic picture constraining future defense and international aid budgets, has necessarily diverted resources and high-level attention away from China and the Asia-Pacific, forcing the U.S. to essentially operate in the region with one hand tied behind its back. Washington's focus elsewhere, and a relatively stable strategic environment with no military threats, reinforces Chinese perceptions of the current period as a "window of opportunity" allowing China to focus on its own economic growth and development.

To date, China's leaders have not commented directly on the implications of the U.S. involvement in extended occupations in Iraq and Afghanistan. Beijing continues to view the United States as the world's most powerful nation and China's most important relationship, and does not want to jeopardize US-Sino relations with unvarnished criticism or harping about the ongoing wars. However, since the U.S. invasion of Afghanistan in 2001, official Chinese media has not hesitated to emphasize indications of instability, reports of civilian deaths, and questions about U.S. will to preserve stability in Afghanistan and Pakistan. China highlights problems in Afghanistan and Pakistan for several reasons. First, China perceives itself as the leader of the developing world and is therefore charged with highlighting what they see as victims of U.S. hegemony. Second, China seeks to cultivate positive relations with Muslim-majority countries for their natural resources and their votes in multilateral fora.

Another key driver of China's perspective on Afghanistan and Pakistan is concern about ties between Islamic militants in Afghanistan and Pakistan and the the Uyghur Muslim minority population in Xinjiang province. China is concerned that the militant Islamist ideology in Afghanistan could bleed into China's Uyghur population and feed what many in Beijing see as a terrorist problem. The difficulty for U.S. policymakers is distinguishing between terrorist groups and legitimate resistors against the Chinese Communist Party. China claims that a Uyghur separatist group called the East Turkestan Islamic Movement (ETIM) has had contacts with Al Qaeda, and the U.S. has designated ETIM as a terrorist organization. That being said, ETIM's true size and the accuracy of its reported connections with Al Qaeda remain unclear.

However, Beijing's concerns about its Uyghur population and possible connections with extremists in Afghanistan and Pakistan raise questions about China's willingness to tolerate U.S. military forces in these countries as a tool to keep extremist forces pinned down and focused away from China. Chinese strategists are uncomfortable with a large U.S. military presence along China's border, and some analysts have expressed concern that U.S. bases in the region supporting operations in Afghanistan are part of a plot to perpetuate U.S. domination of the region. At the same time, however, the U.S. presence in Afghanistan prevents Al Qaeda from focusing on China and helps suppress Islamist groups along China's periphery.

China's Approach to Afghanistan

China's interests in Afghanistan are both economic and strategic. China was largely disengaged from Afghanistan until President Hamid Karzai's government opened up its energy, mineral, and raw materials to foreign investors. In 2007, China was Afghanistan's fifth-largest trading partner, behind Pakistan, the EU, the U.S., and India. China has developed significant portions of Afghanistan's infrastructure, including telephone networks, irrigation projects, public hospitals, and several other construction projects. The crown in jewel in China's investments is the $3.5 billion stake in Afghanistan's Aynak copper field, one of the world's largest with the potential for $88 billion worth of ore. This investment was coupled with the construction of a $500 million electrical plant and the development of a railway from Tajikistan to Pakistan for distribution. Equally important for Kabul is the project's potential need to employ 10,000 Afghans and the $400 million of projected royalties it would accrue yearly, representing more than half of its current annual state budget.

Also important to China is Afghanistan's potential as a source for raw materials. China's booming economy is fueled by foreign natural resources like oil, natural gas, and other minerals. China's iron-ore demand increased close to 15 percent in the first 8 months of 2007, while copper demand surged by almost 35 percent in the same period. This is driving an approach to the region focused on maintaining access to foreign resources and markets. Afghan oil reserves were recently upgraded 18 times by a U.S. geological survey, estimates standing at an average of 1,596 million barrels, while Afghanistan's natural gas reserves were upgraded by a factor of three, standing at a mean of 15,687 trillion cubic feet. Afghanistan also has large iron ore deposits between Herat and the Panjsher Valley, and gold reserves in the northern provinces of Badakshan, Takhar, and Ghazni. Major copper fields also exist in Jawkhar, Darband, and in abovementioned Aynak, located around 30 km southeast of Kabul.

Also of great important to Beijing is Afghanistan's geographic location, which sets it at the triangular cross-roads between China, energy suppliers in the Middle East, and key Indian Ocean transit points from Pakistan. As the easiest transportation route for the exploitation of the estimated 23 billion tons of oil and 3 trillion cubic meters of gas in the Central Asian Republics, Afghanistan plays a central role in China's attempts to diversify its access to foreign resources.

CHINA'S APPROACH TO PAKISTAN

Pakistan is a tremendously important country in China's foreign policy calculations. China sees Pakistan as its primary partner in South Asia, with a 50-year history of political and military ties. Pakistan serves as a conduit for China into South Asia and the

Indian Ocean and, most importantly, as a foundation of its regional strategy to counter to Indian regional preeminence. For Pakistan, China has been a steady and (mostly) dependable provider of money and weapons and a deterrent against Indian regional domination.

It should be noted that China's interest in Pakistan is purely strategic, and not economic. In 2005, bilateral trade was $4.26 billion. By October 2008, annual trade between Pakistan and China had already surpassed $7 billion, and the two sides set the target of $15 billion in trade by 2011. To put these numbers in perspective, the target 2011 trade level between China and Pakistan ($15 billion) is 4% of US-China trade in 2008 ($333.8 billion).

China's military relationship with Pakistan is deep and robust, including joint exercises, arms sales, and defense industrial cooperation. Beijing transferred equipment and technologies to Pakistan's nuclear weapons and ballistic missile programs throughout the 1980s and 1990s. China is currently Pakistan's largest weapons supplier, and Pakistan is by far China's primary customer for conventional weapons: 36% of China's arms sales from 2003 through 2007 were directed to Pakistan (the next-largest customer was Sudan with 7%). Sales include the co-developed JF-17 multi-role combat aircraft and related production facilities, F-22P frigates with helicopters, jet trainers, tanks, the F-7 fighter, anti-ship cruise missiles, missile technologies, small arms, and ammunition.

The JF-17 program has important geopolitical ramifications beyond providing Pakistan with an improved combat aircraft. Pakistan has a longstanding, yet unfilled, order for American F-16s. The U.S. decision to not fill the order, while prudent, hurt our ability to cultivate closer relations with the Pakistani military. More important for this discussion, however, is that the JF-17 would primarily be useful to Pakistan in an India contingency. China's continued selling of the JF-17 reinforces Pakistan's focus on India, which the U.S. has been attempting to shift to the insurgents in Pakistan's West.

For China, the relationship with Pakistan is also important because of its easy access to the Indian Ocean. China is building a major port in Gwadar that would enable support of a military presence closer to the Middle East and along vulnerable sea lanes of communication. Road and rail links would need to go through Afghanistan. Pakistan is interested in exploiting its geography as a Trade and Energy Corridor (TEC) for China. In February 2008, Pakistan's then-President Musharraf told an audience at Tsinghua University in Beijing that "Pakistan is very much in favor of a pipeline between the Gulf and China through Pakistan and I have been speaking with your leadership about this. I am very sure in the future – it will happen".

Implications for US Interests

As elucidated in President Obama's "white paper," the new U.S. strategy toward Afghanistan and Pakistan involves several military and civilian initiatives intended to degrade terrorist networks, train indigenous security forces and focus them on counter-insurgency operations, establish economic alternatives to the insurgency, and improve the effectiveness, accountability, and popular legitimacy of the Afghan and Pakistani governments.

The United States has long called on China to be a responsible international stakeholder that helps solve common problems. China has contributed, to a degree, on international attempts to address problems with Iran and Darfur. Yet, even with Afghanistan and Pakistan on China's periphery, Beijing has too long been on the sidelines of the international effort to defeat terrorism and improve stability in the region. China has often pledged its support for international counterterrorism efforts, and has even participated in some counterterrorism initiatives with the United States, such as the Container Security Initiative. However, some of China's other actions, such as it's pressuring of Central Asian military bases being used to support operations in Afghanistan, suggest a less-than-total commitment to contributing significantly to international counterterrorism operations. The renewed effort by the Obama administration to stabilize Afghanistan and Pakistan and defeat terrorism in the region gives China a new chance to demonstrate their substantive commitment to the international effort against terrorism. As a neighbor to Afghanistan and a close partner to Pakistan, China potentially has a significant role to play. As already discussed, defeating terrorism and promoting stability are shared U.S. and Chinese interests. Yet, China to date has not yet joined the international effort toward Afghanistan and Pakistan, primarily because Beijing probably calculates that it can free-ride on the stability brought by the U.S. and its coalition partners. U.S. should initiate a sustained dialogue with their Chinese counterparts to emphasize shared interests and highlight the important role China can play in achieving our shared objectives.

RUSSIA'S STRATEGIC PARTNERSHIPS WITH CHINA AND INDIA

The Sino-Russian strategic partnership predates the Indo-Russian strategic partnership, which was finally realized with President Vladimir Putin's trip to India in October 2000. In the first half of the 1990s, the United States and the Russian Federation described their relationship as a strategic partnership, but by the end of the decade this term was discredited in both Washington and Moscow. Since coming to power in January 2000, President Putin and his administration have increasingly referred to the European Union and/or Europe as a strategic partner, but that relationship has not been endorsed in official documents in the same way as Russia's relationships with China and India.

The Sino-Russian and Indo-Russian relationships share a number of common features, but there are some important differences as well. In each case there is strong rhetorical support for a multipolar world order not dominated by the United States. As a declining power—experiencing, in fact, the most rapid and precipitous decline in peacetime in modern history-Russia is coming from a very different place in supporting multipolarity than are rising powers like China and India. Russia has witnessed its power and significance erode tremendously in the last decade, while the United States has enjoyed nearly a decade of unprecedented economic growth. Russia warily regards globalization as a fig leaf for the extension of U.S. hegemony throughout the world. U.S. economic strength is outstripped only by its military advantages, and the Russians can find no comfort in comparing the performance of U.S. forces in Iraq and Kosovo with that of Russian forces in Chechnya in the 1990s. After the hopes of a U.S.-Russian partnership dissipated with a series of disappointments in the last decade, former foreign minister Yevgeny Primakov and the majority of the Russian foreign and security policy elite increasingly supported Russia's strengthening its relations with China, India, Iran, and major European powers to stem what Moscow views as the overbearing dominance of the United States in international affairs.

Russia, China, and India all support an enhanced role for the United Nations, and Russia has specifically endorsed India's candidacy to join the UN Security Council. All three denounced the NATO action in Kosovo as a violation of international law since it did not receive a UN mandate. All three are also very sensitive to violations of national sovereignty and are reluctant to support international mediation of civil conflicts because of challenges to their own territorial integrity in Taiwan, Kashmir, and Chechnya. Both Russia and China share a strong aversion to U.S.-led alliances' taking such action, because to a greater or lesser extent they fear the prospect of U.S. intervention in their own territory. During the Kosovo war, the sense grew among Russians that today NATO was taking action in Yugoslavia, but tomorrow it could be in Chechnya or elsewhere in Russia. Although that seems quite unrealistic, the growing relationships of former Soviet republics such as Georgia, Ukraine, Azerbaijan, and others with NATO are viewed nearly unanimously by the Russian foreign and security policy elite as contradictory to Russian national interests.

For China, recovering Taiwan is about as high a policy priority as promoting economic development. The prospect of U.S. intervention to support Taiwan in the event of a conflict is the most likely scenario for great power conflict in the early twenty-first century. China has regarded the broadening of the geographical scope of the U.S.-Japanese security alliance at the end of the 1990s with the same trepidation with which Russia has viewed the expansion of the NATO mission to include out-of-area activities. The most recent Chinese white paper on national defence, issued in fall *:woo,* views the United States in very threatening terms, and Chinese defence thinkers now talk more openly about the increasing likelihood of conflict with the United States. The Indian/Pakistani conflict over Kashmir may present the world's most imminent danger of nuclear conflict.

China, Russia, and India share sensitivities about Islamic threats, as each country has large Muslim populations and each shares borders with states containing Muslim majorities. India has cause for the greatest concern because the Kashmir problem has the potential to escalate into a nuclear conflict with archrival Pakistan. In a little over fifty years since independence, India and Pakistan have already fought three major wars against one another, and there has been continual fighting in Kashmir during at least the last decade. In the last two decades, Russia has fought only Muslim foes. In Afghanistan in the 1980s and Chechnya in the 1990s, Russian forces have performed poorly, and each war has sent shock waves through Russian society. With large Muslim populations reaching into the heart of the Russian Federation in the Volga region, Russian sensitivities about Islamic threats focus more on the potential for state disintegration than interstate conflict. As China is the most ethnically homogeneous of the three states and its Muslim population is more isolated in the west of China in Xinjiang Province, China's concern about Islamic separatism is more muted than that of Russia and India, but it is real nonetheless. In particular, all three governments fear that the increasingly weak and failing states of Central Asia will serve as conduits for more radical Muslim groups, terrorist activities, and drug trafficking, which will erode their authority in peripheral territories. Each country also views Afghanistan under the Taliban as the dangerous hub of these activities.

India and China have increasingly relied on Russia as a source of conventional weapons and possibly other weapons technologies. They are the two biggest clients of the struggling Russian military-industrial complex—each now purchases about $1 billion worth of arms a year-and the relationships are growing. Since domestic Russian procurement virtually dried up in the 1990s, arms sales to China and India are a vital, if controversial, national security interest for Moscow. Three basic rationales explain much of the Russian enthusiasm for arms sales to China, India, and others-notably Iran, since Moscow's announcement in December 2000 of the decision to resume sales of conventional weapons to Tehran.

The first reason is simply economic. The Russian economy has floundered badly since the Soviet collapse (and before the collapse, for that matter), and aside from natural resources, weapons systems are one of the few areas in which Russia can compete with some success in the global marketplace. The Russian military-industrial complex also benefits from U.S. sanctions against sales to China after the massacres at Tiananmen, to Iran for more than two decades after the hostage crisis, and to India after its nuclear tests in 1998. In 2000, Russian arms sales amounted to about $4 billion, which represents a modest increase over the previous five years, when arms deliveries averaged a bit over $3 billion. Even at $4 billion, Russian arms sales amount to only about 15 percent of U.S. arms transfers, and they run considerably behind France's and Great Britain's. This is a far cry from the height of Soviet arms sales in the 1980s, but much of that income existed only on paper, as many Soviet clients were unable or unwilling to pay in hard currency or the equivalent. Still, the basic story for Russian arms sales after the collapse of the USSR is one of massive market loss. Powerful domestic industrial and institutional lobbies, including the Ministry of Atomic Energy, strongly promote Russian weapons systems and related technologies sales.

The second reason is also economic, but with a national security slant. Because Russian procurement nearly came to a standstill in the last decade, without sales abroad the struggling Russian military-industrial complex would have collapsed entire!y. In 1999 and 2000, Russian arms sales averaged about four times the level of domestic procurement. For Russia, losing all of the human and industrial capital invested over many decades in the Soviet weapons complex would have catastrophic implications for future Russian national security. No doubt excessive allocations to the military during the Soviet period were a major factor in Soviet economic decline and consequently detrimental for long-term national security. But even the most liberally inclined Russians understand that Russia must maintain a military-industrial complex, albeit one that commands a far smaller portion of the national product than in Soviet days. Already the erosion of their military-industrial complex raises serious questions about Russia's ability to deliver on arms sales agreements, as increasingly Moscow is offering to sell new systems, such as the Su-30MKI superfighter, that have not gone into serial production before. 16 Most of the conventional arms transfers in the 1990s consisted of off the-shelf systems that had been in production for years. Although Russian enterprises can still build impressive prototypes, the subcontracting networks of the Soviet military-industrial complex have deteriorated to the extent that serial production is very difficult.

The third rationale is directly tied to Russian perceptions of its medium-and long-term security interests, which must be defined to some extent by geography. Although international security may not fully subscribe to the first three rules of real estate, "location, location, location," Russians have historically and culturally attached great importance to the role of geography, and after the ideologically imposed hiatus of the cold war, the study of geopolitics has once again become quite popular in Russia. Russia is surrounded by a belt of weak, and in many cases failing, states to the west and south (former Soviet republics), and just beyond the territory of the former Soviet Union are rising powers China and India and other states with regional aspirations such as Pakistan, Iran, and Iraq; these states have varying interests in international stability and the international system as currently construed. Russia has chosen to use its role as a supplier of weaponry as a means to maintain some leverage and influence on the rise to power of many of these states. In an ideal world Russia would probably prefer to be surrounded by countries that did not seek to develop weapons of mass destruction and their means of delivery, and the official Russian position supporting the nonproliferation regime is not exactly disingenuous. But the reality is that Russia is not surrounded by, let's say, Canada, Mexico, and two huge oceans, but rather by a number of countries that have developed or likely will develop weapons of mass destruction and their means of delivery. By maintaining a shadowy role on the periphery of those weapons programs, Russia maintains some control over their development as well as knowledge about their status. Thinking hypothetically, if you are in Moscow and you have concluded that Iran will eventually, with or without your involvement, develop weapons of mass destruction, the rationale for some degree of involvement becomes more understandable. Determining precisely what that role is without access to classified intelligence reports is virtually impossible, and even with such access, reaching clear conclusions must not be an easy task. 18

The combination of the economic and national security factors driving Russian weapons and weapons technology sales to China, India, and other states suggests that this will be an enduring feature of Russian foreign policy, and there are a number of indications that the Putin administration has made a strategic decision to promote Russian arms sales more aggressively despite the objections of the United States and others. However, there is a competitive aspect to Chinese and Indian conventional purchases from Russia, since Beijing and New Delhi to some extent regard each other as security threats.

EVOLUTION OF RUSSIAN-CHINESE STRATEGIC RELATIONS

Towards a bilateral partnership

The first years of transition in Russia were dominated by radical economic reforms and desire to integrate rapidly the occidental community. However, this period soon left the place for a more auto-centric approach, which meant a retreat of radical economic reforms and a more equilibrated foreign policy between its Western and Eastern axis. Since the normalization of Soviet-Chinese relations announced by M. Gorbachev in 1989, the Presidents B. Yeltsin and Jiang Zemin announced for the first time "constructive partnership" in 1994, and "strategic partnership" in 1996.

Strategic relations between Russia and China should be seen as a part of the triangle including both countries and the US. Promoting a multipolar world and the desire to counteract the dominance of the US in the post-cold war world are among the common objectives of Moscow and Beijing. Another element is the refusal of interference in internal affairs, notably for the human rights and local separatism issues. So, Russian policy towards China (and *vice versa*) is inversely correlated with the policy towards the US. Consequently, the political or strategic factors play a dominant role in the conception of Russian policy in Asian-Pacific region.

The Russian-Chinese Treaty of Good-neighbourliness, Friendship and Cooperation between Russia and China was signed in 2001. It partially repeats the Sino-soviet treaty expired in 1980, precisely, concerning the respect of territorial integrity and sovereignty, Russian engagement for the "one-China" policy (non-recognition of Taiwan independence), and expansion of links in numerous domains (of which the military one).

Further, two articles of the new treaty indicate the military alliance, even if the parties deny this fact and the Treaty doesn't contain a clause of mutual defence. Finally, the treaty mentions actual problems related to countries economic inequality issues revealed especially at the regional level. So, Russia and China should renounce any form of pressure and facilitate cooperation in frontier regions (art.14), and cooperate to combat illegal immigration (art.20).

The bilateral Treaty (2001) consolidated the basis for Russian-Chinese political partnership. However, in spite of the proclaimed strategic partnership, Russian and Chinese interests diverge on several aspects of regional policy in Central Asia.

Convergence and divergence of interests at the regional level

In Central Asia, China and Russia interact in the framework of the Shanghai Cooperation Organisation (SCO). The SCO was formally created in 2001 by Russia, China, Kazakhstan, Kyrgyzstan, Tajikistan and Uzbekistan. In reality, the SCO is the continuation of the Shanghai Forum, created in 1996 by the above-mentioned countries except Uzbekistan aiming to stabilize the post-soviet Central Asia. The main goals were the demarcation and protection of the common border and also, for China, solution of ethnic minority problems in the frontier zone. So, regional security is the first objective of the SCO. However, one can note that Shanghai Forum was founded in 1996, a period of tensions in both Russian-American and Chinese-American relations. Later, the regional preoccupation of the SCO will not exclude the orchestrated action of the organization against the US. Moreover, the acceptance of Mongolia, Pakistan, India and Iran as observers reinforces the international role of the SCO.

At the same time, the SCO reveals the conflict of interests between Russia and China as both countries are searching to increase their presence in Central Asia. On the one hand, China demonstrates a growing interest towards this zone which was submitted to its influence in the past. The SCO is the only structure at China's disposal to promote its interests in the region, rich in hydrocarbons. In this way, China and Russia become rivals for access to oil and gas reserves of Central Asia.

On the other hand, the SCO is one of several organizations serving to promote Russian interests in the region. Russia is present through the CIS and panoply of sub-regional blocs and treaties concluded between different CIS states. In this context, the activation of the Eurasian Economic Community (EurAsEC, regrouping Russia, Belarus, Kazakhstan, Kyrgyzstan, Tajikistan and, since 2006, Uzbekistan) can be viewed as an attempt to oppose the growing influence of China in Central Asia (Facon (2006)). The reinforcement of EurAsEC arrives when China stresses the importance of economic issues within the SCO. More precisely, the Framework Agreement to enhance economic cooperation (signed in September 2003; and also the action plan approved in September, 2004) fixes the main orientations for 2020 aiming to establish a SCO free-trade zone.

However, the economic mission of the SCO remains weakly defined, while the non-coordinated accession of its members to the WTO puts into question its emergence as a trading bloc.

Moreover, the growing competition of Chinese goods in such a case could have negative effects on Russian producers. The latter puts a strong limit for the development of regional trade integration within the SCO. In this context, the Russian Ministry of Economic development and trade officials propose to limit the scope of economic partnership within the SCO. Russian economic interests should be promoted through the EurAsEC while the SCO should be limited to security issues only.

Nevertheless, in spite of numerous discrepancies, the global framework of Russian-Chinese relations creates a favourable context for the development of economic cooperation and the creation of costly energy exports infrastructures.

SOUTH ASIA'S MANIFOLD CHALLENGE

The concept of "the international community", if it is to have practical meaning and encapsulate the notion of "solidarity without borders" instead of being an empty slogan, must come to terms with the multitude and gravity of the challenges confronting the peoples and nations of South Asia (Bangladesh, Bhutan, India, Maldives, Nepal, Pakistan and Sri Lanka). The scale of the problems faced in the region and the numbers of people involved are so huge that success or failure in South Asia pose defining challenges to the core mandates of the United Nations as the global arena for problem-solving. South Asia by itself accounts for one-fifth of "We the peoples of the United Nations". Developments in South Asia cut across the major faultlines of the UN system with respect to the challenges of economic development, environmental protection, food and water security, democratic governance and human rights, nuclear war and peace, inter-state and internal conflicts, and new security issues such as AIDS (acquired immune deficiency syndrome) and international terrorism. What happens in South Asia will surely shape the contours of the global community in the decades ahead.

Two of the central purposes of the United Nations as expressed in the UN Charter – to maintain international peace and security and to promote social and economic advancement – make it imperative for the organization to address these issues in South Asia. The United Nations University (UNU), in collaboration with the UN agencies in Japan, organized an international conference in May 2002 on "The United Nations and South Asia". UNU in Tokyo is particularly well suited as a forum for discussing these issues as the major UN agencies are located in its headquarters building in Tokyo, "UN House". The South Asian embassies in Japan offered their support for the conference and collaborated in its organization. The conference was well timed in that 2002 marked the fiftieth anniversary of the establishment of diplomatic relations with Japan by India, Pakistan and Sri Lanka. But it was ill timed in that on that date India and Pakistan were in the middle of the biggest and most tense mobilization of their full military mights along the full length of their border. Yet, by presenting a forum for communication between different actors within the various sectors, the conference helped to alleviate the substantial lack of interaction and thus contributed to improved efforts at addressing the problems in South Asia.

The chapters in this volume are revised versions of the papers presented at that conference. Their emphasis is on discussing issues of particular relevance to the region and exploring the potential for improvement in both domestic and international efforts at alleviating the problems of South Asia. If and where appropriate, the role that the United Nations can play in this respect is also underscored.

One of the more interesting features of this volume is the divergence of cultures and writing styles of the scholars and the practitioners (officials, politicians, generals). Academics are addicted to notes, whereas practitioners are allergic to them. Many academics have to be reined in so that their contributions form chapters in a book instead of mini-tomes in themselves, whereas some practitioners have to be coaxed into extending their brief vignettes to a length and intellectual weight suitable for publication by a university press. Two of the UNU's five mandated tasks are to serve as a bridge between the normally isolated worlds of scholarship and policy and to serve as a platform for dialogue. This volume is testimony to the need for dialogue not only between participants from the different nations and societies of a deeply divided region of the world, but also between the different professional cultures in the modern world.

Former prime minister of India, I. K. Gujral, expresses the hope that the recent international interest in South Asia is not temporary and based solely on the threat of terrorism and nuclearization, but rather reflects a realization that the world community cannot be safe or happy unless it involves the billion-plus people of South Asia in the critical decisions regarding peace, security and development. According to Gujral, the most serious current challenge facing South Asia is terrorism. But the fight against terrorism cannot be won by force alone. It is of course necessary to fight the jihadi culture. But, even without jihad, there would still be manifestations of terrorism in all South Asian countries in the form of insurgency movements. Therefore there is an urgent need to address the root causes of terrorism, such as lack of good governance, low levels of human development, and new threats such as drug trafficking and the spread of AIDS. Although the main responsibility for the problems and their resolution lies with the South Asian countries, the region has not been brought into the global developmental mainstream by the international community. The international community needs a peaceful, cooperative and dynamic South Asia; it is in its interest to facilitate this.

Gujral sees great potential for development in South Asia in the fields of science and technology, as well as in traditional industries such as chemicals, pharmaceuticals, heavy industries, steel and electronics. For this potential to be realized, however, regional cooperation is necessary. India, as the leading power, can afford to be accommodative to promote such cooperation. Sartaj Aziz, while calling for a comprehensive programme to reduce poverty in South Asia, also asks for UN action to reduce tension between the region's two nuclear powers. There is an urgent need to accelerate the pace of economic and social progress in the region and to meet the challenges of globalization. The United Nations must assume and discharge its responsibility to focus on the inequalities of the globalization process and regain a leadership role in providing a level playing field.

Nor can the international community continue to overlook the security problems in the region. International assistance is needed to fight terrorism and extremism in the region as well as to stabilize Afghanistan. At the same time, Aziz calls for the United Nations to curb "liberal imperialism", that is, the notion that the so-called "postmodern" world can use force, pre-emptive attack or even deception to violate international boundaries with impunity.

Peace and Security

An immediate concern of the international community is the region's impact on international peace and security. South Asia poses many potential threats to regional and global peace and security: it has two nuclear powers engaged in a major territorial dispute; there are several dominant insurgency conflicts here; terrorism is pronounced; and the refugee situation has the potential to be deeply destabilizing. There are also significant cross-regional linkages with respect to relations with China (one of the five permanent members of the UN Security Council), Central Asia (and Russia beyond), the Middle East and South-East Asia. How can domestic and international efforts at resolving conflicts in the region be improved?

Inter-state Conflict

Since the end of the Cold War, the global pattern of conflict has shifted from inter-state to intra-state conflicts (many of which have transnational regional links), yet one of the remaining potential inter-state conflicts is found in South Asia.

The situation is aggravated by the fact that the two potential belligerents are armed with nuclear-armed weapons. Whereas the stability of the nuclear deterrence between the superpowers during the Cold War was itself somewhat suspect, the relationship between Pakistan and India is qualitatively different and even more volatile. The two countries share a long border, which allows little time to decide whether to "use or lose" nuclear weapons in response to a perceived threat.

Furthermore, Pakistan and India are involved in a territorial dispute over Kashmir. This dispute has already resulted in two wars between the countries and the possibility of armed conflict has not yet been eliminated. Neither country has second-strike retaliatory capability, which makes both of them more vulnerable to a pre-emptive strike than was the case between the superpowers during the Cold War. South Asia's relationship with and ties to neighbouring countries also have implications for the involvement of the international community in the region. A complicating element is India's disputed border with China, a third nuclear power with tangible interests in the region. Resurgence of Islamic fundamentalism in the region is also a cause for concern for regional stability. The disruptive nature of this potential conflict is exacerbated by domestic political volatility in all South Asian countries. It is imperative for the United Nations to contribute to a de-escalation of this conflict in order to maintain international peace and security. Stephen Cohen cautions that, in light of the failure of past predictions, it is impossible to predict future use of nuclear weapons by India and Pakistan with any confidence. It is likely that the future will look much like the current situation – a stable relationship between China and India and a rocky one between India and Pakistan, but with innate common sense or external mediation preventing an outbreak of nuclear conflict. However, Cohen also acknowledges the large number of political and military variables that might affect possible outcomes with regard to the nuclear future of South Asia, only some of which can be influenced or controlled by outside powers. He offers two suggestions: the international community should assist in managing crises; and security planners in the region should avoid overconfidence in deterrence and keep their arsenals low so as to reduce the scale of the catastrophe if there should be a regional war.

Echoing many of the same themes, Christophe Carle emphasizes that the future security of South Asia depends on the relationship between Pakistan and India; the other security threats of the region pale in comparison. He points to the elements of instability in the subcontinent's nuclear deterrence. Contiguity undermines the development of effective and reliable command and control systems and, with ballistic missiles, decision-making time may be reduced to 5–10 minutes. The nuclearization of South Asia and the inherent volatility of the nuclear equation in the region mean that external actors, particularly the United States, have become increasingly important. Thus South Asian (in)security has been internationalized.

INTRA-STATE CONFLICT AND TRANSNATIONAL LINKAGES

Most of the countries in South Asia have insurgency movements. The level of violence is variable, but several of these conflicts have been classified as high intensity. The separatist Tamil Tiger movement in Sri Lanka is one example, where an ethnic group seeks territorial withdrawal from the state entity. The Kashmir dispute feeds on and exacerbates political instability in both India and Pakistan.

India faces further challenges in its northeastern regions. The Maoist movement in Nepal impedes effective government in a similar way, and over the past few years commentators have expressed concern about the possible Talibanization of Pakistan. With these threats to political stability and territorial integrity, South Asia remains a region with a high potential for violence and conflict. How can the international community contribute to the peaceful settlement of these disputes? And what can be done domestically to defuse these conflicts?

Nepal has been much in the news in the past couple of years or so, in part because of the palace massacre of the royal family, but mainly because of the ferocity and intractability of the Maoist insurgency. Lok Raj Baral's chapter illustrates the close link between intra-state and interstate conflicts. He points to the transnational elements of the conflict in Nepal, noting that India is often dragged into domestic issues in Nepal, a landlocked Himalayan kingdom sandwiched between two Asian giants with porous and open borders. Weakened states and enfeebled political institutions and leaderships are increasingly incapable of dealing with domestic crises in South Asia, which, in turn, breed inter-state conflicts. Cross-country migration and refugee flows, as well as the issue of treatment of one's own nationals in neighbouring countries, have the potential to trigger inter-state conflict. Conflicts occur over the exploitation of natural resources such as Nepal's water, and over transit rights for a poor and small country seeking an outlet to the sea for its products. There are also challenges with respect to new security issues such as trafficking in drugs and women.

The insurgency in Sri Lanka has been going on for much longer and is also more ferocious: it is the Tamil Tigers, after all, who introduced and perfected the gruesome art of suicide terrorism. Kingsley de Silva notes that South Asia's record of violence in public life is unusual even compared with other post-colonial states. One special feature is the high number of public figures assassinated. Rajiv Gandhi was killed on Indian soil but in the context of Sri Lanka's bitter civil war. The Kashmir conflict has clearer external factors in its origin than Sri Lanka's but, once the conflict in Sri Lanka erupted and persisted, it was prolonged largely because of Indian intervention. In the Kashmir conflict, terrorism became a distinctive factor in the mid-1980s. The two principal protagonists remain inflexibly resistant to any change in their attitude on this issue. In Sri Lanka the Tamil movement was transformed from a relatively peaceful one until the 1960s into an extraordinarily violent struggle with regional ramifications in the 1980s. Assassinations and suicide bombings became central means of terror. Once terrorism becomes a major factor in the political struggle, de Silva notes, the prospects of negotiating a settlement become all the more difficult. A similar central trait is the marginalization of the so-called moderates.

It is argued by some that the major locus of international terrorism has shifted to South Asia. Terrorist acts are committed in relation to both internal and inter-state conflicts, and the level of violence is alarming. Allegations are also frequently made that governments may support cross-border terrorism to undermine neighbouring states. The phrase "aid, abet and harbour" terrorists has entered the international policymaking agenda since 11 September 2001. How can terrorism be curbed; how can domestic and international actors work to decrease terrorist violence? Is terrorism a purely security problem with no significant political dimensions? Can the challenge of "political terrorism" be met without addressing the fundamental political issues that may underlie it?

Peacekeeping

If South Asia poses a challenge to international peace and security, it is also true that the region contributes strongly to the

UN efforts at peacekeeping. The chapters by Lieutenant General Satish Nambiar and Brigadier-General Syed Roomy must be read in the context of three of the world's top four UN peacekeepers being currently from South Asia: Bangladesh, Pakistan and India. Of the total of 44,715 military observers, civilian police and military troops involved in UN peacekeeping operations (PKOs) in July 2001, 12,590 (28 per cent) were from South Asian countries.

As of March 2002, Bangladesh was the biggest contributor to UN PKOs, Pakistan was in second place, India third and Nepal eleventh. What accounts for their continued commitment to UN peace operations in the light of the marked reluctance of some Western countries to accept the burden of UN peacekeeping? South Asian countries contribute with unique and useful skills, for example the Indian army's experience in counter-insurgency operations. Are there wider lessons to be drawn from their experience in peacekeeping operations? One might be improved cooperation on training and perhaps institutional cooperation in the future. In the light of the contributions by South Asia to the United Nations and the size and importance of the region, one may ask also if South Asia has gained the influence in international forums that it ought to have. The generals call for adherence to recommendations from the Brahimi Report on UN Peace Operations, especially that troopcontributing countries must be involved in decision-making on mandates for missions. In addition, though, should South Asia have permanent representation on the Security Council?

2

Strategic Triangle in 21st Century: China, India and Russia

THE RUSSIA-CHINA-INDIA TRIANGLE MOVES FORWARD

Soon after Russian Prime Minister Yevgeni Primakov arrived in New Delhi on Dec. 21 for a two-day official visit, a sensational piece of news sounded across the globe: Primakov had publicly called for the formation of a "strategic triangle" among the three giant nations of Russia, India, and China. Encouraging India to see itself more as a world power, and calling for closer relations not only between India and Russia, but also between India and China, Primakov reportedly stated, "A lot in the region depends on the policies pursued by India, Russia, and China.... If we succeed in establishing a triangle, it will be very good." As the Indian newspaper The Hindu commented, "The concept of a 'strategic triangle' covering India, China, and Russia, spelt out by the visiting Russian Prime Minister, Mr. Yevgeny Primakov, is of immense significance since this is perhaps the first time that a senior leader from Moscow has made such a statement."

Wasting no time to research the real background of Primakov's remarks, Western and other media were quick to impose their own distorted, mechanistic interpretation. The new "strategic triangle"—they intimated—was Russia's reply to the U.S.-British bombardment of Iraq, the attempt of the weakened and frustrated former superpower to put together a new, anti-Western bloc. When a spokesman of the Chinese Foreign Ministry, reacting to such press reports, emphasized China's strictly independent foreign policy and China's policy not to participate in any sort of blocs or alliances, the headlines of the British press proclaimed triumphally: "You see! China rebuffed Primakov"!

In reality, the Russia-China-India triangle is no new invention made under the pressure of the Iraq crisis, but a crucially necessary feature of the entire Eurasian Land-Bridge development strategy, as repeatedly emphasized by Lyndon LaRouche and others in the pages of EIR. For competently informed persons, the actual emergence of the "strategic triangle" Russia-China-India, became virtually inevitable no later than Chinese President Jiang Zemin's historic speech at the Russian Science City Akademgorodok in Novosibirsk on Nov. 24, 1998.

There, Jiang Zemin put forward the basic principles of a policy to harness Russia's enormous scientific and technological potential, as typified by the "closed cities" of the military-scientific-industrial complex, for the economic development of the entire region. This policy, as Jiang emphasized, is integral to creating a "new, just, and rational world economic order," guaranteeing the sovereign economic rights of the world's developing countries. That same concept was affirmed in the official declarations of both the Chinese-Russian and Russian-Indian summit meetings.

The most appropriate comment to these developments, interestingly enough, came in the pages of China's official foreign press review, Reference News (Can kao xiaoxi) on Dec. 24. Reference News published on its front page a detailed summary of a speech given by Helga Zepp-LaRouche in early December at a conference in Mexico City.

Her speech laid out the background and implications of Jiang Zemin's Novosibirsk speech, and predicted that Primakov would push for the inclusion of India in the new China-Russia development partnership during his (then forthcoming) visit to New Delhi.

What was most significant in the Reference News coverage of Mrs. LaRouche's remarks, however, was her emphasis on the difference in attitude between the Chinese government—which paid attention to LaRouche's analysis and warnings on the financial crisis—and the attitude of most other governments. That fact, indeed, uniquely coheres with China's role as a centre-point of a growing circle of nations

devoted to real development around the Land-Bridge policy, at a time when the United States and western Europe are plunging toward a self-imposed "dark age" of financial and socio-economic collapse.

Collision ahead?

It is only in this context, and not from some mechanistic geopolitical standpoint, that can one speak of the Russian-Chinese-Indian triangle as an "answer" to what is increasingly perceived in Asia and elsewhere as a dangerous pattern of insanity coming from the West. The turning-point in that perception was doubtless the outrageous, disgusting performance of Vice President Al Gore at the Kuala Lumpur meeting of the Asian Pacific Economic Cooperation (APEC) forum on Nov. 17. Gore's "globalist" ravings and his brazen attack on Malaysia for asserting its sovereignty against international speculators, are increasingly viewed in Asia as a signal for the same insane, destructive policy and mind-frame, which characterize the Anglo-American attack on Iraq and the closely related escalation of the fraudulent "legal coup" against U.S. President Clinton. All add up to an unprecedented assault against the very institution of the sovereign nationstate—including, emphatically, against the constitutional system of the United States itself. Going handin-hand with a major escalation of British geopolitical destabilizations in the Near East and elsewhere, and a coming, new global financial earthquake of unprecedented dimensions, that assault has already brought the world closer to nuclear war, than anyone could have imagined a mere 12 months ago.

One should not forget, that it was China and India's stubborn insistence on maintaining their sovereignty in the face of "financial globalization," that has so far permitted those two countries to weather the so-called Asian financial crisis, while less prudent nations went under. The striving to restore to Russia a modicum of national sovereignty, is key to the constellation of forces behind the Primakov government. It is above all this issue of national sovereignty and economic development that is placing China, Russia, India, and other Asian nations—despite the repeated, and doubtless sincere affirmations that their growing partnership is not directed against any third party—on a collision course with the "globalist" policy championed by Gore.

The sharp reaction to the Iraq bombing, by Russia and China particularly, is a mild foretaste of what may come. Unequivocal condemnation of the Iraqi bombing was a major point of the Russian-Indian joint declaration signed during Primakov's visit. In an unprecedented action, Russia recalled its ambassadors from the United States and Great Britain, while at the same time calling a limited military alert. Soon afterward, Russia gave the world a pointed reminder of its continued existence as a nuclear superpower, by deploying the first of its new generation of mobile, high-precision ICBMs. China's representative at the United Nations did not mince words in ripping apart the fraudulent basis for the whole operation, naming UNSCOM director Richard Butler in public. And after the Dec. 28 incident in which U.S. planes enforcing the so-called "no-fly zone" fired on an Iraqi anti-aircraft position, the speaker of the Chinese Foreign Ministry, Zhu Bangzao, declared: "The Chinese side has many times declared that the sovereignty, territory, and independence of Iraq must be fully respected. China regards the action of creation of a 'no-fly zone' in Iraq as contrary to the United Nations Charter and to standards of international relations." Another, increasingly angry message is implicit in the sharp statements and actions of the Chinese government, in dealing with the Western-supported political opposition movement in China itself.

A growing community of interest

Russia, India, and China make up 22% of the world's land area and over 40% of its population. As the world's largest and most populous developing nations, whose very maintenance requires enormous inputs of science and technology, India and China have a strong common interest in stabilizing and developing Russia. Russia, for its part, can only survive by bringing its scientific and technological potentials into full economic play, which in turn requires large and stable markets for the kinds of industrial goods it can best produce. All three nations have a vital joint interest in Central Asia, and so forth.

They also share, in different ways, the experience of significant joint development in the 1950s. At that time, both India and China profitted greatly from close scientific and technological cooperation with the former Soviet Union—a partnership which was also key, in its direct and indirect effects, to the relatively rapid rates of industrial growth in the Soviet Union in that period. In a limited, but significant way, the transfer of industrial technology and know-how from the Soviet Union to China and India, in that period, helped shape the Non-Aligned Movement's later striving for a "new, just world economic order."

For all these and other reasons, a profound community of interest now exists among the three giant nations. That community of interest is by no means limited to the three alone, but explicitly includes the concept of joint cooperation in other developing countries. It should be noted, for example, that the Russian-Indian agreements signed during Prime Minister Primakov's visit, provide for joint exploration and exploitation of oil and gas resources not only on each other's territories, but also in Kazakstan, Central Asia, and Iraq. Iraq has already been an important oil supplier to India, and India and Russia both have considerable interest in developing petroleum resources there.

But the pathway to consolidation of the Russia-China-India triangle is by no means an easy one. It will be necessary to overcome a long heritage of British geopolitical manipulation in Eurasia. That heritage is lodged above all in false axioms and habits of thinking among the elites, which have permitted the nations of the region again and again to be manipulated against each other in the name of falsely defined, so-called "competitive national interests." The earlier triangle was effectively smashed in the late 1950s and early

1960s, by geopolitical manipulations whose fruits included the Sino-Soviet split, the Sino-Indian war, the apparently "insoluble" Indo-Pakistan conflict, and so on.

One of the notable tools in those British-directed manipulations, incidentally, was none other than the late Armand Hammer, sponsor of the Gore family and supposed "great friend" of the Soviet Union. Some painful rethinking of old mistakes will be needed on all sides, if Russia and its partners want the "Great Triangle" to succeed today. That means above all gaining a more competent under-standing of the historical conflict between the United States and Britain—or in other words, why Lyndon LaRouche has the friends and foes he has.

STATUS, PROBLEMS AND PROSPECTS OF RUSSIA-INDIA MILITARY-TECHNICAL COOPERATION

Russia is a major exporter of arms and military equipment to India. Russia accounts for 55.3 percent of all purchases made by India in this area in 2008-2011. Overall the portfolio of orders contracted for March 2013 amounts to $10.3 billion.

For reference. The United Kingdom was the second-largest exporter of military equipment to India in 2008-2011 at $2.007 billion. Orders booked in 2003-2010 comprise $4.094 billion. Israel ranks third at $1.839 billion and has an order book of $3.452 billion. The United States ranks fourth with $1.144 billion (and $3.986 billion on order), while Italy comes fifth with $690 million (and an order book of $4.23 billion). Overall, India imported armaments from 14 countries in 2008-20116.

In 2012-2015, Russia's share in the Indian arms market will fall to 37.5 percent, whereas maintaining leadership in absolute figures. This is related to several factors:

- India's diversification policy;
- Russia's inability to compete with other countries on a full range of purchased arms and military equipment (while India increases the number of areas for MTC);
- Our main competitors' consent to supply licenses for military production and the most advanced weapons to India (which they often refused to do previously);

- Indian armed forces' efforts to acquire the most combat-effective systems with payment issues being moved to the background.

The Indian party has consistently raised issue of state control over the quality of products and after-sales services exported expressing dissatisfaction with the "superfluous" (intermediary) links in the Russia-India military-technical cooperation.

MTC with India may have a favourable effect on the industrial structure of the national economy due to the programs' long-term nature and consistently significant purchase volumes. There is a clear need to approach the Indian market with unique solutions and technologies on operations and sub-strategic levels (in the area of missile defence, missile warning systems, nuclear-powered submarines, and missile technology) along with the opportunity to link these deliveries with conventional arms procurement. Russia may also join the Indian program to build INS Arihant nuclear submarines (multiple flaws were identified after the first submarine was built).

It is necessary to find a breakthrough branch in military-technical cooperation with India. This could be a major project for a national missile warning system and air defence development (the Indian system is based on outdated Soviet technology). The Indian party is very interested in developing a modern AMD system. This is an area in which the Russian Federation is in a position to offer India new developments, particularly in long-range air defence systems demonstrating extensive anti-missile potential, such as the Antey-2500 military air defence system, the Tor-M2E-2 and Buk-M2E anti-aircraft missile systems, and new modifications such as the C-400 (C-500 for the future). The Russian party could facilitate the joint design and production of a fifth-generation light fighter, given the advanced aviation know-how that already exists in the national defence complex.

The two countries' participation in joint projects involving third countries (chiefly Israel) seems a promising and profitable avenue for both parties to explore. Criticism consistently levelled by the Indian side over delays in spare parts delivery for imported Russian military equipment is largely caused by the Russian side's cumbersome bureaucracy. Claims to Russian enterprises go through Rosoboronexport, resulting in delays that may last several months. Reputable companies should be selectively allowed to perform independent operational interventions. The time schedules followed by Western competitors should be used as benchmarks (replacing a unit normally takes 3-4 days). There is also a clear need to align servicing operations and provide technical maintenance for Russian equipment through to the end of service life, as other vendors do when dealing with India.

It would also be advisable to establish and finance an adequate and aggressive information support strategy for military cooperation, neutralizing the negative propaganda funded by Russian companies' competitors. Particular attention should be paid to Indian professional defence and technology sector magazines, while special emphasis should be placed on working with them. These magazines play a crucial role in shaping the opinion of the national military elite and that of the individuals that make decisions on MTC.

CROSS-CUTTING AND MITIGATING FACTORS IN TRIANGULAR RELATIONS

On nuclear security, the triangular dynamics between Russia, China, and India become far more complicated. Both Russia and China denounced India's nuclear tests in 1998, although Russia's criticism was milder, and both have urged India to sign the Comprehensive Test Ban Treaty and the Non-Proliferation Treaty. If the nuclear rivalry between China and India intensifies, Russia's nonpartisan stance as strategic partner to both may become less sustainable.

Possible U.S. deployment of national and/or theatre missile defence systems also elicits different kinds of concerns from Moscow, Beijing, and New Delhi. Russians are concerned about the deployment of a national missile defence system that could eventually compromise the Russian strategic deterrent. Although it is difficult to imagine that happening in the next ten to fifteen years, even if Russia reduced the size of its arsenal to one thousand deployed warheads, Moscow would incur some unwanted additional costs in developing countermeasures to defenses. The Chinese strongly oppose U.S. deployment of theatre systems in Asia and especially the potential sharing of such systems with Taiwan. But Beijing is also concerned about so-called "thin" national defenses designed to address small attacks and accidental launches, because those defenses would compromise existing Chinese deterrent capabilities. India is opposed to U.S. deployment of a national missile defence because it will likely hasten Chinese efforts to modernize and expand their nuclear forces, thus compelling India to deploy a more robust nuclear deterrent than it might otherwise do. All three states, however, share a dim view of the prospect that U.S. deployment of national and theatre defence systems to defend the homeland and U.S. troops will possibly allow it to deploy U.S. troops more liberally with less fear of reprisal.

The missile defence issue presents Moscow with tremendous challenges and difficult choices that affect the management of its relationship with China. If Russia were to reach agreement with the United States about modification of the Anti-Ballistic Missile (ABM) Treaty to allow for the deployment of a limited national missile defence system, the Sino-Russian relationship would suffer. The U.S.-Russian agreement at the June 2000 Clinton-Putin summit to explore cooperation on missile defence and to jointly monitor missile launches, followed by Putin's proposal to the Europeans in Rome the same month to cooperate on the development of a joint European theatre missile defence system, elicited serious concern from China.

Presumably Putin had some explaining to do when he met with Chinese leader Jiang Zemin twice the next month, once in Dushanbe for the Shanghai Forum summit and once in Beijing. He was at least somewhat successful, as the two sides concluded with a more unified stance, once again denouncing U.S. plans for missile defence and upholding the ABM Treaty as a bedrock of strategic stability in the world. In the past, the Chinese and the Russians have discussed cooperation in taking joint measures to oppose U.S. missile defence, although apart from joint denunciations of U.S. activities and plans it is not clear what form such cooperation would take.

Moscow must beware of damage to the Sino-Russian relationship resultimg from a potential U.S.-Russian agreement on ABM Treaty modification, but Russian strategic thinkers are also concerned about catalyzing a more rapid Chinese nuclear build-up. With deployed Russian nuclear forces on a downward trajectory, the emergence of a more robust Chinese nuclear deterrent in the future is unsettling. Russia's choices will not be made easier by the new Bush administration in Washington, which has made very explicit its desire to deploy a national missile defence system more robust than that planned by the Clinton administration. As of February 2001, the Russian security establishment still appeared undecided about whether it would agree to accept modification of the ABM Treaty should the Bush administration seek to pursue one. President Clinton's decision to postpone a decision on national missile defence deployment, followed by a review by the Bush administration of economic and technical feasibility, provides a welcome breathing space for diplomatic efforts on a number of fronts. Nevertheless, Moscow will eventually face a fundamental decision on missile defence that will lay down a very significant marker in the consolidation of its post-cold war strategic approach. Should it jump on the bandwagon with the dominant global power or align with its rising power neighbor to balance against the hegemon?

Although far less likely than national missile defence deployment-but hardly unimaginable-Sino-American conflict over Taiwan could also potentially put Moscow in an awkward position. Moscow has consistently upheld a one-China policy, and at the July summit in Beijing Putin stated that Russia firmly supports China's efforts to reunify with Taiwan. But what would Moscow do if actual fighting broke out over Taiwan? Rumours circulated in Asia that before his trip to Beijing last summer Putin offered the Chinese direct military assistance in the event of a crisis in the Taiwan Strait. Supposedly the Russians would send their Pacific Fleet to cut off U.S. naval access to the strait. The rumour seems hard to believe since Russia stands to benefit little by actual involvement in a Taiwan crisis involving the United States-which speaks to the larger phenomenon that China seems to benefit more from the Sino-Russian relationship than does Russia. It would seem that Russia's interests are best served by continuing U.S.-Chinese tension over Taiwan because it increases Moscow's leverage with Washington and Beijing. It also seems slightly fantastic that the Chinese would take such an offer as credible given the decrepit condition of Russia's Pacific Fleet. Still, the story was not denied by Russian or Chinese officials, and there was no comment on the rumour either by top U.S. officials or by major media.

Currently the Russians and Chinese are negotiating a new treaty that would define and further elevate the status of the bilateral relationship. Although it series very unlikely that the new treaty would include security guarantees, it has been reported that it would broaden and deepen Russo-Chinese security cooperation in the fields of arms sales and weapons research and development. Reportedly, Moscow and Beijing are envisioning a fifteen-year cooperation plan that would include two stages. In the first stage (2000-05), China would be able to purchase up to $15 billion in weapons from Russia while expanding joint exercises and military training. In the second stage (2005-15) China and Russia would engage in joint research and development of new generations of military technology.

Although the Russian military-industrial complex could certainly benefit from the infusion of Chinese capital, it is not clear what technological benefit for Russia there would be in such extensive cooperation. In addition, it seems unlikely that Russian industry could quickly ramp up by a factor of three its current arms deliveries to Beijing.

Economic cooperation and trade between China and Russia continue to be sluggish. The announced goal of reaching $20 billion in bilateral trade by the year 2000 not surprisingly proved to be wildly unrealistic, as the overall figure failed to reach $8 billion last year. There is long-term growth potential in the energy sector, but it will require years to develop any major multilateral investment Like much in the Sino-Russian relationship, the rhetoric of partnership outstrips the reality. The overall relationship is better than at any time since the 1950s, but the foundation remains rather shaky. A measured and balanced look at the relationship would suggest that the two countries continue and even increase strategic cooperation, to meet the security interests of both without compromising their primary focus on economic development, which also requires cooperative relations with the West for both Beijing and Moscow.

Although Moscow has emphasized the long-term nature of its shared interests with China and India, the Sino-Russian relationship is controversial among Russian policymaking elites in a way that the Indo-Russian relationship is not. Russia shares a long border with China and a long history of often bitter and complex relations. There is an implicit Russian hedge position on China that is amplified by a growing sense of the economic and demographic vulnerability of the Russian Far East and, to a lesser extent, of Moscow's "sphere of influence" in Central Asia. Perhaps for the near future China will focus on its interests in Taiwan and the South China Sea, but there exists a barely veiled Russian fear that continued Russian weakness will invite Chinese infiltration and eventual control of some Russian territory. Russia shares no border with India, and despite the wild designs of nationalist politician Vladimir Zhirinovsky and the like for Moscow's "drive to the South," it is nearly impossible to foresee circumstances that could lead to conflict between Russia and India. This is not to say that conflict with China is at all likely, but rather that Russia's sensibilities toward China and India are different.

Initially giving longtime friendly partner India the cold shoulder after the collapse of the USSR, Russian diplomats fairly steadily sought to strengthen ties with New Delhi through the 1990s. This process culminated with Vladimir Putin's trip to India last October, when the "strategic partnership" between India and Russia was formally established. Despite this achievement and the signing of a number of arms sales agreements that amounted to more than $3 billion in new deals, however, reports in both the Indian and Russian press indicated some difficult discussions that suggest underlying tensions in this relationship.

It was reported in the Russian press that India played hardball in the arms sales negotiations by demanding further price reductions, and that Russian defence officials were not fully satisfied with the deals, which consisted of agreements of intent rather than contracts. But even with arms transfers to India amounting to about $1 billion annually, the over-all Russo-Indian trade relationship over the past decade has fallen from $5.5 billion a year to about $1.5 billion. One Russian commentator, on the eve of the October summit in New Delhi, concluded that unless Russia and India can revitalize their trade relationship, the agreement about their strategic partnership "will be nothing but words on paper."

It was also clear from the summit and events around it that Indian and Russian interests do not precisely coincide regarding Pakistan or the Taliban. Just a week before Putin travelled to India, Sergei Yastrzhembsky went to Pakistan as a presidential envoy. His letter from President Putin addressed Russian concerns in Central Asia, Afghanistan, and Chechnya, including the role of camps on the Pakistani-Afghan border that are training soldiers to fight in Chechnya, Tajikistan, Uzbekistan, and Kyrgyzstan.

Acknowledging that Pakistan and Russia do not agree on everything, Yastrzhembsky explained that Moscow hoped that Pakistan could play more of a stabilizing role in the region. Although Yastrzhembsky denied that the trip to Islamabad was designed to reach out directly to the Taliban, at a minimum Russia hoped that Pakistan could influence the Taliban to curb some of their activities. The trip also sent a message to the Indians that Russia intended to exercise all of its options, and it may help explain some of the chilliness of the meetings in New Delhi.

The Russian press also reported that Putin made a significant political concession to the Indians to seal the arms agreements by condemning terrorism and noting in his speech before the Indian parliament that the same people were instigating terrorist acts "from the Philippines to Kosovo, and from Kashmir to the Caucasus." Putin also supported India's position that the Kashmir conflict should be resolved only by Pakistan and India and should not involve international mediators. Just after Putin made these very public statements effectively supporting India in its conflict with Pakistan, the arms agreements were: finally signed. Much of the Russian press concluded that India got the best of Russia in their summit deliberations, and that this reflected a shift in the balance of power of the Russo-Indian relationship in favour of New Delhi.

The Russo-Indian summit provoked some discussion in the Russian press about the prospects of a Sino-Russian-Indian alliance and especially its role in addressing religious "extremism" and terrorism, a popular theme of the Putin administration. Vladimir Lukin, deputy speaker of the Russian Duma and a veteran Asia hand who accompanied President Putin on his trip to India, described the trip as promoting the "emergence of a new centre of influence in Asia with the participation of Moscow, New Delhi, and Beijing." But he also noted the significance that "this tripartite interest is not negative in any way, i.e., it is not directed against anyone and is not anti-European or anti-American." In fact, Lukin went on to say that "the threat of international terrorism could help establish a kind of regional alliance of Moscow, Delhi, and Washington, crucial for maintaining stability in Asia." In his interview with Indian journalists, President Putin made some interesting remarks that emphasized the importance of maintaining transparency:

But everybody will understand us if we are going to say that India, China, and Russia have some common interests as countries located in that region, interests that we want to pursue jointly. I do not see anything special in this, nothing dangerous. But what is necessary is that all our proposals in the sphere of cooperation, both bilateral and multilateral, should be open for all our partners, understandable and transparent. I think this is something we can achieve.

Russian support for multilateral security institutions in Asia has a long history, going back at least as far as Brezhnev's proposal more than thirty years ago for a collective security pact in Asia. During the Gorbachev years these calls acquired more of a genuine positive-sum rather than zero-sum character when the Soviet Union improved relations with both China and the United States. Since the collapse of the Soviet Union, Russia has continued to support multilateral frameworks for addressing key Asian security issues. In that regard the Shanghai Forum, which grew out of the border and demilitarization agreement talks between China, Kazakhstan,

Kyrgyzstan, Russia, and Tajikistan, is emerging as an interesting Asian multilateral institution with some potential to address regional interests in dealing with terrorism, drug-trafficking, and other common problems.

RUSSIA, CHINA, AND INDIA OVERCOME FRICTION IN THEIR RELATIONS

The Russia-China partnership has clearly helped to foster bilateral relations after more than two decades of tension and hostility. This partnership has also enhanced the international standing of both countries. At the same time, however, political trust is still rather weak. Moscow and particularly the Russian Far East are clearly worried that the further economic decline of that region will lead to its abandoning by Russians and even Chinese occupation.

China is not perceived by the majority of Russian experts as an immediate military threat, because it is not expected to close the gap with Russia in nuclear and conventional weapons anytime soon. However, more and more Russian commentators, including in the military, are worried about the consequences for Russia of arming China with sophisticated Russian weapons while the Russian army itself cannot afford to have them.

Russia's growing political, economic, and military dependence on China has provoked a certain alarm and anxiety in Russia's academic and political circles. Alexei Bogaturov believes that in spite of impressive rapprochement, Russia and China remain countries that have historically been in conflict and that the geopolitical source of the conflict has not been removed or reduced. Hence, he argues against attempts to pick China as an ally or key partner in the region. Such views are not rare in Russia, even among government officials, in spite of a general official euphoria and an informal taboo on anti-Chinese comments. Common views toward US politics and close military cooperation may not be enough to sustain and enhance the "strategic partnership" between Russia and China. To make it complete, the two countries will have to get rid of their traditional suspicion of each other and engage in a stable and long-term economic cooperation.

The relationship between India and China also has an important influence on the character of regional order and significant geopolitical implications. Friction in this bilateral relationship could have direct effects on China's relations with other neighbours. Stable and cooperative relations between India and China build trust and contribute to Beijing's own sense of security and confidence, providing a counterbalance should other important relationships deteriorate.

The near-rapprochement of relations (driven by the mutual consensus that economic development should have priority) between India and China diffuses, but does not dispel, three decades of friction. Four of the five primary causes of disquiet in India-China relations have been addressed by both powers: India's values-driven Tibet policy has ceased;

Chinese support for secessionist insurgents in Assam and the North East has been withdrawn; the collapse of the Soviet Union reduces Chinese fears of a containment-driven strategic nexus; and, most important, tensions stemming from border disputes between India and China are addressed, though not resolved, through the negotiation of confidence-building measures and agreements. The principal friction in contemporary relations between New Delhi and Beijing is India's belief (apparently well-founded) that China provides nuclear-related military technology and hardware to Pakistan. This abrasion is compartmentalized from India's overall bilateral relationship with Beijing. (New Delhi may be reassured by China's decision to join, and work constructively with, the Non-Proliferation Treaty Exporters Committee [or Zangger Committee].) New Delhi's preference for longer-term prudence in its relationship with China is one consequence of China's military nuclear exports to Pakistan.

India's approach to the management of tensions with China offers important lessons for other regional actors in how to manage relations (especially on sensitive issues) with China. New Delhi has handled Beijing more successfully than Washington has during the corresponding period. India and China have established and maintained regular reciprocal high-level personal visits between political leaders. Both states have improved trade relations and take care to compartmentalize intractable issues that continue to irritate long-standing tensions. Such a policy has perhaps returned dividends of its own with China in turn assuming a "position of `careful neutrality' on Kashmir." In contrast to recent US policy on China, India takes care to respect the principle of noninterference in the internal affairs of another state and eschews a values-driven foreign policy. These developments are especially significant given the depth of India's embedded longer-term strategic concerns with China and the record of mutual tension that has only eased in recent years. India's democratic status also may make it an attractive partner to those East Asian states condemned by the United States for abusing human rights or for falling short of democratic standards.

The renewed Russian-Indian strategic partnership, fuelled by common concern regarding Islamic revivalism, has thwarted Moscow's initial intention to follow a more balanced policy in South Asia, improving in particular its relations with Pakistan. Instead, Moscow-Islamabad links have further deteriorated, especially because of the latter's pro-Taliban role in Afghanistan prior to recent events.

Moscow's strategic interest in India motivates Moscow to promote India's inclusion into the leading forums and institutions of the Asia-Pacific. Having become a member of the Asia-Pacific Economic Cooperation (APEC) organization, Moscow is now backing New Delhi's bid for membership in this regional body. During consultations with the Indian Foreign Ministry in November 1998, Russian Deputy Foreign Minister Grigory Karasin noted that "Russia will try its best to help India develop ties with APEC and eventually to join the organization."

Although Russia and India have renounced an openly anti-Chinese policy, both countries continue to share suspicion and fear toward China. In spite of Moscow's public denunciation of India's nuclear tests in 1998, Russia appreciates India's concern about adequate military preparation in case of Chinese aggression. Moscow supports India not only morally, but also through the resumption of arms supplies, which, after a brief pause in the early 1990s, have been steadily increasing.

Challenges to US International Strategy

Some US officials admit that closer ties between Moscow and Beijing are cause for concern. They say, at the very least, debates are more complicated now on the UN Security Council, where Russia and China frequently make common cause against interventionist initiatives favoured by the United States and Britain. Deadlock on the UN Security Council reminiscent of the Cold War era is becoming a regular occurrence.

For instance, knowing that both Russia and China would probably veto military intervention in Kosovo, the Clinton Administration decided to work through NATO. Both Moscow and Beijing were concerned about external intervention on humanitarian grounds, which would be relevant to conflicts within Russia such as Chechnya, and within China such as its claims over Taiwan. Further, NATO was again conspiring to force the US value system on a Third World state.

Russia, China, and India watched the United States in conflicts throughout the 1990s and each learned the same lessons. Indian military and political sources were among the first to react to the Kosovo operation and to speculate on preliminary lessons to be learned. "We are studying what's going on there [in Kosovo] and drawing our lessons from it." A common theme in Indian, Russian, and Chinese thinking since Operation Desert Storm has been the importance of "force multipliers" provided by information technology, AWACs, mid-air refuelling, unmanned aerial vehicles, and electronic warfare capabilities. Analysts in all three countries believe their armed forces can succeed against a high-technology foe if they use these force multipliers in combination with clever low-technology tactics, urban guerilla warfare, financial terrorism, computer hacking, media warfare, diplomatic actions, and psychological warfare.

In light of the new "interventionist-oriented NATO doctrine" and the new capabilities of long-range precision conventional weapons, Indian military thinkers recommend upgrading its nuclear arms to deter Western intimidation and attack. This is a prime example of the drive toward nuclear weapons and its cascading effects predicted by

General Makmut Gareyev, President of the Russian Academy of Military Science. He believes that countries, including Russia, that are unable to match an opponent in high-technology conventional weapons will resort to nuclear weapons in order to deter conventional strikes. Until 1998, India held the principled position that nuclear deterrence was abhorrent to human sentiment, since it implies that if required to defend its own existence, a state will act with pitiless disregard for the consequences of its own and its adversary's people. But in remarks made on 15 March 1999, Prime Minister A. B. Vajpayee asserted: "The nuclear weapon is not an offensive weapon. It is a weapon of self-defence. It is the kind of weapon that helps in preserving peace. If in the days of the Cold War there was no use of force, it was because of the balance of terror." It is also true that India has begun revamping its conventional forces to push the nuclear threshold upward, creating more options with those conventional forces before resorting to nuclear weapon use.

In his article titled, "Nuclear Shadows on High Tech Warfare," Major General Wu Jianguo, former associate professor and dean of the Antichemical Warfare Academy, sums up the Chinese view of its nuclear capability: "When countries possessing nuclear weapons and high-tech conventional weapons are involved in a war in which the conflict is intensifying, the possible use of nuclear weapons cannot be ruled out. Nuclear weapons, therefore, are still a trump card in the hands of nuclear nations."

Many scenarios that would present a challenge to the United States could arise from the triangular strategic partnership. One possible conflict scenario is that of China and Taiwan. This is a possible conflict for several reasons. First, China is going through an economic modernization. This is good over the long run for encouraging political liberty. In the short run, however, as large state-owned enterprises are disestablished, the Chinese may have unemployment of millions to tens of millions and social and political disruption of one kind or another.

For thousands of years dictators have responded to domestic problems by playing the nationalism card and focusing attention on a foreign enemy or foreign problem. Taiwan will be front and centre because now it is a thriving, prosperous, free-enterprise democracy. Taiwan inescapably disproves those people in Southeast Asia and in the PRC who have said for years that Asians do not have an aptitude for democracy and need to be ruled with a firm hand. Taiwan is an affront to the leaders in Beijing the same way Poland's Solidarity movement in the summer of 1989 was an affront to the leaders in the Kremlin and the dictators in Eastern Europe. The Taiwan Strait is one of the most likely places over the next five to ten years where the United States might end up in a clear confrontation with another nuclear power.

How would such a conflict evolve? Top echelons of the PLA officer corps do not necessarily share a common point of view with regard to Taiwan, and the advice they give is not necessarily militaristic. However, a Western intelligence source surmises that high-ranking naval and air force officers support a militant stance in Taiwan. They, rather than the ground forces, have received the benefits of increases in the defence budget and are eager to test their new capabilities.

Beijing is not likely to haphazardly lob a few missiles over to Taiwan and see what happens. Beijing would have a plan and expect to win. The more probable scenario would be for the Chinese to effect simultaneous crises to distract the United States, forcing the Americans to choose between Taiwan and another ally. This quote from Chinese ultra-nationalist author He Xing lends credence to the "simultaneous crises" theory:

China must pay close attention to those countries that are opposed to American interests, or are potential strategic enemies. It must be borne in mind that the enemies of enemies are one's own allies.... Know this: the more the United States encounters trouble in other places in the world, the more difficult it is for it to concentrate its power on dealing with China and the greater the opportunities for China's existence and development.

Hypothetically, Beijing might cooperate with Moscow on the timing of an attack on Taiwan. Moscow could simultaneously start a conflict with emerging democracies in the Baltics or the Caucasus. Or Beijing and New Delhi could cooperate on timing, with India engaging Pakistan, perhaps with the support of Moscow. Both

Russia and China are arming other enemies of the United States such as Iran and Iraq. Iraq could be persuaded by Beijing or Moscow to simultaneously start a conflict with Kuwait, Saudi Arabia, or Israel. China could concurrently attack Taiwan and stop the food flow to North Korea, forcing millions of refugees into South Korea, and causing the United States to choose between helping Taiwan and assisting South Korea.

The possibility of a nuclear dimension to a conflict between China and Taiwan is all too real. On 2 December 1998, the Defence Intelligence Agency (DIA) reported that the PLA had conducted exercises that included simulated nuclear missile attacks on Taiwan and on US military forces in the region. DIA analysts determined that the missile units were conducting mock nuclear attacks on Taiwan and against US Army troops based in South Korea. US marines on the Japanese island of Okinawa and mainland Japan also were targeted.

The missile exercise directly threatened the 37,000 troops based in South Korea and the 47,000 troops in Japan, including about 25,000 marines on Okinawa. All of these China-Taiwan scenario options are conjecture, but they are not beyond the realm of possibility and are worth considering. That may be particularly so in the aftermath of the terrorist strikes on the United States on 11 September 2001 and the US response. The volatility of the current situation calls into question many of our previous assumptions about stability and the likely course of international and regional relations.

THE SINO-SOVIET RAPPROCHEMENT IN THE CONTEXT OF STRATEGIC TRIANGLE

It is rarely disputed that enmity and mistrust toward the Soviet Union brought China and the United States together in the 1970s. American diplomacy, actuated in accordance with Henry Kissinger's realist ideals, sought to play the "China" card in its fight against the Kremlin. The China factor in U.S. foreign policy thus played an important role in calculations about how to manage the United States' adversary relationship with the Soviet Union (Talbott, 1981: 82). China, for its part, was seeking to pursue normalization with the United States in order to counterweight the Soviet Union. Galenovich (2001) noted that China's posture vis-à-vis the Kremlin in the 1970s was openly aggressive. Beijing called for creating a joint front against the USSR, ceased to recognise the 1950 treaty of Friendship, Solidarity, and Mutual Assistance, and repeatedly demanded the Soviet Union withdraw its forces from Mongolia, halt assistance to Vietnam, and reduce the troop presence along the Sino-Soviet border (Galenovich, 2001: 1). Beginning in 1979, the first talks between China and the Soviet Union were terminated when the Soviet Union conducted the invasion of Afghanistan (Hyland, 1981: 138).

In the early 1980s, a shift in the power balance occurred. The Soviet Union's deteriorating relations with the United States, troubled economy, and declining defence capabilities made the Kremlin seek ways of invigorating its relationship with China. At that juncture, the Chinese leadership was discontented with U.S. foreign policy toward the Taiwan issue (i.e. increased contacts and arms sales), U.S. criticism of the human rights situation in China, and Washington's unwillingness to provide industrial technology so coveted by Beijing. The above-mentioned factors played a key role in bringing China and the Soviet Union together after 1985 when the Sino-Soviet rapprochement commenced.

In March 1982, the then Soviet leader, Leonid Brezhnev, in his Tashkent speech opined upon China as a "socialist state" and strongly criticized the U.S. "two China" policy, thus sending a signal to Beijing that Moscow was ready for renewing a dialogue (Wishnick, 2001a: 75). In response to Brezhnev's appeal, the Chinese leadership subsequently announced its determination to conduct "independent foreign policy" aimed at improving relations with both the Soviet Union and the United States without attaching itself to any big power (Goldstein, 1990: 122). As a consequence, the Soviet Union and the People's Republic of China began a round of talks devoted to the normalization of Sino-Soviet relations and resolution of border disputes.

The results of negotiations, albeit not as fruitful as parties had envisioned, had a significant impact on the increased levels of trade between the two nations. The volume of trade, for instance, skyrocketed from $300 million in 1982 to $1.2 billion in 1984 (Voskressenskii, 1999: 244).

However, three crucial challenges, the so-called "three obstacles," which had been thwarting rapprochement between Moscow and Beijing since the beginning of the 1980s, remained. Beijing still expressed its dissatisfaction with the deployment of Soviet troops along the Sino-Soviet border, the Soviet Union's support for Vietnam's occupation of Cambodia, and the Soviet invasion of Afghanistan in 1979. The Soviet leaders Andropov and Chernenko fell short of achieving any substantial progress on these issues largely due to the short tenure of their offices. It was Mikhail Gorbachev who gave impetus to the normalization of Sino-Soviet relations after ascending to the Communist Party's leadership in 1985.

The Soviet response to addressing the "three obstacles" in Sino-Soviet relations was reflected in Mikhail Gorbachev's speech in Vladivostok on July 28, 1986. In his speech, the new Soviet leader signalled his willingness to resolve the main points of contention between Moscow and Beijing. Gorbachev announced his decision to reduce the number of troops along the Sino-Soviet border and withdraw a considerable part of the Soviet contingent from Mongolia and Afghanistan by the end of the year. The Soviet leader, however, stopped short of giving concessions on the Soviet support of Vietnam's occupation of Cambodia. Only two years later when the Soviet Union began withdrawing forces from Afghanistan, Moscow suggested Hanoi should follow suit (Su, 1989: 115), and in December of that year Vietnam withdrew its troops from Cambodia. Thus, by the end of 1980s China and the Soviet Union made significant progress in overcoming the impasse in the relationship and were gradually moving toward full normalization.

Nevertheless, the two countries had different motives underlying their pursuit of better relations. While China was seeking to establish a peaceful milieu within the strategic triangle in order to focus on its economic development, the Soviet Union sought to restore the ideological nexus between the two communist countries (Voskessenskii, 1999: 247) with an intent to avert a possibility of a two-front conflict, and boost the Soviet economy.

During Gorbachev's first visit to China in 1989 for the Sino-Soviet summit in Beijing, Chinese and Soviet leaders reached a mutual understanding on how to improve the Sino-Soviet relations.

Accordingly, Mikhail Gorbachev and Deng Xiaoping agreed that the new relationship would be based on the principles of peaceful coexistence and mutual respect, would not be aimed against any third country, and the ideological factor would not play any role in the normalization of Sino-Soviet relations. The aforementioned goals were reflected in the joint Sino-Soviet communiqué of 1989. According to the document, the Soviet Union and People's Republic of China agreed to develop their relations on the basis of the five principles of peaceful coexistence, including respect for international norms such as sovereignty, noninterference, and peaceful resolution of disputes (Wishnick, 2001a: 105). Further, any attempt or action by any country to impose its own will on others and seek "hegemony in any form" would be discarded by Moscow and Beijing.

The end of Sino-American confrontation following the decay of the Soviet Union removed the main rationale behind U.S.-Chinese cooperation, and the image of an opening China was replaced overnight by an image of a defiant China ruled by dictators (Zhu, 2006: 90). A month after the Sino-Soviet summit, the Chinese leadership witnessed a hitherto unseen degree of public discontent. The Tiananmen crackdown sparked harsh criticism from the United States which imposed sanctions against China. The Soviet Union, on the contrary, issued a response stating that the events in China were an internal affair, and suggested political dialogue as a means to resolve social problems. Besides, it was not in Gorbachev's interests to undermine the overwhelming progress in Sino-Soviet relations achieved during the previous four years of his tenure. Socio-economic problems in the Soviet Union (mass protests in Tbilisi, Georgia and other Soviet republics) also made Gorbachev refrain from open criticism of China's violent quelling of the protests in Beijing.

In the final analysis, the events in China made the Soviet leadership consider the consequences of liberalization that had been gaining momentum since the beginning of *perestroika,* while a fragile rapprochement between the two countries after two decades of confrontation dissuaded Gorbachev from taking a more assertive stance towards Beijing.

The Soviet Union soon became embroiled in painful process of disintegration, and Sino-Soviet relations were no longer atop the Kremlin's agenda. The Soviet Union and the communist bloc in Eastern Europe subsequently began to unravel.

In sum, the Sino-Soviet rapprochement in the second half of the 1980s was caused by important power shifts within the strategic triangle between the USA, USSR, and PRC. The United States under the Reagan administration was determined to economically exhaust the Soviet Union, thus eliminating it as a major geopolitical threat, while engaging China in order to maintain a strategic advantage in containing the USSR. In light of the worsening economy and political stagnation, the Soviet Union began to reverse its course toward China in the early 1980s for economic, political, and security reasons (Tucker, 1995-96: 518). China, for its part, was also looking forward to resolving disputes with the USSR because of the security threat emanating from the troop presence along the Sino-Soviet border and around China (i.e. Vietnam and Afghanistan). Although the "three obstacles" constantly stymied negotiations between the Soviet Union and China under Brezhnev, Andropov, and Chernenko, Sino-Soviet relations began to mend after Mikhail Gorbachev's ascension to power, and by the end of the 1980s most disputes were resolved.

The normalization of Sino-Soviet relations did not have a long-lasting impact, however, for the Soviet Union and China failed to achieve substantial progress in their economic cooperation. Because Sino-Soviet trade was markedly lower than trade between China and the United States, China considered U.S.-Chinese relations more important. The volume of Sino-Soviet trade amounted to $2 billion by 1985, whereas Sino-U.S. trade had already reached $6 billion by 1984 (Mills, 1986: 543). Thus, although the strategic triangle by and large lost its military component after the end of the Cold War, its political and economic implications remained important well into the following decades.

A RUSSIA–INDIA–CHINA TRIANGLE: 'PRIMAKOV'S TRIANGLE'?

Apart from the Indian and Pakistani nuclear tests, another major event made 1998 a watershed year: the Anglo-American bombing campaign on Iraq to punish Saddam Hussein for obstructing U.N. inspections of his alleged development of weapons of mass destruction elicited a much more dramatic response from Russia than international criticism of India's nuclear tests. Russian President Boris Yeltsin's Prime Minister Yevgeny Primakov called for the establishment of a *'strategic triangle'* among India, Russia and China to ensure peace and stability in the world. Primakov strongly criticized the air strikes by the United States and the United Kingdom on Iraq as being conducted without the mandate of the United Nations Security Council. Primakov's 'triangle' was variously described in US media as 'a coalition of the weak great powers pitted against its one superpower' or the *'Anti-NATO Axis'*.

China immediately rejected Primakov's call, saying that China pursues an independent and peaceful foreign policy, and furthermore kept a low profile. However, Russian diplomats said that China and Russia both feared that the US attacks against Iraq would become a model for unilateral action taken and carried out by Washington against the Democratic People's Republic of Korea and other countries. The Clinton administration had been close to attacking North Korea in 1993 and peace was saved only by the surprise self-styled mission of former US President Jimmy Carter.

Within one year of the bombing of Iraq, the Clinton presidency had set the trend for unilateral action in disregard of the United Nations with two large-scale aerial bombardment campaigns: first in Iraq; and then in Kosovo. Russia, and particularly Primakov himself, had strong links with Iraq, whereas China, having just entered into a 'Strategic Partnership' with the United States during Clinton's July 1998 visit to China, had no specific interest to defend there. However, Kosovo was to Serbia/Yugoslavia what Taiwan was to China and thus China went all the way in criticizing US and NATO policy in further dismembering the Yugoslav Federation. Russia had multiple interests in Kosovo, foremost in Huntingtonian terms as the core nation of Slavic-Orthodox civilization and secondly as the erstwhile leader of the Communist bloc to which Yugoslavia had once belonged. The weakened Russian military wanted to show that it still had some muscle and guts, and had taken a short cut to the airport of Pristina, Kosovo's capital, which stirred NATO Supreme Commander General Wesley Clark into ordering the British local commander, Lieutenant-General Michael Jackson, to evict the Russians with American air support. Jackson refused and the showdown between the American four-star and British three-star generals is recorded on dozens of websites. Jackson asked Clark: "What is your authority, Sir?". Clark smugly said: "Me, I am a four-star general, Michael". "I am a three-star general", Jackson thundered, "but I am not going to start World War III for you". Although a direct US–Russian confrontation was avoided, bilateral ties never recovered. After appointing five different Russian prime ministers in 1998 and 1999, and in failing health, Yeltsin abruptly resigned at the turn of the millennium. His chosen successor, Vladimir Putin, decided to await the outcome of the 2000 American presidential election before re-engaging with the United States.

The Chinese suffered even more dramatically from American transgressions in Serbia/Kosovo, when US B-2 bombers under NATO's command 'erroneously' dropped five guided bombs on the Chinese Embassy in Belgrade, killing three Chinese and injuring twenty. US President Clinton telephoned China's President Jiang Zemin to make an instant apology, but Jiang refused to take the call. A spate of presidential, ministerial and ambassadorial apologies followed during the next few days, but no Chinese could believe that the bombing had been accidental. The whole episode is described in detail in a book by Susan Shirk, who as US Deputy Assistant Secretary of State for East Asian Affairs was then directly in charge of US–China relations. She writes that at the time of the bombing, the Chinese leadership was in a state of high alert because two weeks earlier, Zhongnanhai, the main compound of the ruling elite, had been surrounded by a surprise peaceful sit-in of Falun Gong, a Buddhist-inspired sect of yoga-type meditation and health exercises. Shirk quotes an insider source as saying that President Jiang stayed up on the night after the bombing to write a long memo, not on how to deal with the United States, but how to crush Falun

Gong by means of ludicrous over-reaction. Media reporting about the bombing demonstrated how much control the Communist Party had lost over Chinese society since the proliferation of semi-independent commercial newspapers and the internet, which both sensationalized dramatic news events for higher circulation figures and profits, adding extra pressure on the government to adopt a hardline stance towards the United States. An investigation coordinated by Susan Shirk blamed the *'horrific blunder'* of the bombing, as she called it, on the CIA, using the wrong method to locate a targeted Yugoslav military agency and using outdated databases. Still, very, very few Chinese believed the Americans could make such a stupid mistake. In the minds of many, it must have been some lower-level anti-China conspiracy. Anyway, the Chinese domestic pandemonium had further complicated US–China relations: China no longer only perceived itself as an on-and-off adversary or 'enemy of the future' of the United States, but also the victim of today. In New Delhi, an academic security consultant with access to military intelligence also dismissed any American account of errors or blunders as a cover-up and is absolutely convinced that it was a premeditated attack on Chinese electronic devices and technicians, hidden in the embassy to help the Milosevic regime's air defences against American bombing:

Why did they, the Americans, bomb the embassy? Only those two rooms were targeted. I have very concrete information [about] what these two rooms were doing, what the people in those rooms were doing. The Yugoslavs brought down a B-117 stealth bomber and transferred it to the Chinese. The Chinese were developing a stealth bomber. Stealth technologies you get nowhere. Russians refuse to part with any of these technologies. There is no way they can get it from the EU because of the arms' embargo. So the only way to get it is through 'stealth!'

So, after eight years of volatility but with regular improvements, US–China relations under President Clinton ended on a sour note, and it would get worse. US President George W. Bush and his coterie of neo-con warriors were in no mood to continue the sweet-and-sour tactics that Clinton had played with the Chinese – and the Russians. Bush downgraded America's tentative 'strategic partnership' for the 21st century with China – agreed by Presidents Clinton and Jiang Zemin in 1998 – to one of *'competition'*, and talked of upgrading Taiwan and supplying it with any arms that it needed to defend itself.

Before '9-11' the Bush administration's policy towards China was one of 'congagement' – a blended strategy that transcends both containment and engagement and should embrace neither but should contain elements of both.

The Bush administration continued Clinton's policy of ending India's isolation by lifting the remaining sanctions for its 1998 nuclear tests. This conformed to the administration's de-emphasis of non-proliferation in favour of 'counter-proliferation' by means of the National Missile Defence. Interest in India had grown considerably in the US Congress against the backdrop of the 'rise of China', the spy-plane crisis and new escalating tensions over giant arms' sales to Taiwan. The Bush administration's public assertion that its new fervour for India had nothing to do with any anti-China strategy was dismissed by most observers as just diplomatic talk.

Nevertheless, Chinese Foreign Minister Tang Jiaxuan rejected the 'Primakov Triangle' and said that time had not yet come for a strategic alliance between the three countries: 'We are for discussion on issues of mutual interests, but it is premature to set up any mechanism at the government level'. By May 2001, China had just gone through its first crisis with the Bush administration over the EP 3 spy-plane incident near Hainan and the rearmament of Taiwan, but it chose to avoid confrontation with the new US president. A senior scholar, Sun Shihai, Deputy Director of the Institute of Asia-Pacific Studies under the Chinese Academy of Social Sciences, said that the trilateral partnership should not become a strategic triangle with military components that could be aimed at a third country, especially the United States. But he did emphasize the countries' convergence of interests on issues like the establishment of a multi-polar world, a just and equitable international political and economic order, as well as opposing neo-interventionism in the name of human rights.

The most important factor that kept the idea of an 'India–Russia–China triangle' alive was the broader *'Bush Doctrine'* – the embodiment of neo-conservative determination as divulged in their bible, the 'Statement of Principles' of the The Project of the New American Century. The manifesto advocated a

'Reaganite' foreign policy of military strength and moral clarity, more specifically a significant increase in defence spending and the need to strengthen ties with democratic allies and to challenge regimes that were hostile to American interests and values. Translated into action at the outset of the Bush administration, this meant a series of unilateralist priorities such as missile defence, withdrawal from the Anti-Ballistic Missile (ABM) Treaty, creation of a high-tech rapid-reaction military with overwhelming scope and power and a revitalization of the American nuclear weapons' industry. Bush first made his intentions firmly clear and then expressed willingness to talk, but as consultations, not as negotiations – in other words, you can express your opinion and we will listen but it will not affect our plans.

Renewed Russia–China Friendship Treaty

After US President Bush met with Russian President Putin in Slovenia on 16 June 2001, Russia and China signed a fully fledged bilateral friendship and cooperation treaty in July 2001, which stressed that its aim was not to recreate the old Cold War military alliance while also insisting that it was not directed against any country. Since the Mao–Stalin Pact of 1950, which had so scared the West, had quietly lapsed in 1979, it was the first time that Russia and China had concluded a major bilateral treaty. Yet analysts on both sides acknowledged that they saw the current relationship as a counterweight to the United States' status as the world's only superpower. Liliya F. Shevtsova, an analyst at the Carnegie Moscow Centre think tank, viewed Moscow's recent moves towards Beijing – at least in part – as a message to the Bush administration: 'The Kremlin is sending Washington a warning that if there is no change for the better in relations between Moscow and Washington – now at their coolest in years – Russia is quite ready to strike a closer alliance with Beijing', she said. India was not part of the project at that time because it had shown early enthusiasm for Bush's 'new concepts of deterrence, moving beyond the constraints of the 30-year-old ABM treaty and work[ing] toward deploying a ballistic-missile-defence system'.

According to one analysis, Putin mulled over China during his visit: whether to strike some kind of loose alliance with Beijing – and India? – to counter US supremacy. 'There was a month or two when it could have gone either way', one senior US official said during the negotiations about a new treaty to be signed by Putin and Bush on 24 May 2002, 'until Putin figured out that the Chinese didn't have a lot to offer'.

After the airborne assaults on the World Trade Centre and the Pentagon on '9/11', Putin was the first foreign leader to get through to Bush on the telephone. Condoleezza Rice, then National Security Adviser, conveyed to Washington Post columnist Jim Hoagland that there had been a steady evolution towards a strategic Russian choice that this crisis seems to have confirmed: 'That Russian choice is seen at the White House, as I understand it, to be one of pursuing alliance with and integration into the West rather than flirting with a Third Way strategy built on partnership with China and others who want to reduce American influence abroad'. The US design was clearly to bring Russia into a unidirectional – that is, subservient – partnership with the United States so as to lessen China's leverage on global questions, including missile defence. Sensing that Russia had a special role to play in Bush's 'war on terror', Putin seized the opportunity to recast US–Russia relations after ten years of decline and succeeded in reclaiming Russia's place at the big table. When Bush formally abrogated the ABM Treaty on 13 December 2001, Russia's response was to state pragmatically that it was no longer bound by the 1993 accord known as Start II, which outlawed multiple-warhead missiles and other especially destabilizing weapons in the two nations' strategic arsenals. Putin realized that it was better to accept grudgingly, rather than to resist NATO expansion as Yeltsin had done, and then later to back down.

Beijing responded in a very different way to Bush's ABM announcement. The Chinese considered it as targeted at them, not at the Russians. The Russians would under any subsequent missile agreement always retain enough warheads to overwhelm any future US National Missile Defence, whereas the Chinese only had a very small nuclear arsenal.

China said that the US plans to develop a multi-billion dollar defence system that would shoot down incoming missiles would undercut the deterrent value of its own small nuclear arsenal – about two dozen missiles capable of reaching the United States – and a successful missile umbrella could be stretched to protect arch-rival Taiwan.

The United States, however, has told China repeatedly that it is developing the missile shield to counter surprise attacks from 'rogue states' like North Korea and Iraq [sic!] and that the policy was not being pursued with China in mind. Beijing also feared that the Bush administration's action will mean that nations will no longer agree to any nuclear disarmament control treaties. This could push China into a regional arms race with India and Pakistan. "We have enough domestic concerns. An arms race is only a rich man's game. A poor man cannot play", said Professor Niu Jun, US foreign policy expert at Beijing University's Institute of International Studies. In the end, China's muted response showed that it had decided that there was nothing that it could do and that it was intent on maintaining stable relations with the United States.

While Russia's new Friendship and Cooperation Treaty with China, which was signed in July 2001, seemed to set both on a new strategic course, '9/11' had clearly turned Russia's priorities around. Despite Bush's initial ABM shock, Presidents Putin and Bush in May 2002 opened an entirely new relationship with the signing of a treaty that committed both countries to reducing their nuclear arsenals from about 6,000 warheads each to no more than 2,200 by the end of 2012. With the renewed Russo-American rapport, China appeared to be the loser, as reflected in Chinese President Jiang Zemin's reminder of the first anniversary of the new Sino-Russian strategic partnership, which should have paved the way towards a multi-polar world. China was the leading member in the newly founded Shanghai Cooperation Organization (SCO), and now in the wake of '9/11' US military bases were at China's doorstep in Uzbekistan and Kyrgyzstan, with Russia's approval.

'China–Russia Relations Remain Better than Russia–US Ties'

In December 2002 Russian President Vladimir Putin visited China to reassure the Chinese about the relevance and validity of the Russian-Chinese strategic partnership (first agreed in 1996 and consolidated by their Friendship Treaty in 2001). Despite recurrent frustrations about US hegemony, Putin wanted to maintain good relations with the United States while disagreeing with US President Bush's approach to terrorism. On the day of Putin's arrival in Beijing, the People's Daily published an article under the headline 'China–Russia Relations Remain Better than Russia–US Ties'. The Pravda newspaper explained that Putin himself had complained to Chinese journalists about NATO expansion, which under the current global situation of terrorism and nuclear issues was a negative development. Another new cloud above the US–Russia relationship was the imminent Anglo-American invasion of Iraq, which Russia energetically and China ephemerally tried to block.

After Beijing, Putin went to India where he again tried to sell the idea of a strategic partnership or 'strategic triangle' in Asia for Russia, China and India – with Moscow taking the lead. Putin tried to convince India of the compatibility of the triangle with good bilateral cross-relations between all involved, defining the triangle not as an anti-US coalition but just as a *'counterpoint'* to the US. Putin's aim, analysts say, is traditionally Russian – to centre Moscow solidly between East and West, Atlantic and Pacific, NATO and China.

Putin defined terrorism's main danger as secessionist movements that challenge state sovereignty. While Russia's main concern was Chechnya, China viewed the Muslim separatists in its western Xinjiang region as terrorists, and India maintained that the core problem of Kashmir was Pakistani-based terrorism. Putin supported the Indian view, but the United States viewed Pakistan as an indispensable ally in its wider 'war on terror' and China would also never renege on its key geostrategic alliance with Pakistan. From its defeat of India in the 1962 Border War, Pakistan was China's tool for keeping Soviet ally India off-balance and, more recently, China's back door to the Indian Ocean, Arabian Sea and the Persian Gulf.

The heart of Indo-Russian relations is defence cooperation and it embraces the joint production of Brahmos cruise missiles and the joint manufacture of advanced submarines. The SU-30 project is engaging almost all of the production capacities of Hindustan Aeronautics. Consequently, the aviation industries in both India and Russia have acquired the capacity to undertake the joint development, production and marketing of medium-range transport aircraft.

After the Anglo-American invasion of Iraq there were – not surprisingly – renewed calls for a 'Moscow–Beijing–New Delhi triangle', a potential alliance of three nuclear-armed countries of some 2.5 billion people that would theoretically be able to balance US power in coming years. Indian Prime Minister Atal Bihari Vajpayee had just concluded a successful visit to China and the two countries had expressed similar views on the American war on Iraq. All three countries were disturbed by the blatant disregard of the United Nations and protested against what they viewed as a rejection of the rules of the international game.

Russia, China and India still back the primacy of the United Nations Security Council in solving crises, and support the principle of non-intervention in the internal affairs of sovereign states. Apart from shared concerns over US dominance, the three have other common interests and mutually reinforcing needs. All three are weary of militant Islamic groups and want stability in Central Eurasia. The main weakness in the triangle, however, comes from China's and India's competitive relationship, with both holding conflicting visions of regional dominance, with China so far the winner. While Russia and China are opposed to US Theatre Missile Defence (TMD), which is in clear violation of the ABM Treaty, India offered its enthusiastic support to the United States. China, too, has a stake in Kashmir in the areas bordering Xinjiang and is a major arms' supplier to Pakistan. In short, Sino-Indian relations would continue to remain a stumbling block for materialization of the strategic triangle for which Russia had been canvassing.

But the arms' sale relationship between Russia and the two Asian countries was growing steadily. The trade provides Moscow with billions of much-needed dollars and important arms' export markets, while Beijing and New Delhi get sophisticated armaments ranging from combat aircraft to submarines. In 2003, Russia and India held their first joint naval exercises in the Indian Ocean, when a large task force of Russian surface ships and nuclear attack submarines simulated attacks on aircraft-carrier groups. The naval exercise was coordinated with a mission by long-range bombers. On 13 May 2003, several Russian strategic bombers – Tu-95 Bears and Tu-160 Blackjacks – flew from a base in Central Russia to the Indian Ocean to simulate an attack by long-range cruise missiles.

It has, however, been argued that the trilateral axis could hardly be feasible because the Indian nuclear and missile programme is not so much aimed at Pakistan, but is in fact deterrence against Chinese nuclear warheads. The would-be triangle is also seen as implausible because India and China also happen to be competing economies. Moreover, Russia and China have already solved their border disputes, while China and India are still divided by a chunk of barren terrain and the granting of asylum to the Dalai Lama and thousands of his followers. There have also been warnings that a well-armed and strong China may one day not just make Russia its junior partner, but even pose a threat to Russia's resource-rich Far East.

The 'Trialogues': No 'Equilateral' Triangle

On 3 September 2003 the first *'trialogue'* of the foreign ministers of Russia, China and India took place in New York. The three countries together represent the vast majority of the global population and theoretically could be able to balance US power in coming years. After the US invasion of Iraq, there was again more shared opposition to US policies than in previous years. India had new doubts about a closer relationship with the United States. As a counterweight to Islamic terrorism and at the behest of the United States, India had growing military ties with Israel, which were a very divisive issue in a country with the second largest Muslim population in the world after Indonesia. Bush had failed to condemn or even to mention terrorism in Kashmir in his UN speech earlier in the week. At the official level 'the dialogue between Moscow, Beijing and New Delhi will continue', said Russian Foreign Minister

Igor Ivanov, adding that the three nations have a shared interest in a 'multi-polar and just world'.

Russian President Vladimir Putin had been particularly insistent upon the triangle during his December 2004 visit to India. But China had so far resisted, and it is unlikely that India will be a party to overt anti-American actions in Central or South Asia, even though it will clearly collaborate more with China on trade and energy issues and for anti-terrorism purposes may even liaise with the Shanghai Cooperation Organization (SCO) now that China has offered it such an opportunity.

In April 2005, when China's major cities were shaken by violent anti-Japanese demonstrations, Chinese Premier Wen Jiabao was on an official visit to New Delhi. Wen used the occasion to pledge Chinese 'support for India's aspirations to play an active role in the UN and international affairs'. Part of the Indian media 'over-interpreted' this as Chinese support for Indian permanent membership of a reformed United Nations Security Council. Wen and his Indian counterpart Manmohan Singh signed a broad-based 'India-China Strategic and Cooperative Partnership for Peace and Prosperity', of which the main content was a five-year pact for cooperation in five high-tech sectors, in which these two fastest growing 'elephant economies' (that is, mammoth versions of 'tiger economies') have optimal synergy: India in software; China in hardware. The hope of China's Prime Minister Wen Jiabao was that an India–Russia–China axis will 'democratize international relations', a pointed indictment of US hegemonism. India, for its part, wanted improved cooperation with the dynamic economies of East Asia, a bigger regional role and a counterweight to Chinese and US sponsorship of Pakistan. Indian Prime Minister Manmohan Singh observed: 'India and China can together reshape the world order'.

The April 2005 Sino-Indian strategic partnership followed less than one decade after the establishment of the Sino-Russian strategic partnership, which was triggered by the United States dispatching two carrier-led task forces to the Taiwan Straits in 1996 in response to Chinese missile tests, and as a warning to the Taiwan electorate not to vote for independence. (Then) Chinese Premier Li Peng stated that the strategic partnership between the two countries would help to correct the 'balance of forces' in the world. This went in tandem with the 'Shanghai Declaration', to set up a security body of China, Russia and three former Central Asian Soviet republics, initially named the 'Shanghai Five', which aimed to counter further inroads by the US and NATO into the region and which in 2001 was renamed the Shanghai Cooperation Organization.

India and Russia had also concluded a strategic partnership in 2000. Under the accord, the two countries agreed to develop a common strategy in dealing with Afghanistan. Both New Delhi and Moscow were concerned that the radical Islamic agenda of the Taliban was having an impact on areas such as India's Kashmir and Chechnya in Russia. President Putin stressed Russia's unqualified support for India's bid for permanent membership of the UN Security Council, something that China was ambiguous about in 2005 and explicitly opposed in subsequent years as India moved closer to the United States. Nevertheless, China, India and Russia were now tied together by three bilateral strategic partnerships, of which two, Russia–China and Russia–India, had a robust arms' supply relationship as the strongest component, and the third, the Sino-Indian, had the least military–strategic content.

Vladivostok: Russia's Far Eastern Metropolis

Soon after this promising improvement in India–China relations, the new Russian Foreign Minister Sergei Lavrov met with his Chinese and Indian counterparts, Li Zhaoxing and Natwar Singh, in June 2005 in Vladivostok, their first meeting outside of a multilateral forum. They discussed security and this time also energy security and especially regional stability, considering the waves of instability that were engulfing Uzbekistan and Kyrgyzstan, which were allegedly instigated by Western-inspired *'orange revolutions'*. The symbolical event, the signing of a China–Russia border agreement that had been negotiated for four decades and that concerned two per cent of the 4,300-kilometre border, should set an example for China and India. China and Russia had fought a short border war on an island in the Ussuri River in 1969 but were reaching a final settlement now. Why couldn't China and India ? In terms of concrete results, the meeting produced a communiqué that did not mention the term 'strategic triangle' but stressed that it is in the interests of the three countries to strengthen their trilateral partnership, and that the mutually beneficial cooperation will contribute to the consolidation of peace and stability in Asia and the world at large. The selection of Vladivostok as the venue can be viewed as emphasizing Russia's status as an Asian power along with India and China.

A commentator in the Russian magazine Kommersant wrote that former Russian Prime Minister Yevgeny Primakov's dream had come true, as his 1998 'triangle' was designed to curb US influence, specifically the 2005 fight against 'colour revolutions' in former Soviet Republics:

In fact, yesterday's meeting in Vladivostok witnessed that Russia and China agree to create their own alliance to fight 'colour revolutions' in Central Asia. Lavrov stated that the uprising in Andijan was nothing else than 'the operation of Islamic extremists, Taliban leftovers and some Chechen terrorists'.

By putting responsibility for the Andijan events on international terrorists, Lavrov expressed solidarity with Beijing's official position. China is a most ardent supporter of Uzbek President Islam Karimov's 'fight with terrorism', including the slaughter in Andijan. This means that Russia is ready to share responsibility with China for everything that goes on in the region. This would be the first step to create a joint military bastion of Moscow and Beijing, which would be protecting Central Asian regimes from 'colour revolutions' and excessive American penetration into the region.

It would soon be clear, however, that Lavrov's and the commentator's rhetoric were too premature and way over the top. India was improving its relations with China, but far more substantially with the United States. The US is a huge trading partner for India and China, and Russia will not be able to compete at this point, at least not for the foreseeable future. Moreover, the Bush administration had in the meantime lifted restrictions on arms' deliveries to India, which was going to cause problems for Russian defence exports to India, and Washington did not have intentions of making such a concession to China. In addition, Sergei

Karagonov, the Chairman of the Presidium of the Russian Council for Foreign Defence Policy, was convinced that Primakov's idea was not viable. He emphasized that none of the three countries would want to join a coalition in direct opposition to the United States.

Nevertheless, the 'Vladivostok Trio' had given some other substance to Primakov's triangle. The trio stressed the primacy of the United Nations, which the United States is sometimes inclined to bypass, and the need to reform it. The demand for 'consistent, sustained and comprehensive opposition to terrorism without any double standards' was a warning that India, Russia and China consider murderous secessionists in Kashmir, Chechnya or Xinjiang as dangerous as the US considers Osama Bin Laden and al-Qaeda. They also wanted the global oil economy to recognize Russia as one of the world's largest fuel producers, and India and China among the biggest consumers. To that end, India, which has put US$ 1 billion in Russia's Sakhalin-I project and might invest more, would host a meeting in October 2005 of Asia's principal oil producers and buyers. This would be another feather in the cap of India's Minister of Oil, Mani Shankar Aiyar.

In the energy sector, China and India for a long time seemed to become rivals that might get into armed conflict over oil and minerals. In January 2006, India and China put aside their energy rivalry. The two states' oil majors – CNPC and ONGC – signed a mega-pact for joint bidding in Central Asia, the Caspian Sea Region, Africa and Latin America. Indian Minister of Oil M.S. Aiyar explained that fierce Sino-Indian competition had driven prices up further: "Wherever the Indians have gone, the Chinese are already there", wrote Madhu Nainan, chief editor of Petrowatch, a market intelligence newsletter in India. "Mostly, it is India that needs cooperation with China – and not the other way around." The biggest energy issue between the US and India is the construction of a 2,775 kilometres (or 1,725 miles), US$ 7.5 billion gas pipeline from Iran through Pakistan to India, which has already been under negotiation for fifteen years. India adamantly rejects any US pressure over its millennia-old relations with another ancient Asian empire: Persia, or Iran.

When Indian Prime Minister Manmohan Singh announced in March 2006, with the visiting US President George Bush at his side in New Delhi, that the two had reached agreement on a 'historic' civilian nuclear pact, China and Russia felt that their reluctant triangular partner was compromising its 'independent foreign policy' and that India felt that it had to reinforce its credentials that it was not a second Japan and would not subordinate its foreign policy autonomy to Washington. The countries' three leaders – Manmohan Singh, Hu Jintao and Vladimir Putin – met in a so-called 'outreach session' during the G8 summit in St. Petersburg in July 2006, which underlined that the latter two had now been accepted as crucial players in the world. But the three also held their first trilateral summit, the first of its kind among the three countries. The current G8 have 45 per cent of the world's GDP, whereas inclusion of China and India would move this to the 60 per cent level, thus enhancing the forum's ability to influence global political and economic relations. "Our approaches to key international problems are very close or, as the diplomats say, they practically coincide", Putin said in his opening remarks. Putin threw his support behind proposals to expand the G8 by including India, China and other outreach countries that Russia had invited to attend the summit: "Without such countries as India and China it is impossible to solve global economic and financial problems", he said. Putin outlined a new political agenda for the G8 to help mould a new multi-polar world. "Our world has not become safer after the collapse of the bipolar world", he said. "On the contrary, it has become less predictable. [...] We do not have the tools and instruments to address the challenges of today". An expanded G8 may become such a tool: "What mankind is concerned with today, what we are doing in G8 is to try and work out a new architecture of international relations", Putin concluded.

THE SINO-RUSSIAN RELATIONSHIP IN THE 21ST CENTURY

Since the end of the Cold War, Russia and China have been the only permanent U.N. Security Council members, whose political systems are undemocratic (Grant, 2012: 16). This is one of the main reasons why China and Russia cooperate on a wide range of international issues in an effort to counterbalance the United States and other Western countries. However, there is one important difference in these countries' statuses in global affairs. China's increasing role in world politics is widely associated with its extraordinary economic growth, whereas Russia's assertive posture in the international arena stems from Moscow's nostalgia of its former superpower status and relatively high energy prices, which allowed the Kremlin to salvage its faltering economy after 2000 (Larson and Shevchenko, 2010: 64). Thus, internal weaknesses and fears of U.S. power make Russia and China hold similar positions on many global issues. Moscow and Beijing remain strongly committed to the principle of noninterference in internal affairs of sovereign states mainly due to domestic problems and regional separatism. Further, both countries maintain relations with the pariah states, including North Korea, Iran, Cuba, Myanmar, and Syria, and object to Western sanctions against these regimes. For instance, in 2005, China and Russia blocked U.S. sanctions against Myanmar the Security Council, labeling such efforts as "meddling in internal affairs." The same held true for China and Russia's position on sanctions against Burma (2007), Sri Lanka (2009), Zimbabwe (2008), and, most lately, Syria (2012). With regard to regional affairs, Russia and China cooperate on trade and security issues within the Shanghai Cooperation Organization, but the latter is far from being considered a substantive body, in part, due to disputes between Moscow and Beijing over leadership in the organization (Scheineson, 2009).

The economic partnership between Moscow and Beijing remains the weakest aspect of bilateral relations. Although the volume of bilateral trade has been growing steadily throughout the previous decade reaching $60 billion in 2010, it is still far below its potential. One of the reasons underlying slow progress in establishing closer economic ties between Russia and China is the difference in patterns of economic growth. Accordingly, the strengthening of Russian national currency and a rise in international energy and raw material prices fuelled Russia's economic growth in the 2000s. These developments had a positive impact on Sino-Russian economic relations (Moshes and Nojonen, 2011: 43). However, bilateral trade during 1996-2010 was marked by the decrease in Russia's exports of machinery and transport equipment from 17.7 per cent to 1.3 per cent, whereas exports of raw materials to China increased from 7.1 per cent to 20.6 per cent. By contrast, China's exports of machinery and transport equipment increased from 5.7 per cent in 1996 to 35.4 per cent in 2010, while manufactured goods started to constitute 18.6 per cent of China's exports to Russia as opposed to 7 per cent in 1996. Despite the fact that Sino-Russian trade has been growing remarkably in the last decade (Itoh and Kuchins, 2011), the above-mentioned economic disparity in trade capacities raises grave anxieties that Russia is gradually becoming a "junior partner" in Sino-Russian economic relations, or a natural resource appendage (*pridatok*) to China (Kutchins, 2010: 33). Russia's exports of energy resources to China are likely to either remain on the same level or may even increase in light of Russia's inability to reform its economic structure and China's growing demand for natural resources.

Conclusions

The strategic triangle among the United States, China, and the Soviet union has undergone a host of vicissitudes throughout the last four decades of the Cold War, culminating in a unipolar world order based on U.S. dominance in international relations. The collapse of the power balance within the triangular system in 1991 had a consequential impact on Sino-Russian relations and U.S.-Chinese relations alike. As regards the U.S.-Russian relationship in the new millennium, both powers attempted to forge closer ties with China, albeit not simultaneously, when relations between Washington in Moscow deteriorated. By the end of the 1990s China and Russia began to express their dissatisfaction with U.S. unilateralism, and such a stance was reflected in the countries' shared vision of a multipolar world and the concept of the "strategic relationship directed towards the 21st century." Despite grandiose proclamations of the "strategic partnership," shared vision of a multipolar world, and increased diplomatic cooperation, Sino-Russian relations are utterly lacking in substance. Much like during the Cold War, the relationship between Moscow and Beijing is based upon counterbalancing the United States in global politics, for cleavages within the strategic triangle among the three powers have generally led to the reorientation of China and Russia's foreign policies in the 1990s and late 2000s.

In so far as economic relations between Moscow and Beijing are concerned, notwithstanding increased economic interaction, neither country truly regards another as a strategic partner. Russia still considers its relations with the European Union indispensable, while the United States remains priority for China (Kotkin, 2009). This configuration is unlikely to change in the future: besides military hardware and natural resources, there is little Russia can offer to its "strategic partner." Likewise, most joint projects between Russia and China are aimed at enhancing energy cooperation through building oil and gas pipelines in Central Asia. Given the resource-oriented model of Russia's economy, Moscow will likely remain China's resource and weapons supplier for decades to come. China, for its part, has been using its "strategic" alliance with Russia as "strategic" leverage vis-à-vis Washington. Diplomatic cooperation with Moscow has helped China promote the idea of multipolarity as it relates to Beijing's national interests. It can be assumed that China's relationship with Russia will become irrelevant as soon as China becomes an independent power in global affairs.

This, in all likelihood, will mark the end of the "strategic" partnership between the two powers, paving the way for U.S.-China rivalry.

3

China's Military Strategy

It is an excellent time to reassess China's national military strategy. The next wave of significant reforms for the Chinese People's Liberation Army (PLA) is already beginning to unfold. The results of the 15th Party Congress (September 1997) and the 9th National People's Congress (NPC) (March 1998) indicate that after many years of study and debate firm decisions have been made to move forward with structural, organizational and other adjustments to China's armed forces. At the Party Congress Jiang Zemin announced a 500,000-man reduction in force size over the next three years. In the wake of the 9th NPC, a fourth General Department was created—the General Armaments Department—and the Commission for Science, Technology, and Industry for National Defence (COSTIND) was elevated to ministry status with a civilian in charge. We should expect to see more changes, although Beijing's timetable is unknown. Some change may be dramatic and public. Most will be quiet and not easily discernable, given the opaque nature of the Chinese defence establishment.

While the recent party congress and NPC serve as significant benchmarks, we must remember that they are points on a continuum of change that the PLA has been undergoing for almost two decades. *What does the PLA hope to achieve and why? How does it plan to achieve its ends?* These very basic questions, which on the surface seem so simple, are probably the most critical questions one can ask in evaluating the Chinese armed forces. They are critical questions because if one does not address these overarching issues it is difficult to make sense of all other developments: command

and doctrinal issues, organization and force structure, or hardware development and acquisition, to name a few.

To answer these basic questions we must have a framework and a context. This chapter attempts to provide such a context. It will offer a notional national military strategy for China.

There are five major assumptions implicit in this chapter. The first is that China does in fact have a national military strategy. That is, there is a rationale behind the ongoing PLA reforms. A second assumption is that outside observers can adduce that rationale, even if imperfectly, from public domain information. The third assumption is that the PLA remains subservient to the party and the state and therefore China's national military strategy is derived from and mutually supportive of Beijing's overarching national security strategy. A fourth assumption is that while there is much that is unique about China's armed forces, there is also a good deal of universality in how defence establishments go about the business of planning at the national level. A fifth assumption is that Western models can sometimes help structure a discussion of Chinese phenomena even to the point of using Chinese terminology comfortably within those constructs.

The U.S. Army War College (AWC) model of military strategy as developed by Colonel Arthur Lykke, USA (Ret.) serves as the superstructure of the following analysis of the PLA. While the PLA would certainly *not* use an American construct to articulate its national military strategy, this model is nevertheless a useful tool for the descriptive and analytic purposes of this chapter. I have also borrowed useful frames of reference from the planners on the Joint Staff who produce the Pentagon's national military strategy (which in turn is based upon a derivative of the Army War College model), as well as several universal military concepts such as "centre of gravity" and others. Into these "frames" we shall place Chinese "lenses" to articulate a vision of the bigger picture.

National Military Strategy

Before proceeding there are three terms which should be addressed: strategy, national security strategy, and national military strategy.

Strategy. Strategy is an easy word to use but is difficult to define. Most standard dictionaries are more confusing than enlightening on that particular entry because a strategy refers to a holistic system and process. Our interest in the word strategy will focus on its component parts because of their utility in analyzing the whole. The U.S. Army War College utilizes a simple but powerful formula to express what a strategy is and what its critical component parts consist of: *Strategy = Ends + Ways + Means*. In this equation "ends" are our objectives or goals, "ways" are the courses of action we choose to achieve those goals, and "means" are the resources either at hand or which must be developed to enable the courses of action.

There are three important aspects of this model to keep in mind. The first is that the three components of a strategy—ends, ways and means—are interdependent. All of the components must be appropriate to the whole and in proper balance with the others if the strategy is to be successful. The second point to keep in mind is that when we attempt to study someone else's strategy, such as the PLA's, focusing on only one component of the strategy without an understanding of the other two may lead to incorrect or incomplete conclusions. The third point is the utility of this model as an analytic tool. It is almost universal in its applicability and is not limited to military affairs. One can easily use this equation to craft, describe or analyze political or economic strategies. Also, in the realm of military planning it is applicable across the three levels of warfare—the strategic, operational and tactical levels.

National Security Strategy. American analysts often use the term "national security strategy" or "security strategy" in the context of a nation's military concerns or military-related issues. This chapter adopts a variant of the much broader definition used by the U.S. Joint Chiefs of Staff. A National Security Strategy (NSS) will refer to the development, application and coordination of all the elements of national power (political/diplomatic, economic, informational, military, sociological/cultural) to achieve a nation's objectives in domestic and international affairs in peace as well as in war. In pursuing the national objectives set forth in a NSS, multiple strategies co-exist: an economic strategy, a political strategy, a diplomatic strategy, a social strategy, and a military strategy, at the very least. There are two points to make about this definition. First, Lykke's equation is still a valid construct. A national security strategy will have to articulate ends (objectives), ways (courses of action), and means (resources). Also, it should be noted that the military element of national power is a subset within the broader national security strategy. This brings us to a description of a national military strategy.

National Military Strategy. A National Military Strategy (NMS) is the military component of a nation's overall National Security Strategy. Its objectives are derived from those within the overarching NSS. It is the role of the national military leadership to ensure that the military element of national power will be available to contribute to the NSS in both peace and war, in the here and now and in the future. The NMS is the vehicle through which the national military leadership articulates, revalidates, and adjusts the ends, ways, and means of the armed forces to comport with changing NSS objectives, a changing security environment, or changes in the availability of national resources to be applied to the armed forces. A national military strategy is usually influenced by civil political and economic decisions. Consequently, national military strategies are dynamic and require constant review, revision and updating. At the national level of military planning—the level at which a NMS is generated—direction, guidance and policies are articulated in broad terms to steer the armed forces in the correct direction. Specific decisions, programs and detailed planning follow in due course.

Once again, the equation is still valid. A NMS must articulate ends, ways and means. In the case of a NMS, the equation is rewritten to reflect the national level of military strategy: *National Military Strategy = National Military Objectives + National Military Strategic Concepts + National Military Resources*. National Military Objectives (NMOs) will be derived from the NSS. The National Military Strategic Concepts (NMSC) will articulate the courses of action that will be undertaken to achieve the ends. The National Military Resources (NMRs) describe the types of capabilities that will be required to be on hand or be developed to enable the NMSCs.

The starting point for crafting a NMS is the articulation of NMOs. From these are developed NMSCs and NMRs. But before articulating NMSCs strategic planners first must use a critical "strategic filter" that identifies the imperatives of conflict and the possible constraints planners may have to consider. At minimum, the strategic filter: (1) considers political decisions handed down to military planners or brokered between military and civilian leaders; (2) assesses the current and projected security environments (conflict with whom? when?); and (3) performs an analysis of the operational environment (what kinds of conflicts?).

The synergistic relationship between the three elements of a NMS is readily apparent. If the resources are not available to enable the NMSCs, then weighty political-military decisions are in order: either adjust the NMOs and NMSCs or commit the resources (usually funding) to develop the NMRs. But such a zero-sum set of decisions is usually unacceptable for political reasons and impractical for reasons of national security. Consequently, at the national level of military planning, the NMS often encompasses multiple substrategies for different time frames. At a minimum, one strategy must be focused on current capabilities and near-term contingencies. Another should consider the requirements of coping with future potential security problems. Crafting military strategies for the here and now while accounting for over-the-horizon problems is a conundrum that is encountered almost exclusively at the national level of military planning and, save success in war, is probably the ultimate test of a nation's generalship.

With the preceding discussion behind us we can now move on to consider the case of China. To do so we will take the iterative and dynamic process that is used to *craft* an NMS, which is a cyclical process, and artificially stretch it out in linear fashion in order to be *descriptive* of its components.

China's National Military Strategy

The national military strategy that will now be discussed finds its roots in the late 1970s and early 1980s, when Deng Xiaoping reassessed the international security environment and made the decision to make economic modernization the central task for the coming decades. Deng's decisions not only sent the Chinese nation down a new and different path, but sent the PLA down a new road as well. It stands to reason that a modernizing, outward-looking China seeking a leading role in the mainstream of the international order would require a new type of defence establishment and a new military strategic direction than that of a previously autarkic China seeking to lead the "Third World." What follows then is a description of what Chinese strategic planners might term the general thrust of the national military strategy "during the new historical period" and into "the cross-century period." It is current to the extent that the latest policy decisions coming out of the 15th Party Congress and 9th National People's Congress are incorporated as adjustments. But we should bear in mind that the general direction of China's NMS has been evolving for more than a decade. Consequently, there is both continuity and change to report.

National Military Objectives

China's national military strategy seeks to achieve three sets of national military objectives: *Protect the Party and Safeguard Stability, Defend Sovereignty and Defeat Aggression,* and *Modernize the Military and Build the Nation.*

These three objectives not only define what it is the PLA must achieve as a military force, but highlights the unique role it plays in the political economy of the PRC. Significantly, these three national military objectives are derived from and are mutually supportive of China's three national security objectives. The formulation of these three national military objectives are strictly those of the author's and not authoritative PRC formulations. However, they should be familiar to students of the PLA because China's top military leaders often allude to them or aspects of them in public statements.

For example, in the April 1998 issue of *International Strategic Studies,* Deputy Chief of the General Staff Lieutenant General Xiong Guangkai states that the "basic objectives" of China's armed forces are to "consolidate national defence, resist aggression, defend the nation's sovereignty over its territorial land, sea, airspace as well as its maritime interests, and safeguard national unity and security."

In May 1998 Chief of the General Staff Department (GSD) General Fu Quanyou provided this iteration: "the PLA's mission is to strengthen the national defence, fend off aggression, safeguard territorial sovereignty and the rights and interests of territorial waters, and maintain national integrity and safety." As yet another example, in 1996 Defence Minister Chi Haotian offered that the "basic objectives" of China's national defence are to "solidify the defensive capacity, resist foreign invasion, and safeguard the unification and security of the country."

Although the three national military objectives that this chapter posits are seemingly self-explanatory, it is worthwhile to briefly discuss each because through them we achieve a greater appreciation of just what it is the PLA is attempting to achieve, the challenges it faces, and a flavor for the organizational culture of this massive defence establishment.

Protect the Party and Safeguard Stability. The first and foremost mission entrusted to the PLA, and a national military objective, is to be the guardian of the CCP. The past two decades of professionalization and modernization have not altered the fundamental fact that the institutional loyalty of China's armed forces and the personal commitment of it top leaders is to the maintenance of the regime and the primacy of the CCP. The PLA remains the party's army. China's "national command authorities" are the leaders of the Central Military Commission (CMC), which is a party organization under the Central Committee. It is worth remembering that it has only been 71 years since the "Red Army" was founded. The revolutionary heritage of that army and its roots as a communist insurgent force that saved the fledgling CCP from annihilation in the 1920s and 1930s is not too distant a memory for some of the current PLA leaders. Minister of Defence and CMC Vice Chairman General Chi Haotian (66 years old) joined the PLA as a young man in the early 1940s during the "twin struggles" against the Nationalists and the Japanese and he spent a good part of his later career as a senior political commissar. The constant self-propagandizing within the PLA to remind the troops that the party is the focus of their loyalty has not abated as the Chinese armed forces have attempted to become a more proficient military force.

Indeed, the first among the "Five General Requirements" issued by Jiang Zemin for all PLA soldiers is to be "politically qualified."

It is often argued that today the party and ideology mean less and less in China. For the general populace and even some civil cadre that may be truer than not. However, the party and ideology still count for quite a lot in the PLA. The "new nationalism" that has been ascribed to the PLA is not necessarily at the expense of the Party and it may just be that in today's China the PLA is the only institution over which the CCP "centre" in Beijing still has near total control from one end of the nation to the other. The constant public affirmations of the PLA's top leaders of the primacy of the Party is no more empty rhetoric than the statements of the top U.S. military leadership affirming the primacy of the Constitution and the principle of civilian control over the military.

In August 1997, PLA Academy of Military Sciences Commandant General Xu Huizi encapsulated many of the above thoughts in an article in *China Military Science*.

> After entering the new historical period, Deng Xiaoping repeatedly stressed that our military situation is that of the party commanding the gun, instead of the gun commanding the party; the military must follow the party's instructions, and must not at any time wave its own flag.... Comrade Jiang Zemin referred to the principle of the party commanding the gun as our military 'soul.'

For these reasons, the PLA must be prepared to defend the CCP with military force against domestic challenges as well as external threats. Over the past few years much of the internal security mission of the PLA has passed to the People's Armed Police (PAP). However, the PAP is ultimately under the control of the CMC and the "regular" PLA has not been absolved from its requirement to provide for the defence of the party. One of the many reasons the PLA was called upon to converge on Beijing in the Spring of 1989 was because the PAP was incapable of handling a situation that was viewed by the CCP leadership to be burgeoning into a direct threat to the rule of the regime and the CCP. The PLA also pursues the related military objective of safeguarding internal stability. Some domestic challenges and threats may be aimed at the state, not the party per se. Examples would be acts of violence by separatist factions in non-Han China such as in Tibet or Xinjiang. Still other threats to stability with which the PLA must deal are natural disasters and manmade disasters. In these situations the PLA is often called upon to provide disaster relief, internal humanitarian assistance, as well as fight back the forces of nature such as floods or large-scale fires.

At the risk of being guilty of unsubstantiated generalization, I would offer that the top leadership of the PLA remains a very conservative group, which is virulently opposed to any domestic circumstance that could lead to instability (*luan*). The up-and-coming generation of leaders (colonel and above) are probably no less so. The chaos of the Cultural Revolution touched many of this latter generation personally and tragically and they fully understand the cost China paid in terms of development and modernization. And if in their hearts some dismiss as irrelevant Communist ideology, they may still see the CCP as the only political force in China that can successfully keep the nation together and lead it into the future.

Defend Sovereignty and Defeat Aggression. This national military objective brings us to the classical warfighting mission of the Chinese armed forces. Militaries exist to fight and so does the PLA. It is worth pointing out that the PLA considers itself a defensive force. Its leaders often declare that China since 1949 has never fought a war of aggression and has gone to war only when other nations have attacked China first or threatened its territory. Officially, Chinese will argue that their intervention in Korea (1950), the war against India (1962), the Sino-Soviet clashes of the late 1960s, and the incursion against Vietnam (1979) were all conflicts foisted upon China in defence of its sovereignty. Hence, they would couch their warfighting objective in terms of defence against aggression and the preservation of the nation's sovereignty. Moreover, the PLA rejects the notion of fighting as part of a formal alliance, proudly claiming that no Chinese combat troops are stationed on foreign soil, nor does Beijing desire to do so.

However, as mentioned earlier, China's definition of "sovereignty" is much broader than just the sanctity of its borders. The PLA defence of China's sovereignty also includes being capable and prepared to employ force to achieve national unification and assert Beijing's maritime rights. Chi Haotian has commented directly on these points in the past. In a May 1996 interview he was reported to comment that China's national defence policy "is aimed at protecting China's territorial land, waters, and air space as well as China's maritime rights and interests against foreign aggression. It is also aimed at safeguarding China's unity.... In the last decade, Beijing's use of the PLA to assert its claims to resources in the South China Sea has raised a great deal of concern within the region and beyond. As far as China's unification goes, only the issue of Taiwan remains unresolved. Although Beijing claims it prefers to settle this issue in a peaceful manner, China's leaders will not renounce the use of force. This puts a tremendous amount of pressure on the PLA for obvious reasons. As we review China's analysis of its security environment later in this chapter, it will become clear just how much the PLA must accomplish as a professional military force.

Modernize the Military and Build the Nation. The modernization of the military deserves its own place among the PLA's national military objectives. The top civilian and uniformed leadership of the PRC consider China's overall modernization and the modernization of the military (often referred to as "army building") to be mutually dependent and supporting national objectives. "Strengthening national defence and army building," declared Jiang Zemin at the 15th Party Congress, "is the basic guarantee for national security and the modernization drive."

The Chinese believe that without a modernizing and capable military the nation will not be able to enjoy the security from external threats it requires to continue to concentrate on economic reform. Without a capable military China cannot secure the internal stability it requires to modernize in the civil sector. Without a capable and modernizing military China cannot hope to secure any of its national security objectives in the realms of sovereignty or unification. Finally, without a modern PLA whose capabilities ultimately comport with China's (anticipated) economic, technological, and political strength, the PRC will not be able to take its seat at the table of world leaders in Beijing's much hoped for multipolar international order. While both civil and military leaders subscribe to these views, the tension in the system revolves around the fact that military modernization is not proceeding at the same pace as economic modernization. Moreover, by long-standing political fiat going back to the beginning of the Dengist period, the decision *not* to invest state treasure in military modernization at the expense of economic reform still stands. Jiang Zemin reaffirmed this tenet at the 9th NPC in March 1998. Speaking to a full session of the PLA's delegation to the NPC, Jiang lectured that:

It is also very important to correctly handle the relationship between economic development and the building of national defence. Building a modernized army and national defence is a guarantee for the country's safety and modernization drive. This is something the whole party and the whole nation always care very much about. The level of China's productive forces is still not high, and our economy is not that strong. Therefore, we must concentrate our energies on economic development. *Without a highly developed economy, it is also impossible to promote the modernization of national defence and the army. We must always insist on taking economic development as the central task while paying adequate attention to modernizing national defence...*

Outwardly, at least, the top PLA leadership supports this basic line and does not question its validity. A serious challenge to the party leadership on this account should not be anticipated. Yet, as the men who are responsible for modernizing the military in a world (as we will later see) which they view as basically hostile, they do evince concern about how far behind economic development military modernization can lag. For example, General Xu Huizi has cautioned that "we must also understand that national wealth does not equate to military strength; there are many examples both past and present, in China and overseas, where a nation has been wealthy while its military was weak. We must try to keep our military quality development level at a level compatible with national defence security; keeping it at a level appropriate to China's international status as a great nation is a choice on which we must insist." Defence Minister Chi Haotian made a more direct commentary on this point in 1996 in a lengthy article in *Qiushi*. "The building of national defence," stated Chi, "cannot exceed the limitation of tolerance of economic construction, *nor can it be laid aside until the economy has totally prospered*."

As a result of this contradiction, the leadership of the PLA is going to have to be very focused in how it approaches the modernization of the military. The decisions they make (and are making) in this regard will to a large extent drive some of the major national military strategic concepts in their overall NMS.

The corollary to "modernizing the military" is "building the nation." Not only is the PLA's modernization expected not to be a drain on the state's coffers, but military modernization is also expected to enhance the economic, scientific and technological level of the state. The military, says Chi Haotian, is expected to do so by leading and participating in "key state projects," by bringing science and technology to the rural areas of China, by transferring superior military technologies to the civilian sector, by providing the nation with a pool of PLA veterans who are technically advanced relative to their civilian counterparts (the PLA as a "big school"), and providing infrastructure to the hinterlands.

These, then, are the broad national military objectives the PLA seeks to achieve. To achieve these goals China's military planners need to articulate strategic concepts, or courses of action. Before they can do that, however, they must think through the environment in which they must operate, now and in the future. They must employ a "filter" that highlights both challenges and opportunities.

China's National Security Objectives

China's national security strategy has been apparent and quite public for over two decades and there is no need to detail it here. The political reports from the 13th,14th and 15th Party Congresses, the work reports associated with meetings of the National People's Congress (NPC), and a good number of key decisions and policies emanating from Central Committee plenums and NPC Standing Committee meetings have all become increasingly public over the years. From the time Deng Xiaoping consolidated his power in the late 1970s, observing and analyzing the ends, ways, and means of that strategy has defined the essence of China-watching. The "Four Modernizations," "Reform and Opening Up," "Economic Construction as the Central Task," and other phrases coined by the Chinese to describe *aspects* of their strategy are all quite familiar even to the casual student of Chinese affairs. But because we are slowly working toward developing a national *military* strategy for China, we must posit and articulate Beijing's national security objectives since they will drive the PLA's national military objectives. If one were to distill all of the statements of China's national security objectives, both explicit and implicit, that have been publicly declared or adduced over the last few years they could be distilled to three simple words: *sovereignty, modernity,* and *stability*. These words encompass the totality of everything the Chinese nation is determined to achieve. Moreover, these objectives are not only those of the People's Republic of China (PRC), but capture the essence of the Chinese Revolution.

That revolution has been in motion since the last decades of the Ch'ing (Qing) Dynasty. The Chinese proudly proclaim over five thousand years of continuous civilization, and rightly so. But China is new to the business of developing a nation-state—less than one hundred years, less experience than the United States. The history of the Chinese Revolution has been, and continues to be, the story of the difficult transformation of an ancient traditional civilization into a modern nation-state. Every stage of the revolution has more or less sought the same three objectives: sovereignty, modernity, and stability. From K'ang Yu-wei to Dr. Sun Yat-sen to Republican China under Chiang Kai-Shek, to Deng Xiaoping and now Jiang Zemin— all have attempted to achieve these goals. Where there has been divergence has been in the "ways" to achieve those "ends." The great exception was, of course, Mao. While he embraced sovereignty and modernity as legitimate national security objectives, he rejected stability as a goal in his later years. By substituting "perpetual revolution" for stability and by making "class struggle the key link," Mao set back China's progress immeasurably. Consequently, the history of China under Deng Xiaoping is in great measure the story of Deng's efforts to reverse the damage and find a new path to progress. And there is little doubt that China under Jiang Zemin embraces these three national security objectives as well. Let us explore each a bit further.

Sovereignty. One would think that sovereignty, "freedom from external control" to cite *Webster's*, is so fundamental to nationhood that it need not be articulated as a national security objective. For China, this is not the case. Beijing's right to assert and defend its sovereign prerogatives as a nation-state is an enduring preoccupation that even today's leadership brings with them to office. It is not surprising of his political report to the 15th Party Congress in September 1997 Jiang Zemin made explicit references to the Opium War (1840), the Eight Power Intervention (during the Boxer uprising, 1900), the war against Japan (1937–1945), and China's "Hundred Years of Humiliation." The prominent position of these references is not mere rhetoric. It underscores that sovereignty is one of the enduring national objectives of the PRC under the Chinese Communist Party (CCP) just as it was for Republican China under the Kuomintang (KMT). This is the result of more than a century of foreign military, political, and economic intervention from without, warlordism and regionalism from within, and the difficulties all Chinese regimes since the fall of the Ch'ing have experienced in just defining and securing the geographical scope of the Chinese nation-state. Consequently, as portrayed by Beijing, Hong Kong's retrocession to China in July 1997 was as much an emotional event for the people of China as it was a political event.

In the context of 1998, how Beijing defines sovereignty is now much broader than merely being the master of its own nation. Today, issues related to sovereignty encompass at least six categories of issues. First, of course, is concern over the return of territories Beijing considers part of the PRC, but over which it exercises no jurisdiction—Taiwan and Macao, for example. Second are issues related to border disputes China still has with some of its neighbours and the problems of demarcation and control.

This encompasses a series of bilateral problems. Issue number three concerns areas of China over which Beijing does exert control but whose indigenous non-Han population oppose China's rule, such as in Xinjiang and Tibet. A fourth category is one of multiple competing claims such as in the South China Sea, not just for atolls, reefs and islets but for maritime resources. A fifth issue involves what Beijing views as unwanted and unwarranted foreign concern over, or meddling in, Chinese domestic social and political issues. A sixth category relates to international pressure for China to accede to multilateral instruments and protocols which might constrain Beijing's freedom of action whether or not the instrument in question is or is not problematical.

The constant lectures on China's sovereignty to which foreigners, official and private, friends and adversaries, are subjected are tedious, formulaic and almost archaic. But it would be a mistake to dismiss the seriousness of the message because of the medium.

Modernity. During the last two decades China's quest for modernity has probably been the most studied, analyzed and scrutinized of Beijing's three national security objectives. This is especially the case in economic matters. Modernity, of course, encompasses much more than economics. It includes social change, political reform, cultural adaptations, intellectual change, and technological and scientific innovation, to name just a few of the aspects of the modernization process. The leadership in Beijing understands this and in fact does have separate objectives and strategies for each of these areas. But for the purposes of this short discussion, we must condense this vast subject to its essential elements.

In the final analysis, the objective of modernity as defined by today's PRC leadership means increasing the economic strength of the nation, enhancing the technological and scientific capabilities of the state, and raising the standard of living of the population. China's leaders have come to believe that its sovereignty and its place among the leading nations of the world in the future will be secured by, and a function of, its economic and technological strength. Hence the centrality of this objective and the emphasis it receives in China's national security strategy.

The 15th Party Congress and the 9th National People's Congress were devoted in the main to articulating the latest adjustments to China's modernization strategy. The Party Congress provided broad statements of "ends" and "means." The NPC, in turn, announced specific plans and policies to enable them. It is worthwhile to quote Jiang Zemin at the NPC in his role as State President for he offers an excellent example of a broad statement of a national security objective in general and a specific "end" or objective for the national security objective of modernity.

The goals we have set are as follows: When the People's Republic celebrates its centenary, the modernization program will have been basically accomplished and China will have become a prosperous, strong, democratic and culturally advanced socialist country. At that time, our country will rank among the moderately developed countries of the world, the Chinese people will have achieved common prosperity on the basis of modernization and the great rejuvenation of the Chinese nation will have been realized.

Stability. This last of China's three national security objectives is as sacred as the other two. A large dimension of the history of Chinese civilization through the millennia is the history of periods of peace alternating with periods of unfathomable social chaos and violence. Moreover, during the last two centuries stability has been the exception, not the norm. It has been a period of *nei luan wai huan* [domestic disorder and foreign calamities]. The legacies of the White Lotus, Taipings, Nien, Miao Tungan, I-ho ch'uan, warlords, civil war, Red Guards, right through to Tiananmen in 1989 represent what every Chinese regime has feared the most, including the current inhabitants of *Zhongnanhai*. They do not take internal stability for granted.

Today the greatest challenge for Beijing's leaders is undoubtedly the need to balance their bold plans for modernization with the risk of instability, for it is clear that economic modernization has been accompanied by tremendous social dislocations. Over the past year and a half, one is struck with the frequency of press reports citing labour unrest, worker protests, and acts of civil disobedience. The Chinese leadership is acutely aware of the *maodun* (contradiction) which they have set in motion. Again, we quote Jiang Zemin at the 15th Party Congress:... it is of the utmost importance to correctly handle the relations between reform and development on one hand and stability on the other so as to maintain a stable political and social environment. *Without stability, nothing can be achieved.*

But the objective "stability" does not just refer to maintaining the internal peace. A second aspect of stability means regime maintenance; that is, maintaining undiluted the authority and monopoly on power held by the Chinese Communist Party (CCP). The third aspect of "stability" has an outward dimension. It is the firm belief of the Chinese leadership that only a peaceful and stable international environment will permit China to successfully pursue its national objectives. Or, as Jiang Zemin put it, "We need a long-term international environment of peace for carrying out socialist modernization, especially a favourable peripheral environment." And it is precisely because of Deng Xiaoping's great "strategic decision" shortly after the Third Plenum of the 11th Central Committee in 1978 that the world security situation had relaxed and a world war was a remote possibility that he decided the time was right to launch China on its grand experiment in modernization. It is clear that how Beijing chooses to pursue its objective of sovereignty while seeking to preserve a peaceful international environment will also pose a challenge in the future.

These, then, are the three key national security objectives posited as the driving forces behind China's current national security strategy. By striving to achieve these objectives the PRC hopes not only to enhance the state of its domestic conditions but also to be able to strengthen its desired role as the preeminent nation in Asia and as one of five key actors in the future multipolar world order that Chinese theorists argue will revolve around the PRC, the US, Russia, Japan, and Western Europe. We now turn to the question of how the military element of national power is developed to support these security objectives.

The Strategic Filter

At a minimum, the "strategic filter" for military planners at the national level must address three issues. First, they must account for political decisions that have been handed down to them or that have been brokered with civilian counterparts. These decisions usually encompass fiscal decisions and affect allocation of resources. Political decisions can also dictate or constrain military courses of action. Second, military planners must survey the security environment and assess what threats, current and future, must be addressed. Third, the nature of warfare must be examined to determine what kinds of engagements on the spectrum of military conflicts are most likely to occur. We attempt to use a "strategic filter" to look through Chinese eyes and attempt to see their strategic planning environment as they do. In some cases, we have definitive Chinese statements on these issues. In others, we can only try to transform ourselves into a PLA staff officer (*canmouguan*) sitting in the General Staff Department and speculate in an informed manner.

Political Decisions. Three key political decisions made by the top Chinese leadership affect what strategic military concepts are acceptable or possible for the PLA's national planners. These political decisions are not recent developments but long-standing policies. The first is that China does not participate in formal military alliances. This means the PLA must plan on being a "go-it-alone force" when it does go to war or when the military element of national power is employed. It also means that PLA planners do not have to concern themselves with questions of interoperability with potential allies or even temporary coalition partners. This goes for doctrinal issues as well as hardware and combat systems which, in any case, the Chinese would prefer to produce indigenously. It explains as well the deep reluctance of the PLA to accept invitations from foreign militaries to participate in combined training exercises even when these events are couched in terms of serving as confidence-building measures.

A second political decision in effect is that the PLA will not station combat forces abroad (trans., stationed on foreign soil). The reasons for this are a combination of geopolitical reality (who would invite the PLA to permanently station combat troops on its soil?) and budgetary considerations (it is expensive to station troops abroad). Moreover, since China does not engage in formal military alliances, such an eventuality is difficult to imagine. Of greater significance, this policy also dictates that the defence of China must take place close in, on, or near China's actual land borders or off the Chinese littoral. These decisions make "forward presence" for the Chinese a relative concept. It also dictates that the PLA must maintain a certain scale or size, especially in its ground forces, to compensate for vast borders and the need to fight close to them.

The third political decision with which PLA planners must grapple has already been mentioned—that the funding the PLA requires to operate, train, maintain and especially to modernize the armed forces will be subordinated to other national priorities. We will not enter the great PLA budget debate here. The jury is still out on the real value of investments China makes in national defence, especially given the opaque nature of their system, the multifurcated streams of funding that find their way to the armed forces, the obviously low official figures, and the issues surrounding the "hidden budget" that is the result of PLA domestic and global enterprises. The numerical spread in foreign estimates of the real value of the Chinese defence budget continues to inspire an awe of its own. For 1994, the range of estimates ran from about $10 billion U.S. to $149 billion U.S. For our purposes the trend is what matters. The recent "official" defence budget increase the PLA received during the 9th NPC (12.8 percent, for an official budget of 90.9 billion Yuan) indicates that while defence spending is going up yearly, no fundamental political decision has been made to reverse national priorities and provide the armed forces with a massive infusion of state funds. The PLA leadership undoubtedly does not receive the funding it would like (in this regard they have much in common with their brothers-in-arms across the globe). The question that we still have difficulty answering is: Are they getting what they need to fund their key current programs and underwrite their future requirements?

The PLA Analysis of the Security Environment. The basic and oft-repeated Chinese articulation of the nature of the world security environment is well known. Beijing sees the next two or three decades as a period in which the possibility of world war is negligible. The basic trend is toward "peace and development." China faces no immediate major direct military threats and the world is generally at peace. It is this assessment, originally made by Deng Xiaoping, that has impelled China to concentrate on economic reform as its primary national security objective. China continues to have, and continues to need, a window of relative peace to experiment and move forward in this endeavour. Jiang Zemin revalidated this assessment at the 15th Party Congress:

The international situation at present as a whole continues to move toward relaxation, and peace and development are the main themes of the present era.... For a fairly long period of time to come, it is possible to avert a new world war and secure a favourable, peaceful international environment and maintain good relations with the surrounding countries.

At the same time, Jiang also pointed out that there are serious security problems that require China's attention: However, the Cold War mentality still exists, and hegemonism and power politics continue to be the main source of threat to world peace and stability. Strengthening military alliance between various military blocs is not conducive to safeguarding peace and ensuring security. The unjust and irrational old international economic order is still infringing upon the interests of the developing countries, and the gap in wealth is widening. It is still serious that human rights and other issues are used to interfere in the internal affairs of other countries. Local conflicts due to ethnic, religious and territorial factors crop up from time to time. The world is not yet tranquil.

Jiang's "caveat" is a relatively subdued echo of PLA concerns. For their part, Chinese military strategists seem to view the world as a place basically hostile to Beijing's national interests, especially China's sovereignty. It is a world where dangers to national security lurk everywhere. The strategists view competition between nations for advantage as the norm and as a zero-sum equation (*ni si wo huo*). Change in the global and regional security environment is viewed as constant and usually dangerous. The absence of war does not mean the absence of hostility toward China. And, over the horizon, today's much-needed trade partners can slowly transform into serious economic, political, and military rivals. China's Defence Minister General Chi Haotian is Beijing's top military spokesman on these issues and he continues to be quite straightforward and frank in publicly highlighting the dangers that PLA planners see bubbling beneath the surface of a relatively peaceful world. As recently as March 1998, he underscored that pockets of antipathy toward China continue to require military vigilance:

Hostile international forces have never abandoned their strategic plot to westernize and split China, and the great cause of the motherland's ultimate reunification has yet to be accomplished. Under the long, peaceful environment and the situation centering on economic construction, we must be prepared for danger in times of peace and enhance our awareness of hardship. We must not become intoxicated by songs and dances in celebration of peace.

Fair enough. It is the job of defence ministers around the world to remind the troops that preparedness is why they are paid. What is interesting is that in this particular talk to PLA delegates at the 9th NPC Chi couches the need for preparedness not just as a matter of general professional responsibility but as a result of clearly identified security challenges.

In April 1996, General Chi spoke of the competitive nature of world relations when he wrote that "Major countries successively take contending for economic and technological superiority and enhancing comprehensive national strength as their development strategies and try by every possible means to gain the strategic initiative in the 21st century." These types of official statements set the analytic tone for PLA strategic planners. But what are the specific concerns these planners see that might affect the formulation of national military strategic concepts, especially those that must be incorporated into their national military strategy? We will now survey them briefly. What we will find is that if one were a Chinese military planner contemplating the various possible contingencies for which military force might be required now or in the future, there would be very little reason to feel complacent. What does the PLA planner see when he looks around the map? What are the major near-term, mid-term, and long-term concerns and shaping factors?

Geography. Geography continues to be a critical factor for Chinese military planners. China shares land borders with fourteen other nations. All told, the Chinese claim more than 20,000 kilometers of land boundaries and 18,000 kilometers of coastline that must be defended. Moreover, these borders encompass almost every major type of climate and terrain known in the habitable world. Just being able to secure its land borders is an almost staggering proposition for the PLA. It should be pointed out that since 1949 all of China's wars or military campaigns (Korea, India, Indochina-Vietnam, Soviet Union) have been fought either to secure control over disputed portions of those borders (India, Soviet Union) or to preempt a potential threat to those borders (Korea, Indochina-Vietnam). But the new international security environment and proactive diplomacy by Beijing have guaranteed that threats to China's land borders remain minimal. Rapprochement with Russia has alleviated a tremendous pressure on the PLA. Moreover, the dissolution of the USSR broke up what was previously the longest land border in the world. Cautious but steadily improving relations with Hanoi continue to keep the Sino-Vietnamese border pacific. The 1996 five-nation agreement between China, Russia, Kazakhstan, Tajikistan, and Kyrgyzstan is addressing problems in the northwest. If China still has a major potential border security problem it is with North Korea, which we shall come to shortly. But for the most part, China's land borders have never been more secure than they are today.

Defence of the Economic Centre of Gravity and the New Maritime Imperative. The same cannot be said of China's coast. In the last twenty years there have been two significant changes in China's security environment. The first is rapprochement with Russia.

The second, ironically, is the result of two decades of successful Chinese economic modernization. China's economic centre of gravity has shifted from deep in the interior, where strategic industries were sequestered in the 1960s to protect them from a possible Soviet invasion, to its current location on China's eastern coast, where Beijing's new market economy is strongest. This "gold coast," from Dalian in the north to Hainan in the south, defines the current economic *schwerpunkt* of China and its likely future location as well. And, arguably, Beijing's ongoing and future potential success in developing this coastal economy will be a major factor in defining China's importance in the future international order.

This shift has resulted in a profound change in the PLA's security calculus. Previously a large land force was required to protect the Chinese interior and its industries against a protracted land war with invading Soviets. Today, however, this pronounced shift in the economic centre of gravity presents China with a littoral and maritime defence requirement that it probably has not had since the mid-Ch'ing Dynasty. For the PLA today (and more than likely tomorrow) *the essence of defending China will be defined by the PLA's ability to defend seaward from the coast in the surface, subsurface and aerospace battle-space dimensions*. This is precisely the type of warfare that the PLA is currently least well postured to conduct. Hence, the emphasis in military modernization over the past few years has been on naval forces, air forces, and missile forces—the three services whose force projection capabilities are required for and best suited to defend the new economic centre of gravity. Because of this shift it could be argued that even if the PLA did not have a Taiwan "problem" to consider, it would still emphasize force projection capabilities with a maritime (and maritime airspace) control and denial focus.

Defence of Maritime Sovereignty. In line with China's new coastal defence requirements, it is clear that the PLA has other maritime issues to contend with. Besides their 18,000 km of coast, the Chinese claim to have "more than 6,000 islands, and three million square km of territorial waters..." to defend. The PLA must develop the capability to enforce Beijing's claims over disputed areas in the South China Sea and other maritime claims. While the waters have been relatively calm since the "Mischief Reef" incident, China could decide to employ the military element of national power once again if, from its perspective, it feels provoked by the other claimants in the region. Besides the Spratly Islands, China has competing claims with Vietnam over the demarcation of the Gulf of Tonkin and with Japan over the Diaoyu/Senkaku Islands. The issue of the South China Sea also highlights the importance China places on maritime resources (oil, fishing, and minerals) as it proceeds with economic modernization. And it is worth highlighting again that in his articulation of China's national military objectives earlier in this chapter Defence Minister Chi Haotian specifically cites the need of the PLA to safeguard China's "waters and maritime rights and interests." These two requirements—defending China's maritime territorial claims and defending its maritime resources—are specifically included in the articulation of the objectives of the PLA Navy by its commander, Lieutenant General Shi Yunsheng.

Close to Home: The Prospect of Instability. PLA and PAP military planners cannot discount the possibility that their classic internal defence mission will become more important in the next decade. As mentioned earlier, the social dislocations attendant to China's economic modernization are becoming greater and greater. Over the past few years worker protests, sit-ins, and physical attacks on local party officials and headquarters have been reported in the press with increasing frequency. As the social safety net continues to erode, by political mandate or by virtue of poor management, the possibility of increasing social instability cannot be discounted. China already has a "floating population" of some several millions which the state security apparati blame for increasing crime. If Jiang Zemin and Zhu Rongji actually implement the reforms of the state-owned enterprises as they have promised at the 15th Party Congress and 9th NPC, then over the next three years some three to five million additional Chinese could become unemployed and be without any social benefits at all. The "Great Amway Riots" of April 1998, as I like to call them, could be a harbinger of worse situations to come. And should the Asian financial crisis eventually hit China hard, the social chaos could be totally unmanageable.

But beyond the social unrest that could take place, China has other internal problems that must certainly keep PLA planners alert. In Xinjiang, the Uighur separatist movement has not been crushed. It is difficult to determine just how large or minuscule the problem is in fact. Last year several "terrorist" attacks in Beijing and other parts of Han China were reportedly tied to the East Turkistan freedom movement. We do not know if that linkage is true. But for the first time that one can remember (or that has been reported outside of the mainland) China now has a terrorist problem and the Chinese certainly believe the Pan-Turkic problem is potentially serious. This means that the PLA will need to have contingency plans on file if the PAP and other state security forces cannot handle future unrest in Xinjiang Province.

And always there is Tibet. The on-again, off-again unrest in that region is certainly a part of the PLA planning calculus. The issues of Xinjiang and Tibet directly attack Beijing's national security objectives of sovereignty and stability. Consequently, there is no reason to think that Beijing would not employ the PLA in either combat or military operations other than war (MOOTW) in either of these locations if its capabilities were needed to quell serious unrest.

Taiwan. Taiwan represents both a near-term contingency and a long-term readiness problem for PLA planners. Beijing will not renounce the right to use military force against Taiwan. Consequently, the PLA must develop a serious conventional deterrent capability vis-à-vis Taipei. The problem, of course, is that the only credible military deterrent is real conventional capabilities (we assume the political will is there). The next question must be, capability to do what? Whether the March-April 1996 mini-crisis in the Strait was a success or failure for Beijing is still being debated abroad. But one thing is certain; if one were a Chinese military planner, it should be painfully obvious that the PLA needs to develop a more diversified set of conventional military capabilities to employ as flexible deterrent options (FDOs). Relying heavily on missiles as a FDO runs the risk of being too provocative (witness the U.S. reaction). This is true whether the PLA must act against Taiwan or in defence of its claims in the South China Sea. In the 1996 affair, the PLA quickly escalated from "forward presence" (large military exercises on the coast) to "demonstration of force" (missile launches). It appears that either the PLA did not have many other options in between with which to *slowly* escalate or they totally miscalculated the external response. My own inclination is that it was both.

Russia. Russia should probably be viewed as a long-term potential problem for the PLA. In spite of increasingly friendly relations and their new "cooperative strategic partnership," there is no dearth of mutual distrust between Russia and China, especially in Siberia and the Russian Far East. China is still viewed by the Russians as a threat and these views have their political champions on the far right in Moscow. Beijing's economic strength at a time when Moscow is relatively supine is felt most sharply in Russian Asia, and the Maritime Provinces recoil at what they see as

Moscow's kowtowing to Beijing at their expense. For their part, Chinese military planners likely view Russia as a possible "over the horizon" problem. They may worry about the day when the Russians recover their national strength and the imperatives of geography and the legacies of historical animosity act to unleash rivalries anew, not just on their common border but perhaps in Central Asia. These rivalries will probably be driven by competition for natural resources: lumber, oil, minerals, and food from the sea.

Korea. Chinese military planners discount the possibility of an all-out war in Korea á la 1950. Nevertheless, they should be worried about the security problems China could face if the economic and political situation in North Korea deteriorates to the point of a total meltdown. An implosion in the north has the potential to send tens of thousands of North Korean refugees streaming over the border into China's ethnically Korean provinces. This type of chaos on China's border is precisely the type of situation for which the PLA is historically deployed. But in this sort of scenario the PLA would not be fighting a classic war. China's armed forces would be engaged in MOOTW. They would have to secure their borders, deal with thousands of refugees, and possibly keep the Korean People's Army at bay simultaneously. The scenarios are endless. The point is, the PLA must be prepared to intervene unilaterally to secure China's own interests in the event of total chaos on its border with the Democratic People's Republic of Korea (DPRK).

Japan. The Chinese view Japan as the only Asian nation that has the political, economic, technological, and (potential) military strength to challenge Beijing for regional dominance in the next century. Japan is likely viewed by the PLA as the primary mid-term strategic concern. While it may seem irrational from an American perspective, Beijing believes that under the veneer of a generally pacifist Japan lurks an undercurrent of unrepentant Japanese militarism and a strong desire on the part of the Japan Self-Defence Forces to overturn constitutional limits on their roles and missions. Tokyo's reluctance to directly confront its role in World War II and Japanese military participation in United Nations Peace-Keeping Operations (PKOs) in Africa and the Middle East fuel these Chinese suspicions. However, *the* most worrisome development from the perspective of the PLA is the recent promulgation of the revised U.S-Japan Guidelines for Defence Cooperation. This instrument is viewed as a codicil under which the Japanese armed forces, especially the navy, will justify operating even further out from Japan proper while still claiming to be a force purely for the defence of the Japanese home islands. Even more damning, China considers Tokyo the "other black hand" behind Taiwan's drift toward independence. This is because of a variety of reasons that go back to Taiwan's status as an Imperial Colony (1895–1945) and Lee Teng-hui's ties to Japan. These two factors (Chinese suspicions of Japanese military expansion and the Taiwan factor), when combined with maritime territorial disputes, makes for an imposing set of military planning requirements for PLA staff officers.

India. Up until the May 1998 nuclear detonations by India and their accompanying barrage of anti-China rhetoric, relations between Beijing and New Delhi seemed to be on the road to mending. The fact that the nuclear detonations occurred shortly after the visit to India of GSD Chief General Fu Quanyou was a double slap in the face. It is still too early to say what impact these events will have on overall Sino-Indian relations or what impact the Indian detonations will have on China's nuclear policies. These questions notwithstanding, the Indians have handed PLA planners a set of potential problems that encompass both a readiness issue on land in the disputed border areas and possibly a mid- to long-term maritime-aerospace planning problem in the Indian Ocean. At a minimum, India will continue to be viewed as an enduring security concern.

The United States. The United States poses a special conundrum for the PLA. China needs good relations with the U.S. to achieve its overarching national security objective of modernization. But this should not be confused with a shared vision of how the post–Cold War security regime in Asia should unfold. For one thing, the Chinese do not subscribe to the U.S. argument that Washington's bilateral military alliances in the region are necessarily stabilizing. Moreover, from the viewpoint of PLA planners, the forward presence of the American armed forces throughout the Pacific and

Asia on land, sea and air cannot be a happy fact of life. The Pacific Ocean is still an American lake and the looming shadow of the U.S. Navy casts a pall over all others. It is in the interests of China and the PLA to see the U.S. military presence in Asia reduced at some point in the future. There is probably little debate in Beijing on this basic point. Where there may be significant debate is on the timing of a U.S. force withdrawal.

Some Chinese security analysts could argue that the American military presence has some utility for China by acting as a guarantor of the regional stability Beijing must have. They might argue that a quick drawdown by the U.S. would result in Tokyo filling the military vacuum quicker than the PLA could be prepared to credibly face down the Japanese. Others might see utility in the continued U.S. military presence in Korea as a check on instability close to home, although that argument will disappear after Korean unification or reconciliation.

Yet, there is a residual distrust and apprehension in some circles in the PLA about the true intentions of the United States in Asia and the role of its armed forces in the Pacific. The United States, through its forward military presence, has the *potential* to act as the great spoiler to two of Beijing's *core* security concerns: Taiwan and Japan. Because the United States underwrites the security of Taiwan, some Chinese security analysts argue that Taipei can continue to be recalcitrant in negotiating cross-Strait political issues and reckless to the point of provocation in its foreign and domestic policies. Moreover, it is the United States, some PLA planners would argue, that is goading the Japanese to rearm and pressuring Tokyo to expand its military role in the region under the false flag of increased host-nation burden sharing. Moreover, the "China Threat" theory that was in vogue in the U.S. a couple of years ago had its

Chinese analogue. Some PLA analysts seriously believe that the U.S. is attempting to contain China militarily using Japan as the "northern anchor" and Australia as the "southern anchor." And Chinese opposition to NATO expansion is borne of a fear that the Partnership for Peace might spread to Central Asia and exponentially enhance U.S. influence on China's western doorstep.

Consequently, PLA views of the U.S. are highly dichotomous. On the benign side, the U.S. is probably viewed by PLA strategists not so much as a *direct* military threat to Beijing, but as a lumbering but lethal giant that can wreak havoc on China's various national security interests because of (as viewed through Chinese lenses) vacillating American domestic political tacts and ignorance of the greater strategic implications of Washington's ever-changing policies. On the more cynical side, the U.S. is seen as capable of undermining core interests concerning Japan and especially Taiwan. More than likely, the PLA must constantly factor the potential reaction of the U.S. into almost every military contingency plan it may have. Assuming there are a variety of PLA contingency plans targeted against Taiwan, the "U.S. factor" is a significant unknown variable for the PLA. Beijing's suspicions about Tokyo's future path and the vagueness of the phrase "areas surrounding Japan" in the U.S.-Japan Guidelines for Defence Cooperation have probably only heightened concern about the U.S. role.

Nuclear Threats. Beijing's decision to develop nuclear weapons decades ago was in part a function of the desired status that capability conferred upon the PRC in the world order. However, Chinese security analysts are also quick to point out that China had no choice but to possess atomic weapons because China had been subjected to "nuclear blackmail" in the past—first by the United States during the Korean War and later on by the Soviets. For the past thirty years, Beijing has adhered to a nuclear strategy of minimum deterrence and has publicly declared a no-first-use policy.

It would appear that China's leadership has been satisfied with this approach. But whether this will remain the case indefinitely may be open to debate, certainly within China. One reason is the recent nuclear detonations by India. Second, over the past few years there has been growing concern among China's nuclear scientists and Beijing's security policy establishment over the possibility that the U.S. might in fact develop a national ballistic missile defence system and concerns about what China views as U.S. pressure on Russia to amend the Anti-Ballistic Missile Treaty to allow high-capability Theater Ballistic Missile Defence systems.

The prospect of India having offensive nuclear capabilities, and the U.S. possessing highly capable high-altitude ballistic missile defenses cannot be a comforting combination for those charged with responsibility for China's nuclear strategy.

STRATEGY FOR WEAPONS AND EQUIPMENT DEVELOPMENT

Weapons are tools used to carry out armed conflicts. It is an important component of the military's combat power. It is the major element that determines the success and failure of a war. The development of modern weaponry, contained and controlled by national defense science and technology and national defense economic realities, have affected a succession of military scientific theories.

The Development of Modern Weaponry and National Defense Science and Technology

On June 7, 1981, the Israeli Air Force sent out 14 aircraft and bombed a nuclear reactor 20 km southeast of the Iraqi capital of Baghdad. "The bombs landed precisely on the main building where the nuclear reactor was located." On May 2, 1982, during the Falklands War between England and Argentina, England's SSN Conqueror fired two wire-guided TIGERFISH torpedoes and sank the only 13,000-ton large cruiser, General Belgrano, in the Argentina Navy. Two days later, the Argentina air force flying the French manufactured SUPER ETENDARD fighters needed only one EXOCET AM39 air-to-ship missile to sink the large, superbly equipped and costly ($200 million) SHEPHERD class destroyer from a distance more than 45 km away. On May 25, Argentina sank the British Navy's 18,000-ton troop transport, an ATLANTIC SEA TRANSPORT [Daxiyang Yunsongze] class ship. In June 1982, in the air battle above Syria's Bekka Valley, the Israeli Air Force won an important battle by using all types of jamming methods and precision-guided weapons like air-to-surface missiles and television and in 2 days completely destroyed all the surface-to-air missile sites in the Bekka Valley. In the surprise attack on Grenada on October 25, 1983, the United States used many surveillance methods and sent out an E-2C high-altitude, early-warning aircraft with antijamming capability, and hi-tech F-15s and F-16s, which had been remodeled and equipped with infrared sighting equipment, laser-guided bombs, and radar-guided self-seeking air-to-surface missiles, to achieve its predetermined military objectives with very little cost. During the military conflict over the Gulf of Sidra between the United States and Libya between March 24-25, 1986, and in the air attack on Libya by the United States on April 15, the United States used hi-tech weapons such as laser-guided bombs, "Rockeye" cluster bombs, TRIDENT radar-guided, self-seeking air-to-surface missiles and for the first time, used its high speed antiradiation missile "HARM" as well as other hi-tech equipment such as new infrared sighting equipment. The United States lost only one F-111 fighter-bomber and in turn sank and seriously damaged two Libyan cruisers, destroyed one missile launching site, destroyed about 5 to 12 Soviet made MIG-23s and 3 to 5 IL-76 transports, and achieved combat successes on 5 predetermined targets. Since the 1980s, several local area conflicts have vividly shown, and people have clearly understood even before the smoke cleared, that modern weapons have assumed some new characteristics under the impetus given them by the advances made in national defense science and technology.

One is electronics. With the development of microelectronics, computers, satellite communications, lasers, and other technologies and greater improvements seen in communications, navigation, radar, telemetering, remote control, remote sensing, and modern electronic command, control, and communications systems because of electronics and the radio, various kinds of weapons systems are extensively using electronic equipment and technology. From the perspective of the cost accounting of weapons systems, the percentage of the costs of the electronic equipment within each of these weapons systems is relatively sizable. In aircraft, it is 33 percent; in missiles, 45 percent; in space vehicles, 66 percent; in military vessels, 22 percent; and in combat vehicles, 24 percent. Electronic equipment has already become an indispensable component of modern weapons systems. It has also become the nerve center of modern weapons systems. With the development of the fifth generation of computers, artificial intelligence, and robotic technology, it is possible that troops could be equipped with simple artificial intelligence weapons systems in the future.

Second is the change in guidance systems. Since the 1950s, along with the development and discovery of new technologies like wireless, television, infrared, laser, microwave, inertia guidance, photoelectricity, acousto-electronics, sensors, and precision measuring and automation, precision-guided weapons systems (cruise missile, surface-to-air missile, air-to-surface missiles, air-to-air missiles, surface-to-surface missiles, ship-borne missiles and antitank missiles) have appeared along with terminal precision-guided weapons warheads for guided artillery shells, guided bombs, and guided torpedoes. The guidance system changes in these weapon systems have greatly increased their capabilities for automatic searches and identification and attack, and have increased tenfold the precision of these weapons systems, to the point of near perfect accuracy.

Third is covertness. Weapons are tools for the destruction of the enemy but at the same time, they are also the major target of offensives by the enemy. The new technological revolution has searched for and provided advanced equipment, ways, and methods for the modern battlefield, and together with troops, weapons have now become a serious threat. In the history of combat, to increase battlefield survivability of weapons, man has thought of many kinds of decoys and camouflage. With the development of invisible light technology (like infrared, ultraviolet, laser, microwave, and others), surveillance technology and various anticamouflage technology, original camouflage mechanisms have lost a great deal of their effectiveness. To increase their battlefield survivability, weapons systems have begun moving toward the direction of concealment. "Concealment" is the use of various types of scientific technology to decrease detection by radar, infrared, photoelectricity, and weapons sighting systems. It is the adoption of a specialized technology through systems research and design. Major "concealment" methods include:

- Having the weapons system's structural distribution and design be scientifically rational and still be able to decrease the effective reflecting surfaces of radar, electromagnetic spectrum, and laser.

- Decreasing infrared radiation and the noise level of engines within the propulsion system in the weaponry.
- Selecting coatings that will absorb and shield radar waves and infrared radiation as well as effectively reduce radar reflecting surfaces. For coating on surfaces of the weaponry, new wave-absorbing structured materials made of composite materials and electromagnetic spectrum "absorbing material" are now being selected. There is also the use of different kinds of concealment technology and use of different methods for different weapons systems, such as missiles, aircraft, ships, tanks, vehicles, and artillery. The U.S.'s B-1B bomber is a weapons system that uses rather advanced stealth technology. Structurally, it uses swing-wing. The outer shape of the body and wings are designed for radar reflecting surfaces. It uses a turbofan engine and a bypass culvert that dispenses the mixed hot and cold air to decrease the heat radiation strength of the jet. It uses the radioactive isotope polonium 210 and curium 242 as well as ferrite as its surface coating. Cover coating the aircraft surface with these substances decreases the radar reflecting surfaces and will furthermore absorb and shield radar, electromagnetic spectrum, and laser radiation. From what we have seen in localized wars during recent years, covert technology has raised the survivability of weapons systems in close concealed contact with the enemy and in surprise attacks. It has also played a role in decreasing wastefulness in terms of consumption.

Fourth, focused energy, is different from radiation mass destruction weapons like chemical, atomic, and nuclear weapons. A focused- energy weapon directs energy into beam power that kills the enemy or destroys a target directly. (It is also called a directed energy or directed beam energy weapon.) The rapid rise of laser technology, particle beam technology, microwave technology, and plasma technology has provided the foundation for the creation of focused-energy technology. In recent years, there has been rapid development in focused-energy weapons, and at present, the phase of theoretical experimentation has largely been completed and has entered the prototype stage of research. According to reports, the Soviet Union is in the process of researching three kinds of high energy laser weapons for its anti-air defense. It could complete the research work for a practical model against a star wars weapon in the 1990s and deploy a small quantity of them. There is intense research going on for various kinds of tactical laser artillery and guns and the coming of directed-energy weapons in theatres of war are not far away. The combined use of these and conventional weapons systems will result in greater casualties and destruction.

War and the need for the development of weapons power are the motivations for weapons development. As long as war, an abnormal development of mankind, persists, the military will strive to find more sophisticated weaponry and suggest the need for development of weapons. With this "demand as an incentive," opposing sides, all wanting victory, will initiate national defense construction "monitors" for "military expenditures" for large investments in national defense science and technology and support for research work in the leading edge of technology and advanced weapons systems. The greatest "INVESTMENT returns" in weapons development for national security and arms superiority would be a pioneering spirit in new ideas, exploitation, and creation of new technologies. In other words, national defense science and technology could apply all kinds of new technologies to both the research of weapons and their production, thus acting as "technology boosters." In this way, the research disciplines within national defense science and technology could become the "breeding grounds" for high technology development; furthermore, the new achievements of science and technology would most appropriately find their first applications within the military.

Weapons Development and the National Defense Economy

It is common knowledge that modern warfare is not only the competition of weapons on the battlefield but is also, at the same time, an all-out competition of the total strength of the opposing side's politics, economics, military, and science and technology. During the development of weaponry, the four aspects of politics, economics, military and science and technology are completely brought into play. In today's climate of rapid development of national defense science and technology and the daily emergence of new weapons, the material base of the actual national defense economy should be not only strong but also exceptional.

- With the upgrade in the tactical and technical performances of weapons, manufacturing costs would correspondingly be also more expensive. Since the end of WWII, science and technology development has flourished. There has been a multitude of achievements in science and technology that have continuously increased weapon precision, its powers to cause casualties, and its military effectiveness. The explosive power of a small atomic bomb has the same effectiveness as 100 bombers from WWII. The fire power of today's tank is tenfold greater than that of WWII. A mission to destroy 60 percent of the equipment of a tank division would today require only 1 percent of the aircraft used 40 years ago. During the Falklands War between England and Argentina, the EXOCET missile, which cost only $200,000, fired by the Argentinean Air Force was able to sink a British SHEPHARD missile destroyer that costs $200 million. The ratio of the two costs effectiveness is 1:1,000. The precision of precision-guided bombs and artillery shells is 2 to 3 times better than that of non-guided bombs and artillery shells. However, the upgrading of weapons performance has also brought with it the consequence ofmore expensive manufacturing costs. The cost of scientific research and technical components compared to the cost of a system with microcomputer technology, new materials, and new techniques imported in great quantities would appear to be prominently greater. Each of the U.S.'s HELLFIRE antitank missile costs about $28,100 to buy, but the scientific research to produce it costs $310 million. Each of the LEOPARD-II tanks of the Federal Republic of Germany costs $3.58 million to buy, yet the scientific research cost was $360 million. The research cost of Japan's MODEL 61 tanks cost 500 million to research and develop in the 1950s, its MODEL 74 tanks cost 2.5 billion to develop in the 1960s, and the MODEL 88 tanks that currently are under research and development have a budgeted cost that could reach 25 billion. The research and development expenditures of three generations of tanks seem to have increased geometrically. According to statistics, the costs of fighters and tanks increase about tenfold every 20 years and the costs of aircraft carriers increase by tenfold every 30 years. Weapons development has come to rely more and more on the national defense economy, causing great burdens for many countries.

- The increase in weapon power has also created battlefield situations where the consumption of battlefield material and economic losses are immense. It requires a huge quantity of material reserves. The 4th Middle East War lasted only 18 days and both sides, Egypt and Israel, suffered economic losses of over $5 billion. The loss of aircraft by both sides was comparable to the combined loss in aircraft in a year by all of the participant countries during WWII. In the first 3 days after the war started, the total number of tactical missiles launched by both sides was equivalent to the combined total of all the reserves of the countries in NATO. The loss of tanks was equal to one-third the number of those in the possession of NATO countries at that time. Both sides strategic reserves and materials were exhausted a week into the war. We can infer the amount of economic loss that could be created by modern warfare from this. In the Falklands War, the English spent a total of $2.16 billion, about $1.2 million every hour. This kind of consumption, to fight one mid-size modern war, is difficult for even an economically great power to support.

In addition to the above, research and production of weapons, ammunition, technical facilities and engineering equipment all consume large amounts of metal and various kinds of nonferrous metals. They also need the support of the chemical industry and energy resources, as well as military industrial products. According to the statistics from affiliated departments at the United Nations, 15 to 16 percent of the world's copper output and 10 percent of it tin, nickel, lead, and zinc outputs are used for weapons production and toward the building of other national defense installations. The consumption of energy resources is even greater. During WWI, the consumption of fuel by each soldier for each day averaged about 6 kg. During WWII, it was increased to 20 kg for each person each day. In the several local area wars fought in recent years, the fuel consumption of each man each day increased to 90 kg. The consumption level is shocking! This not only raises problems for logistics support, it also increases the economic and energy resources burden.

- The rapid increase and shorter intervals in the updating and replacement of weaponry have sharply increased military expenditures and expenses. The advancements of science and technology have caused new weapons to emerge in an endless stream and greatly accelerated replacement and updating of weaponry. Before and after WWI, the time period for a weapons system to go from research and design, through trial tests and production to its deployment within the service required about 20 to 30 years. At present, this procedure requires only 10 to 15 years or an even shorter period. According to the analysis of a Soviet economist, Maj. Gen. Guluofu, a new weapons system for the Soviet military from research to its deployment in the services requires 10 - 15 years. Since the 1960s, Soviet missiles have already been updated three generations. The majority of its aircraft, submarines, and surface ships underwent updating long ago. Its anti-air defense missiles, radar, command equipment, communications equipment, and other equipment have also been through several generations of updating. The research of new weapons and the updating of existing weapons have greatly increased the military expenditures and expenses of every country. According to an analysis by western observers, "The world economy is already shouldering a burden of massive destructive weapons, poverty, and debt. Militarization will further sap its strength." Since the 1960s, the global expenditure for weapons has been about $14 trillion. In 1985 it was about $800 billion, in 1986 about $900 billion. Every second of every year about $1.7 million are spent. Immense military expenditures have become serious economic problems for each of the world's countries.

- The research and production of modern weapons have made even greater demands on the national defense economy and national defense industries. Since WWII, especially during the 1960s and 1970s, the unceasing discovery of new technology has led to a great revolution in weapons and military-use equipment.

In 1945, the atomic bomb appeared. The research of computers for weapons use came in 1946. In 1952, the first transistorized computer was developed. In 1953, the world's first hydrogen bomb was exploded. In 1955, the first nuclear-powered submarine was launched. In August 1957, the first intercontinental ballistic missile was fired, and in October of that same year, the first manmade satellite was orbited. In 1960, mankind recovered its first satellite. In 1961, the world's first manned satellite did an orbit around the earth and returned to the surface. In 1967, the first integrated circuit was successfully developed. In 1969, man had his first landing on the moon. In 1977, the neutron bomb was researched and developed. In April 1981, the world's first spacecraft flew. The research and production of all these new weapons and equipment and a large portion of the new technology that entered into the sphere of the national defense economy not only greatly changed the production and industrial structure of the national defense economy, it also added a series of new production and industrial sectors. These changes helped to restructure the traditional national defense industries, moving them in the direction of technological improvement, and development of a technological reserve. The diffusion of a large quantity of high technology made it possible to turn a consuming national defense economy into a propagating field of national defense economy.

Weapons development is reliant on the development of the national economy. It also encourages the growth of national defense science and technology. Military high-technology also gave impetus to the development of the economy. Looking at this from two-dimensional space, this big "O" cycle could possibly expand further. Analysing it from a three-dimensional space, this kind of spiraling trend is perfectly suited to the objective laws of material development.

Weapons and Equipment Development and Military Scientific Theory

"Technology determines the tactics." The appearance of large quantities of technical equipment inevitably brings about great transformations in military theory and tactics; this in turn leads to great changes in strategic thinking, patterns of combat, combat style, and military structures:

- Weapons development enhances man's strategic consciousness, deepens his strategic reflections, and increases the emphasis on strategic projections. In today's world, strategic research is extremely dynamic. With the development of strategic rockets and various spacecrafts, as well as the gradual development of energy beam weapons, kinetic energy weapons, and other space weapons systems, war has extended from the surface, air, and sea toward outer space. The areas of man's activities have already extended beyond the earth and moved into space. This has opened up man's field of vision and expanded his modes of thinking. In the wideness of space, the earth is no longer "boundless and limitless," but has become one of the "global villages" in the universe. In the eyes of the strategist, the earth has become small and man's strategic reflection is becoming more profound and his strategic consciousness has been greatly enhanced. Man's heart embraces the whole of the universe. The development of strategic research is even more important than at any time in history and has become an especially important issue for all countries globally. What is coming will be conflicts in space. One of the conflicts will be the military struggle for "control of the high ground in space." The other will be exploitation and use of space, the struggle for the resources of space. For this reason, every country in the world is busily formulating and developing strategic plans. In March 1983, the United States became the first to formulate a "Star Wars Plan." This caused global commotion in strategy research. The Soviet Union responded with "defensive measures" to the "Star Wars Plan." Western Europe came up with the "Eureka Plan." Each of the COMECON countries announced a "Plan for the integrated advancement of science and technology by the year 2000." Japan had its "Policy outline for science and technology;" China had a "Policy for a new technological revolution;" India came out with "Policy statements for new technology;" South Korea had its "Conceptions for long range national growth;" and Yugoslavia had its "National science and technology development strategy." To rank within the world's family of nations, to live and survive in the "global village" in this universe, each nation must come up with ideas for a "grand strategy." "To stand shoulder to shoulder with the giants" one must intensely fix one's eye on the growth of national defense construction and weapons in the next century.

- Modern weapons are not only direct combat strengths between opposing combat opponents, they are also strategic deterrents and tools for international political struggles. The appearance of offensive strategic weapons like missiles, atomic bombs, nuclear-powered submarines, and long-range bombers has caused great changes in military strategy. The research, production, and large stockpiles of strategic weapons are already more than needed to seek out and kill an enemy. It has turned into a tool for political and diplomatic struggle. The large-scale arms race have caused the United States to stockpile over 9,400 nuclear warheads with a total nuclear weight equivalent of over 4 billion tons. The Soviet Union's stockpile of over 8,000 nuclear warheads has a total nuclear weight equivalent of over 5 billion tons.

The quantity of nuclear warheads possessed by these two nuclear powers comprises above 97 percent of the global total. Both have the capacity to destroy the other several times over. Living under these conditions, the military strategy of both sides has gone through many changes; strategic ideologies have been revised about every 10 years. However, pressure from the threat that "destroying the enemy doesn't necessarily mean one's own survival" has kept them from crossing the "nuclear threshold" and taking the next step of pressing the button to launch those nuclear missiles. England, France, and China have independently and on their own developed into national nuclear powers. The limited power of these countries is not enough to compete with the capabilities of the United States and the Soviet Union, but they do play a role in the even development of political, economical, and military affairs within the world. This power is entirely a symbol of a country's independence and its existence within the world of politics, economics, military affairs, and science and technology.

In addition to nuclear weapons, the emergence of strategic weapons has definitely caused reforms within the military, changing past combat theories that we must go through war and campaigns to achieve strategic objectives to the possibility that strategic weapons could directly attack the opponent's strategic targets and achieve the strategic objectives. The development of various space weapons has not only intensified military struggles in space, it has also increased ways in which strategic objectives could be directly achieved.

- Today's weapons systems are very mobile. They also have long range, high accuracy, and great power, causing the time and spatial aspects as well as the intensity of war to change greatly. The development of these weapons and the great number of these weapons being deployed within the services have caused the arenas of war to be extended into deep sea and space, the length of war to shorten, and the suddenness, destructiveness, savageness, and mutation to increase unprecedentedly. In the "blitzkrieg" of the German armored troops during WWII, they could advance only about 30 km daily. Today, under normal circumstances, the Soviets could do 50 km and under nuclear conditions it could reach above 100 km. When the Soviet Union invaded Afghanistan, its push towards Kabul, a distance of 900 km took only 6 days. The time it takes for an intercontinental ballistic missile to travel its whole distance is only slightly more than 30 minutes and there is no more than 20 minutes of early warning for its defense.

During the Falklands War, England's SHEFFIELD class missile destroyer did not even have the opportunity to react before it was hit by Argentina's EXOCET missile. With this short span of time, it is very difficult to react. This has made even greater demands on command and control. The largeness of the battlefield and the number of troops involved have given rise to immense increases in technical weaponry and specialized technology and have caused even greater problems in the coordination of operations and commands. According to reports, there were only 20 different military specialties during Word War I. It grew to 160 during World War II, and at present, the number of military technologies and specializations exceed 2,000. During combat, the army, navy, air force, and the other different service branches are all involved at the same time. The types of weapons used are never less than a dozen and usually are in the hundreds. This alone would demand that the commander prepare detailed plans and coordinate his commands well. There must be no mistakes in differentiating missions, allotting time, and coordinating activities. Any small error could lead to major mistakes and even greater disasters.

First strike has always been the combat phase that militarists attach greatest importance to. The success or failure of the first strike impacts the whole battle. In modern combat, because of the short time needed for combat, the phases of combat are no longer clearly delineated. The long range surprise attack or the counterattack during the preliminary period of the combat has become the main combat model for first strike. Thus, every nation has given special attention to studying the first strike phase of a war. The United States emphasizes that "every preparation must be made to win with the first strike." The Soviet Union also believes that "surprise attacks are the most effective combat opening moves to implement in future wars.... Victory can basically be determined in the first phase of a war." This will demand that commanders make complete preparations for first strikes. Intelligence, reconnaissance, personal observations with automatic and rapid analysis, processing and judgment, decisionmaking, formulating careful plans, and even reactions must be quick and accurate because only then could the "first strike win" objective be achieved.

- The extensive use of modern weapons has caused great changes in military structures. Before WWI, the military was basically composed of land forces that included the infantry, artillery, calvary, and navy. Before WWII, there was a great deal of aircraft and tanks in the military, thus the air force, armored troops and motorized troops came into existence. The air force itself was divided into bomber, fighter, and attack aircraft forces. There were surface vessels, submarines, naval aviation forces and marines in the navy. After WWII, strategic rocket forces, army airborne forces and other service branches were formed. With the development of space technology and the successful development of various spaceflight vehicles as well as the development of various space weapons, the militarization of space will possibly strengthen the military deployment of a new independent military service branch "Space Forces." In 1982, the United States established the Air Force Spaceflight Command (a command comparable to the Strategic Air Force and Tactical Air Force Commands combined), and in 1983, the United States established the Naval Spaceflight Command. In 1985, the two commands and affiliated army commands were combined to form the U.S. Spaceflight Command. Not long after the United States had established the Air Force Spaceflight Command (1982), the Soviet Union appointed Lt. Gen. Sadaluofu as the "Aeronavigation Forces Commander." Some reports have said that "it is possible that the Soviet Union had already established a military spaceflight command like the U.S. Air Force Spaceflight Command and that the aeronavigation force was nothing but a subforce of that command." Various evidence has shown that the growth of the militarization of space has brought about the birth of the "Space Forces." With the advancements made in microelectronics, computers, and artificial intelligence technology, multipurpose robots could soon be used more and more in military applications and in those work areas where the labor is heavy and environmentally dangerous; thus a "robot force" would have to be deployed. The influence of weapons development on military administrative systems and deployment and on the overall structure can be easily seen. At present, the strategic course for overall military development is: a reduction in the overall personnel strength, a rise in the proportion of technical military personnel in the overall structure, a decrease in the proportion of personnel directly involved in combat, and a different scale for the increase in the proportion of logistic personnel (including technical support personnel).

The impact of modern weapons on military theory has been profound and extensive. The various sophisticated tools, means and methods of modern policy decision studies, projection studies, and futures studies have scientifically given impetus to and provided directions for military theories and strategic growth. It has allowed the military to grow scientifically so that it can completely anticipate conflicts and play a better leadership role.

WEAPONS AND EQUIPMENT DEVELOPMENT STRATEGY RESEARCH

The weapons development strategy is dictated by the realpolitik of politics, economics, national defense and science and technology. These situations suggest comprehensive ideas for the development of weapons. Weapons development hinges between the needs of combat and military construction, and what is possible economically and in science and technology. At the same time it is also determined by a country's political system, its national defense strategic policies, and its fundamental appraisal of the international condition. Thus, different countries have different weapons development strategies.

China is a socialist country and a part of the Third World. This is the political basis from which China formulates its national defense development strategy. China espouses a foreign policy of independence and self-determination.

It is against all expansionism and aggression. It supports all struggles and movements for justice. China, together with the rest of the Third World, is a major force for the preservation of world peace. This demands that China have the necessary military strength and an appropriate weapons development program to defend itself against outside aggression.

It also demands that it have the ability to completely protect its territory and rights, to protect its country's unity, legitimate rights, interests and self-respect, to prevent the breakout of world wars and to protect world peace.

China is a country that is still economically, scientifically, and technologically undeveloped. This in itself imposes a limit on the amount of money it can possibly commit to weapons development and makes it even more impossible for it to be involved in an arms race. Thus, the development of China's weaponry must be based on the needs of national defense and military construction and economic strength, the level of potential in construction and its economic strength, the level of potential in the development of its science and technology, and the independent, self-determining and self-reliant road it takes toward developing weaponry.

In the near future, our actions must be firmly directed toward transforming our present weaponry, so that our military weapons will be improved by the end of the century and they will have the ability to meet the demands of a localized conflict. We must also face the future by developing weapons systems for our country, striving to reach world advanced standards in weapons in the next century and carrying out the modernization of our weapons. In order to realize the objectives of the above-mentioned weapons development strategy, our military must develop suitable strategic nuclear weapons and tactical nuclear weapons, strengthen its research for precision-guided weapons and electronic and technological equipment, and work even more toward modifying various conventional weapons.

Strategic nuclear weapons are not only a combat tool of immense destructive power; they also serve as powerful deterrents and an anti-deterrent force.

After our country had successfully exploded its first atomic bomb on October 16, 1964, it went on to successfully explode its first hydrogen bomb in June 1967. With every step China takes in the development of its strategic nuclear weapons, the strength of world peace is also increased by those steps. China's development of its limited nuclear capability is completely for the purpose of defense, for breaking up the nuclear monopoly and nuclear threats of the United States and the Soviet Union, and for preserving long-lasting world peace.

To win time for the world to stabilize within this nightmarish nuclear situation and to provide our socialist modernization greater security in the international environment, to completely destroy the nuclear blackmail of the U.S. and the Soviet Union, to strive for the thorough destruction of nuclear weapons, to proceed toward preventing a world from exploding into war, and to increase the strength for world peace over war so that China and Third World countries can play a greater role in international affairs, China must continue to develop proper strategic weapons and move toward upgrading their precision, lessening their weight, and increasing their mobile combat capability.

Field tactical nuclear weapons are an effective antipersonnel weapon. The extent of their destructive area is above 300 km.

This weapon not only has the superior tactical technical capabilities of long range, fast firing rate, high accuracy, and great destructive power, but it could also be used as a surprise weapon in major field operations to strive for and grasp the field initiative. In its tactical use, in an offensive situation it could directly break up the effective fire power of the enemy and destroy the defense points of the enemy from a distance, or it could attack the depth defenses of the enemy and cut off the enemy's retreat. In a defensive situation it could attack the enemy rear echelon troops, stop the continuous assault of the enemy, and defend against the enemy making a direct deep push.

Coordinated and complementary field tactical nuclear missiles used with various other conventional weapons systems could give the military greater military benefits and battlefield power. In a situation where, temporarily, no global wars are being fought, localized wars will be the major forms of combat for a period of time. In localized wars, the possible use of field tactical nuclear weapons by the enemy cannot be dismissed. Thus, China appropriately and within reason must develop field tactical nuclear weapons in order to further break down the various kind of nuclear threats of the hegemonists and restrain the use of field tactical nuclear weapons by the enemy.

After the implementation of the strategical changes in the guiding ideologies of military construction, the serious research of various weapons systems for localized wars will become the major tasks of our country's weapons system development for a period of time. The effective use in recent years of conventional precision-guided weapons in several localized combat theatres of operations has been followed with general interest by various countries around the world. Our national socialist characteristics have also determined that the major combat form of our military will hereafter still be that of defending our national territory. In a defensive war, the major missions assumed by our military will be defending against the enemy's surprise air attacks and stopping a mass invasion by the enemy's tanks. In our military's conventional arms buildup, the development of different precision-guided weapons for anti-air and antitank defense will be of special importance.

The level of modernization of our weapons directly corresponds to how sophisticated our electronic technology is and this will have a direct impact on victory or defeat in modern warfare. After our forces are equipped with a large quantity of electronic equipment and computers, not only will the electronic command, control, communications and information systems (C3I) within our combat and control become highly automated, and simple platforms and partial electronic equipments of warfare like reconnaissance and antireconnaissance, jamming and antijamming, destructive and antidestruction devices be completely transformed for "electronic wars;" they will also allow electronic technology to spread and permeate into all of the other weapons systems until it becomes the mainstay of our modern weaponry. The energetic development of our country's military use of electronic technology is of utmost importance to upgrading the modernization level of our military weapons and closing the weapons gap with advanced countries.

For a long time, our military had summarized a complete set of combat methods and experience on how to gain victory with inferior equipment over a superiorly equipped enemy. Facing a strong opponent, our military would be inferior in terms of weapons. Our country's economic strength is still very weak, our science and technology is still not very developed and compared to a strong enemy, the gap in our weapons will be difficult to overcome immediately.

After our country implemented the strategic change of "transferring the work emphasis towards economic construction," there has been little possibility that military expenditures will be increased greatly and also little possibility that more money will be forthcoming for the research of sophisticated weapons. Thus, we must begin exploring new ways to develop weapons that possesses Chinese characteristics.

On the one hand, we can track the development of global high technology, build a good technological reservoir, and actively research new weapons systems in order to lay a foundation to close the gap with the advanced standards in foreign countries. On the other hand, we can use what we currently have and what high-technology results we have already achieved to change the low-tech conventional weapons system in our military, and upgrade the tactical technological capability of our present weapons so that with these slightly improved low-tech weapons systems we can still win a victory over our enemy's hi-tech weapons.

A weapons development strategy is an important component of our national defense development strategy.

In the historical situation where our guiding ideology for military buildup is undergoing grave strategic changes, the somber formulation of a military weapons development strategy, the development of military weapons in a planned, focused, and measured way, and the acceleration of the pace of development of our military weapons will all have practical and long term impacts on encouraging our military's modernization and standardization.

4

China's Shadow over South Asia

All the talk of a "new beginning" in Sino-Indian relations notwithstanding, there is little evidence to support the view that China has re-cast its foreign policy to build an accommodative relationship with Asia's other rising power — India. If anything, Beijing has unveiled major strategic moves that will effectively isolate India in South Asia and further squeeze India's traditional strategic space in the region, keeping New Delhi tied down with multiple sub-continental concerns. After Pakistan and Myanmar, Beijing is skillfully employing economic and military means to draw Bhutan, Bangladesh, Nepal, the Maldives, and Sri Lanka into China's orbit. The Chinese military's recent incursions and road construction activity in Bhutanese territory are aimed at coercing the tiny Himalayan kingdom to end its protectorate relationship with India and move into China's orbit "if Bhutan desires peace and development with the world's fastest growing superpower."

Ignoring Indian pleas not to fish in troubled waters in volatile Nepal, Beijing has gone ahead with arms supplies to the beleaguered monarchy. Nepal's King Gyanendra has been openly playing "the China card" to counter Indian and U.S. demand for an early restoration of multi-party democracy in the Himalayan Kingdom. Taking advantage of a sharp downturn in India's relations with Bangladesh over issues ranging from illegal immigration to Islamist terrorism, transit and trade, Beijing has upgraded its ties with Dacca to gain naval access to the Chittagong port, to establish a road link with Bangladesh via Myanmar and to acquire Dacca's immense natural gas reserves. China is already the largest supplier of weaponry to Bangladesh. Chinese Premier Wen Jiabao's recent offer to provide Dacca with nuclear reactor technology has led to speculation as to whether Beijing would replicate in Bangladesh the sort of military, nuclear and missile collaboration it has with Pakistan. Bangladesh and Nepal are also expected to join Pakistan in concluding peace and friendship treaties with China in the near future.

At the 13th S.A.A.R.C. summit held in Dacca in November 2005, India's physical presence was overshadowed by China's invisible presence but growing influence. Nothing highlighted this more strikingly than India's volte-face on the issue of China's induction into the grouping as an observer or a dialogue partner. On the first day of the proceedings on November 12, Indian Foreign Secretary Shyam Saran ruled out China's induction unless it signed a memorandum of understanding for being associated with S.A.A.R.C. However, within less than 24 hours, Indian Prime Minister Manmohan Singh was forced — mainly by the pro-China grouping comprising Nepal, Pakistan and Bangladesh — to come out with a statement welcoming China as an observer. (The only consolation for India was that it managed to extend the same privilege to its friend, Japan.)

India's climb-down occurred in the backdrop of the pro-China grouping threatening to veto Afghanistan's entry into S.A.A.R.C. as the grouping's eighth member, which India supported, unless China was allowed in. The inclusion of China as an observer is seen by most S.A.A.R.C. member-states as a counterbalance to India. Apparently, while India has been preoccupied with fighting cross-border terrorism on its own territory, China has been busy making significant inroads into India's backyard through cross-border economic and strategic penetration of Nepal, Bangladesh, Sri Lanka, and the Maldives.

Beijing's main objectives are said to be access to raw materials, commodities, natural resources and access to South Asian markets for Chinese goods and to expand China's influence in the region. However, China's support for India's smaller neighbours suggests that gaining access to markets and natural resources is not the only reason behind Beijing's South Asia policy: Beijing also wants to make a point on the limits of Indian power.

In fact, aiding "India-wary" countries in South Asia to "concircle (contain and encircle) India" has long been an integral part of China's strategic calculus. As a rising maritime trading power, Beijing is also seeking to once again project force into the Indian Ocean in the manner of the fleets sent out under the command of Admiral Zheng He nearly 600 years ago during the Ming dynasty.

Border Talks End in Stalemate, Again

China's growing presence in South Asia is accompanied by a hardening of its stance on the territorial dispute. This became evident at the last round of border talks held in Beijing between September 26-27, 2005. Defence analysts attribute the Chinese intransigence in resolving the border dispute to the rapidly shifting military balance of power in Beijing's favour on the Tibetan plateau. Since 1999, there has been a constant probing of the line of actual control, via frequent border crossings by Chinese border patrols in a manner designed to test Indian resolve, psychology, vulnerabilities and border intelligence.

With the near completion of the 1,118 kilometer (695 miles) Qinghai-Tibetan railway and other military infrastructure projects in Tibet, China "may be tempted to resort to force or coercion more quickly to press diplomatic advantage, advance security interests or resolve disputes," according to an unnamed senior Indian military officer.

The Chinese have also rebuffed India's pleas for a quick boundary settlement within a fixed timeframe. Even on Sikkim, the Chinese have deliberately decided to "go slow" on the implementation of their verbal promise after obtaining a written commitment on Tibet from India in June 2003 during Prime Minister Atal Bihari Vajpayee's visit to China. From the Chinese standpoint, the concept of give and take vis-a-vis India could also damage China's image in South Asia as the predominant power.

China Opposes India's Bid for U.N.S.C. Seat

Another sign of pro-active containment of India is Beijing's opposition to any move to expand the veto-holding permanent membership of the U.N. Security Council. With the exception of China, the remaining four permanent members have voiced their support for expansion of U.N.S.C. permanent membership, with the United States supporting Japan while Russia, France and Britain are supporting India's bid. The Chinese Foreign Ministry spokesperson has now made it clear that while Beijing is willing to see India occupy a seat in the semi-permanent or non-permanent category, it remains opposed to having its Asian rivals — India or Japan — sitting in the U.N.S.C. permanent membership category. The fact that China has now emerged as the major obstacle to U.N.S.C. reforms can be attributed to divergent world views held by Beijing and other world capitals. Similar to how the U.S. seeks to prevent the emergence of a peer competitor at the global level, China wants to prevent the rise of a peer competitor at the regional level. This stance leads Washington to support a multipolar Asia (with a strong Japan and powerful India to balance China) but a unipolar world (with the United States as the sole hyper-power without any peers). In contrast, Beijing prefers a unipolar Asia-Pacific (with China as the sole superpower without any peers) and a multipolar world (with the U.S., E.U., Russia and China as four major power poles). In contrast with both Washington and Beijing, New Delhi champions multipolarity at both regional and global levels. Beijing's attitude to the expansion of the U.N. Security Council is a clear indication that it will not countenance the emergence of an Asian peer competitor.

The East Asia Summit

In early 2005, Beijing dispatched its diplomats to Laos (then "country convener for India" within the A.S.E.A.N. regional grouping) and other Southeast Asian capitals to dissuade them from lobbying for India's membership (albeit, unsuccessfully) in the East Asia Summit (E.A.S.) scheduled for its first inaugural meeting in Kuala Lumpur in December 2005. However, with the exception of Malaysia, Beijing did not find any takers for its anti-

India stance primarily because nearly all Southeast Asian countries supported India's participation in the E.A.S. seeing it as a useful counterweight to China's growing power. Having failed to keep India (and Australia and New Zealand) out of the new regional grouping, the Chinese Foreign Ministry attempted to dominate the emerging East Asian Community (E.A.C.) by dividing it into two blocs: the core or primary states with China as the leading, dominant player inside the A.S.E.A.N.+3 (China, South Korea, Japan) and the peripheral or secondary states of India, Australia and New Zealand (or, "outsiders" as the People's Daily editorial of December 7, 2005 described them). Beijing remains leery of India's great power pretensions and attempts to extend its influence in China's backyard. Seeing New Delhi's "Look East" policy as part of a wider "congage China" strategy unveiled by the Washington-Tokyo-New Delhi grouping, the thrust of Chinese diplomacy is to confine India to the periphery of a future East Asia Community and to foil India's efforts to break out of the South Asian straitjacket. The People's Daily commentator reacted sharply to the Indian prime minister's proposal for an Asian Economic Community (A.E.C.): "India's proposal is not warmly responded [to] as each country has its own considerations." Apparently, China's "own considerations" are primarily geostrategic in nature. Beijing fears that India's participation in the core group would shift the balance of power and make the E.A.C. less susceptible to domination by China. Therefore, in the run-up to the East Asia Summit in Malaysia and days after obtaining observer status in S.A.A.R.C., China's message to India was crystal clear. Finding India relegated to the outer circle, an Indian diplomat expressed his disappointment over the decision to entrench the A.S.E.A.N.+3 framework within the E.A.S.: "To state that A.S.E.A.N. is in the driver's seat, the passengers have a right to know where they are going."

Energy Fuels Feud

Both face growing demand for energy and are locked in fierce competition for stakes in overseas oil and gas fields in Asia, Africa, Latin America, and the Middle East. In the energy competition stakes, however, China currently has an overwhelming lead because

China has linked energy to its national security policy for longer than India has. Moreover, China has been more successful in diversifying its energy resources, developing a varied network of oil suppliers from Africa to Latin America.

China's superior financial muscle and diplomatic clout also enables it to win friends and contracts for natural resources. As 2005 progressed, Chinese oil firms went out of their way (excessively overpaying for assets) to thwart India's attempts to secure international energy assets in Kazakhstan, Ecuador, Angola, Nigeria, and Myanmar. Clearly, India's efforts to secure supplies cannot succeed unless and until New Delhi creates incentives (arms, aid and diplomatic support) or economic dependencies (via trade) for the supplying country to sell oil and gas to India. Ironically, the day India's oil minister, Mani Shankar Aiyar, left for Beijing to discuss energy-cooperation joint ventures, Myanmar announced that its gas would be flowing east to China instead of north and west to India. Despite the conclusion of energy cooperation agreements, China is likely to go solo in its quest for energy security; energy competition, rather than energy cooperation, will be the norm.

As finding new sources of oil becomes more difficult, there are bound to be areas of friction between Asia's two fastest growing economies. While China views the Andaman Sea off Myanmar's coast as an important source of oil to fuel the economic expansion of China's western provinces, India sees China's presence in the Bay of Bengal an unwelcome development. The Chinese Navy has asserted its legitimate right to operate in the Indian Ocean to ensure security of its oil and trade transiting through the region.

China already has better relations with the two largest energy suppliers — Saudi Arabia and Iran — than does India. With Pakistan as its long-term military ally, China also has closer relations with four important Islamic countries (Saudi Arabia, Iran, Pakistan and Bangladesh) than India, the United States and Japan.

As a major trading country and a future world power, China is now laying the groundwork for a naval presence along maritime chokepoints in the South China Sea, the Malacca Straits, the Indian Ocean and the Strait of Hormuz in the Persian Gulf through acquisition of naval bases in Cambodia, Myanmar, Bangladesh and Pakistan to protect its long-term economic security interests.

Sooner rather than later, China's military alliances and forward deployment of its naval assets in the Pakistani, Bangladeshi and Burmese ports would prompt India to respond in kind by seeking access to the Vietnamese (Cam Ranh Bay), Taiwanese (Kao-hsiung) and Japanese (Okinawa) ports for the forward deployment of Indian naval assets to protect India's shipping and trade routes and access to energy resources from the Russian Sakhalin province.

CHINA'S MISSTEPS IN SOUTHEAST ASIA

As tensions in the South China Sea ratcheted up in 2010, the United States looked on with growing concern that its strategic and economic interests and those of its friends and allies were being undermined. At the Shangri La Dialogue in June, for instance, Secretary of Defence Robert Gates identified the South China Sea as an "area of growing concern for the United States". Yet it was not until Secretary of State Hillary Clinton raised the subject at the ARF a month later that Asia's long-running sovereignty dispute hit world headlines. Clinton reiterated that freedom of navigation was a vital U.S. interest and that it opposed the use of force to resolve the problem. In a departure from past policy, Clinton suggested that the United States stood ready to facilitate talks on implementing the Declaration on the Conduct of Parties in the South China Sea (DoC), the agreement drawn up by ASEAN in China in 2002 to manage the dispute but which the two sides have singularly failed to implement.

Clinton's comments at the ARF were provoked in part by reference to the South China Sea as a "core interest" by Chinese officials, even though the exact context of their comments remains unclear. The subject first surfaced in April, when it was reported that during a visit to Beijing by Deputy Secretary of State James Steinberg and Asia Director of the National Security Council Jeffrey Bader in March, several senior Chinese officials, including Assistant Minister of Foreign Affairs Cui Tiankai and State Councilor Dai Bingguo (President Hu's point man on foreign affairs), had described the South China Sea a "core interest" the implication being that China would brook no interference from the United States (New York Times, April 23; Washington Post, July 30). Whether the PRC officials were referring to the South China Sea as a whole including the disputed Paracel and Spratly Islands or just the Exclusive Economic Zone where China has protested the surveillance activities of the US military is uncertain. Beijing has never officially described the sea as a "core interest" and government officials claim that Steinberg and Bader "misinterpreted" comments made at the March meeting (Interviews, Beijing, October). Yet according to Clinton, at the U.S.-China Strategic and Economic Dialogue in May in Beijing, Dai Bingguo repeated that the South China Sea was Beijing's "core interest" (Interview with Greg Sheridan of The Australian, U.S. Department of State, November 8). Reference to the South China Sea as a core interest was interpreted in Washington as elevating the problem on a par with Taiwan and thus an subject over which China was prepared to go to war.

The United States was not the only country to push back against Chinese assertiveness in the South China Sea. Twelve countries raised the subject at the ARF, including the four ASEAN claimants (Vietnam, the Philippines, Malaysia and Brunei) and Indonesia which has an overlapping maritime boundary claim with China near the gas-rich Natuna Islands. Southeast Asia's anxieties were further fuelled by the Sino-Japanese standoff in the East China Sea in September when the Japanese Coast Guard detained a Chinese fishing trawler that had rammed one of its vessels near the disputed Senkaku/Diaoyu Islands. Even Malaysian Prime Minister Najib Razak, the leader of a country that has traditionally downplayed tensions in the South China Sea, described the PRC as "more assertive than ever before" (China Daily, September 29). Singapore Prime Minister Lee Hsien Loong described Clinton's comments as a "useful reminder" of America's role in Asia, a role "which China cannot replace ... because of America's security contributions in maintaining the peace in the region" (Straits Times, September 24).

Since the ARF, the United States, ASEAN and China have all moved to tamp down tensions over the South China Sea. In

September, Assistant Secretary of State Kurt Campbell denied that Clinton's comments had been aimed at China or that Washington was "taking sides or stoking tensions" and that the Administration's goal was to "create a more stable, predictable environment". A month later, in recognition of the fact that Clinton's offer to facilitate talks on implementing the DoC was strongly opposed by China and viewed as unfeasible by ASEAN because Beijing would walk away from the agreement if a third party attempted to mediate, Campbell told journalists in Tokyo that it would be inappropriate for the United States to play a direct role in the talks. Washington has more pressing problems to deal with than the South China Sea, though Honolulu-based U.S. Pacific Command continues to monitor developments with concern.

The ASEAN states have had to strike a careful balance: they do wish to be seen as siding with America on the South China Sea, but nor do they want to be perceived as appeasing China. Thus while the 2nd U.S.-ASEAN Summit in New York on September 24 provided another opportunity to discuss the territorial problem, member states softened the language in the final communiqué. Prior to the meeting, a leaked draft had made explicit mention of the South China Sea and the importance of freedom of navigation and non-use of force. The final communiqué, however, merely noted the importance of "regional peace and stability, maritime security, freedom of navigation.... and the peaceful settlement of disputes" (White House, Joint Statement of the 2nd US-ASEAN Leaders Meeting, September 24). The White House "Read-out" on the luncheon meeting, however, did make explicit mention of freedom of navigation and the non use of force in the South China Sea.

According to Campbell and Bader, Clinton's comments in July have served to move China "back to a more collaborative approach" on the South China Sea. There is some evidence to support this contention. After the ARF, Chinese officials stopped referring to the South China Sea as a core interest in meetings with their American counterparts, though mainland academics continued to muddy the waters by arguing that sovereignty was, by definition, a core interest and that China had "indisputable sovereignty" over the atolls in the sea (Author interviews, Beijing, October 2010). In recent months, however, Chinese academics have also gone quiet on the subject.

Senior Chinese officials have also sought to play down the subject on visits to Southeast Asia. At the inaugural ASEAN Defence Ministers Meeting-Plus (ADMM-Plus)¯which brought the 10 ASEAN defence ministers and their counterparts from the United States, China, Japan, South Korea, India, Russia, Australia and New Zealand together in Hanoi on October 12 Chinese Defence Minister General Liang Guanglie reacted rather mildly when eight countries raised the South China Sea dispute, even though prior to the meeting he had insisted it was not an appropriate venue to discuss the problem.

During October Chinese Vice Foreign Minister Zhang Zhijun was dispatched to four Southeast Asian countries on a "listening and reassurance" mission, while in November Vice President Xi Jinping Hu's heir apparention a trip to Singapore to mark 20 years of formal diplomatic relations stressed that a "prosperous and stable China does not pose a threat to any country," that Beijing would "continue to undertake its responsibilities for regional peace and development" and in an obvious attempt to counter Yang's statement at the ARF, that "China sees all countries, big and small, as equals" (Straits Times, November 16).

By raising the South China Sea at the ARF and ADMM-Plus, both ASEAN and the United States hoped that Beijing would be forced to recalibrate its position and adopt a more flexible and accommodating stance.

The acid test of this expectation is whether meaningful progress can be achieved over the next 12 months on implementing the DoC. There are cautious grounds for optimism. At the ASEAN-China Summit in October, Premier Wen Jiabao told ASEAN leaders that the PRC was committed to implementing the agreement (Philippine Daily Inquirer, October 30). On December 22-23 the ASEAN-China Joint Working Group on the DoC will meet in Kunming to discuss implementation guidelines, the results of which will be discussed by an ASEAN-China Senior Officials Meeting early in the New Year.

Indonesia took over the rotating ASEAN Chair in December, and Foreign Minister Marty Natelagawa has indicated that meaningful progress on the South China Sea problem will be among Jakarta's "leading priorities" (Straits Times, September 19). Yet acute problems remain in implementing the DoC, including the modalities of the discussions (China objects to ASEAN caucusing on the subject) and the precise definition of "disputed waters."

And although Philippine President Benigno Aquino has called for ASEAN solidarity on the South China Sea, arriving at a consensus will be problematic because membership is made up of claimant and non-claimant states, and some members have close ties to the PRC. Moreover, even though the DoC contains some potentially useful confidence building measures, given that the problem has become overlain by nascent Sino-US maritime rivalry, it remains doubtful whether its implementation will fundamentally change the dynamics of the dispute.

For its part China has been incensed at what it perceives as U.S. collusion with some Southeast Asian states at the ARF. At the time the meeting took place Vietnam occupied the ASEAN chair, and Beijing suspects Hanoi encouraged the United States and other participants to raise the subject so as to "internationalize" the problem. Stepped-up military cooperation between the United States and Vietnam has also raised Beijing's ire, including the repair of a U.S. navy supply ship in April, a visit by the hospital ship USNS Mercy in May, and in August a port call to Danang by the destroyer USS John McCain, the transit through Vietnam's EEZ of the aircraft carrier USS George Washington and high level defence talks between the two countries. Vitriolic commentaries in the PRC press have warned Hanoi of the dangers of becoming a "strategic pawn" of the United States.

As a result, Vietnam continues to pursue multiple strategies with China vis-à-vis the South China Sea dispute. First, it holds regular dialogue with the PRC in an attempt to manage tensions but also assuage Chinese concerns.

In August, for instance, Deputy Defence Minister Nguyen Chi Vinh visited Beijing and reiterated Vietnam's "3 nos" policy: no foreign alliances, no foreign bases and no relationship with another country to be directed at a third (VNA, August 26). Second, Hanoi continues to coax ASEAN to implement the DoC and move forward with a formal Code of Conduct. Third, Vietnam highlights the subject at international forums, including a second most important conference on the South China Sea in Ho Chi Minh City in November.

Fourth, the government has accelerated the modernization of the armed forces, particularly the navy and air force, including an order for 12 SU-30 MKK fighters and six Kilo-class submarines from Russia, the first two of which could be delivered in 2014. Fifth, and most controversially, Vietnam seeks to facilitate the military presence of most important external powers in Southeast Asia.

Thus in October Hanoi and New Delhi agreed to increase the frequency of Indian navy ship visits to Vietnam and, most noteworthy, an announcement by Prime Minister Nguyen Tan Dung that the strategically located former US naval base at Cam Ranh Bay would be opened to foreign navies for repair and re-provisioning, including submarines and aircraft carriers (Bangkok Post, October 31). Dung's announcement thus paves the way for increased US Navy ship visits to Vietnam in the coming years.

After nearly a decade of adroit statecraft, China's diplomatic posturing has substantially drained the reservoir of goodwill it had built up in Southeast Asia, forced ASEAN governments to question anew Beijing's peaceful rise, and pushed regional governments closer to the US. Singapore's Minister Mentor Lee Kuan Yew has spoken of 2010 as marking the beginning of a "decades-long tussle between the US and China for pre-eminence in the Pacific" (Straits Times, October 2). Events this year suggest that tussle will increasingly be played out in Southeast Asia.

CHINA'S UNPLEASANT IN SOUTHEAST ASIA

Most mornings, activity in Phnom Penh all but stops when the morning heat begins to rise. But on that day, the city resembled a festive papal visit to a devoutly Catholic nation. Nearly a hundred thousand Cambodian children lined the streets, many in threadbare school uniforms and waving tiny Cambodian and Chinese flags or small photographs of Jiang's face. The children cheered and screamed for Jiang as his open car toured through the city, chanting as if he were David Beckham or Bono, rather than an elderly politician with thick glasses and an oily, swept-back hairdo. Jiang's route did not take him past one of the city's most important attractions. Only a few blocks from his motorcade, foreign tourists wandered through Tuol Sleng, an old high school that Cambodia's Maoist Khmer Rouge regime had converted into a killing factory in the 1970s. Tens of thousands of Cambodians were brought to Tuol Sleng between 1975 and 1979. Fewer than 10 made it out alive.

During the Khmer Rouge's murderous four-year reign, during which they killed as many as 2 million Cambodians, China served as the regime's most important foreign patron. Beijing sent the Khmer Rouge over 15,000 military advisers and provided the bulk of its external aid. Beijing knew what was going on in Cambodia. Before Jiang's visit, Chinese leaders had actively worked to forestall a special international tribunal for the Khmer Rouge officials still alive.

But standing alongside Jiang that day, Cambodian Prime Minister Hun Sen did not mention the Khmer Rouge era or the tribunal. Instead, he praised Jiang's "historic" visit to Phnom Penh and called China's relatives with Cambodia "a precious gift." A beaming Jiang replied that he was "overwhelmed by friendship and joy" and promised that the relationship would become much closer.

Jiang was right. Within five years, China had become probably the most important foreign influence in Cambodia, and Hun Sen shuttled to and from Beijing constantly. Beijing became Cambodia's most important provider of foreign aid, giving Cambodia one of the largest Chinese aid packages of any nation in the world while also forgiving Cambodia's entire debt to China. Chinese language programs quickly dominated downtown Phnom Penh: one Chinese-language school alone drew over 10,000 students. As a result, although older Cambodians who remember the Khmer Rouge remain suspicious of China, their sons and daughters, who once would have headed to Australia, France, or the United States for higher education, now look to universities in Shanghai and Beijing. Chinese newspapers, films, television, and radio have become increasingly popular. Thousands of Chinese businesspeople have moved into Phnom Penh and northern Cambodia, creating entire villages of recent migrants. Chinese tourists descend en masse on the capital. Today, even when the prime minister has concerns about China's influence, he keeps quiet. Cambodia is hardly unique. Since the late 1990s, perceptions of China in Southeast Asia have shifted significantly, so much so that elites and publics in a most importantity of the 10 members of the Association of Southeast Asian Nations (ASEAN) now see China as a constructive actor—and, potentially the preeminent regional power.

China's image transformation has resulted from a range of factors. China has benefited from missteps by the United States and Japan, ranging from the response to the 1997 Asian financial crisis to Washington's post–9-11 focus on counterterrorism in Southeast Asia. But the transformation also stems from a rise in China's "soft power" in Southeast Asia—that is, China's ability to influence Southeast Asian countries by persuasion, rather than coercion. This growing attractiveness is conveyed through various means, including culture, diplomacy, participation in multinational organizations, businesses' actions abroad, and the gravitational pull of China's economic strength.

When Joseph Nye coined the term soft power, he originally used a more limited definition that excluded investment and aid and formal diplomacy—more traditional, harder forms of influence. But in the context of Asia today, both China and its neighbours enunciate a broader idea of soft power, implying all elements outside of the security realm, including investment and aid. Soft power stems from both governments and nongovernment actors—from businesspeople and pop stars and language teachers. Nongovernment actors do not necessarily operate in concert with the state, and no state can be said to have a completely coherent foreign policy. Still, it is possible to identify broad strategies Beijing has enunciated and policy tools it has used that allow nongovernment actors to more effectively wield soft power. Just as us policies between World War II and the end of the cold war made Washington popular in the region and smoothed the way for American soft power, it is these frameworks that today make it easier for Chinese soft-power actors, from language schools to businesspeople, to have a growing impact on the ground.

The Unpleasant Begins

Nineteen ninety-seven provides a convenient date to mark China's soft-power emergence in Southeast Asia. Whether or not Beijing explicitly recognized that the United States and Japan were fumbling their responses to the Asian financial meltdown that began with the Thai baht's collapse and soon spread across the region, China's own reaction proved savvy. Beijing refused to devalue its currency, which would have exacerbated devaluations in Thailand and Indonesia, and portrayed its decision as standing up for other Asian nations. After the crisis, ASEAN Secretary General Rodolfo Severino announced, "China is really emerging from this smelling good."

Since then, Beijing has begun to employ several strategies to boost its soft power in Southeast Asia. In statements and speeches, Chinese leaders enunciate a doctrine of "win-win" relations, highlighting that Southeast Asians can benefit from their relationship with China even as China benefits from its relationship with them. China will not interfere or meddle: foreign nations benefit because China will not make demands on other nations' sovereignty, economic models, governance, or political culture. "We don't believe that human rights should stand above sovereignty," the head of Beijing's premier state think tank says. China implicitly contrasts its "win-win" philosophy with that of the United States, a non-Asian actor that Beijing portrays as disrespectful of sovereignty, imposing a web of sanctions on Southeast Asia and demanding economic and political concessions.

The Chinese have backstopped this "win-win" rhetoric with real initiatives. Over the past five years, China has ended nearly all of its old border disputes and has signed Southeast Asia's Treaty of Amity and Cooperation, a document that commits the signers to mutual respect for a country's sovereignty and equality. Beijing has committed to creating a code of conduct on the South China Sea. It has enthusiastically signed bilateral cooperative agreements with several Asian states. Beijing seems willing to sign these agreements en masse, leaving details to be hammered out later. (In the lawyerly—and democratic—US political system, this type of sign first, talk later diplomacy would be virtually impossible.)

Beijing also has reversed its previous disdain for multilateral organizations, which older Chinese leaders had seen as constraints on China's power. It has not hurt that, as the United States became less interested in multilateralism between the late 1990s and today, China's participation in multilateral groups has made it look better by comparison.

Again, Beijing has backed up its changing strategy with real initiatives. As a dialogue partner with ASEAN, China works closely with the organization, trying to strengthen it and, according to Asian diplomats, initiating far more joint projects than other partners, such as Japan or the United States.

China's strategy also includes focusing on developing nations whose bilateral relationships with the United States or Japan are faltering. After President Gloria Macapagal-Arroyo pulled Filipino troops out of Iraq in 2004 as part of a deal to win the freedom of a Philippine hostage, the United States cut assistance to Manila. Shortly after, China invited Macapagal-Arroyo for a state visit, and then aggressively wooed Philippine policy makers, offering greater cooperation and aid.

Another most important component of China's appeal to developing nations involves Beijing's portrayal of China as a potential ideal, as a model. China emphasizes top-down control of development and poverty reduction and the sidelining of political improvement for economic improvement. China's model particularly appeals to rulers in authoritarian or semi-authoritarian nations. With the Chinese model, the regime has time to think of ways to co-opt businesspeople and other elites that it needs to keep on its side to remain in power.

Flaking Old Insecurities

Until the past decade, China exerted minimal soft power in Southeast Asia. Following Chinese leader Deng Xiaoping's advice, an insecure Beijing still pursued a defensive foreign policy and focused on rebuilding China's domestic economy from the ravages of the Cultural Revolution. The Chinese public still lacked confidence that Beijing could become a global actor, let alone a regional power. A poll taken by the research organization Horizon Group in 1995 asked Chinese citizens their views of the "most prominent countries in the world": one-third ranked the United States most prominent, with only 13 percent choosing China. The Chinese imperial court's treatment of mainland Southeast Asia as vassal states, and the modern history of Maoist China supporting communists in Thailand, Malaysia, and, most disastrously, Cambodia, left a residue of mistrust in the region. China's limited engagement with Southeast Asia foundered on Beijing's continuing claims to the South China Sea, China's suspicion of ASEAN's multilateral forums, and concern among ASEAN nations that China's continuing economic growth would siphon foreign investment from Southeast Asia. Meanwhile, China's policy tools remained weak. It was not a most important aid donor, its diplomatic corps remained dominated by older envoys, and its public diplomacy was blunt.

In the late 1990s all this began to change. China's breakneck economic growth fostered greater confidence within the Chinese public. By the end of the 1990s, many Chinese urbanites were too young to remember the Cultural Revolution. They no longer shared an inherent distrust of the state's wielding of power and ideology. In 2003, the Horizon Group again polled Chinese citizens. This time, nearly 40 percent picked China as "the most prominent country in the world." America came in a distant second. China's leadership was also becoming more confident. Until the mid-1990s, the generation that had grown up around Mao still dominated China's inner circle. But this generation passed away in the 1980s, or was forcibly retired to make way for younger officials. After the crackdown at Tiananmen Square, the leadership recognized that China could not rely on the United States, but had to develop better relations with its neighbours and become a greater international player.

China recognized, too, that its hard power was still limited. In the mid-1990s, Beijing tried to signal its rising military strength to the world by aggressive moves like sending ships to unoccupied, disputed reefs in the South China Sea. This approach backfired. Provocative military exercises, including missile tests in the Taiwan Strait, frightened neighbouring states and evoked old memories of Chinese military adventurism.

Even as they saw that China's aggressive moves triggered Southeast Asian balancing against Beijing, Chinese leaders could not help but notice another trend. Wang Jisi, director of American studies at the Chinese Academy of Social Sciences in Beijing, one of China's elite think tanks, noted in Chinese publications that America's weakness might be its soft influence, not its unrivaled hard power.

Wang was right. After the finish of the cold war, America had retreated from the world, consumed with its own economic boom, its culture wars, and its political scandals. Significant pluralities of Americans opposed US interventions abroad and called for Washington to slash foreign aid, and the White House listened. Washington cut public diplomacy abroad and merged the United States Information Agency, the main public diplomacy outfit, into the State Department. The Clinton administration sidelined many of the multilateral institutions that America had built after World War II, creating perceptions of the United States as a unilateral actor— a perception that would only increase as the Bush administration eviscerated multilateralism.

Support and Trade Tools

China's economic tools also have become more sophisticated. China's aid has undergone a serious transformation. According to a study by Henry Yep of the National Defence University in Washington, in 2003, China's aid to the Philippines was roughly four times greater than America's, China's aid to Laos was three times greater, its aid to Indonesia was nearly double, and its aid to Cambodia nearly matched US levels. Beijing has revamped its aid programs to better tie assistance to discrete policy goals, including promoting Chinese companies abroad, cultivating important political actors, and bolstering China's benign regional image. In Thailand, for instance, Chinese aid has been used for the kind of lobbying familiar in Washington: to bring important elected Thai politicians to study trips and conferences in China. Beijing has also used funds to purchase surplus Thai agriculture, mollifying Thai farmers worried about the impact of China's free trade agreement with Southeast Asia.

China's embrace of free trade in the region and its promotion of the idea that it will become a most important source of foreign direct investment also bolster its image. In addition to the ASEAN-China Free Trade Agreement, Beijing is negotiating closer bilateral trade ties and economic partnerships with individual Southeast Asian states. By the end of 2006, Southeast Asia's total trade with China probably will eclipse Southeast Asian trade with the United States or Japan. (China-ASEAN total trade in 2005 was roughly $130 billion; US-ASEAN total trade in 2005 was about $150 billion.) By comparison, the United States struggled to complete a bilateral free trade agreement with Thailand.

On visits to the region Chinese leaders set targets for future Chinese investment into Southeast Asia. These targets, usually for five or even ten years in the future, tend to be enormous, and obscure the fact that, at present, Chinese direct investment still lags far behind investment from the United States and other wealthy countries like Japan.

Finally, over the past decade the Chinese government has not only lifted restrictions on migration within China but has also made it vastly easier for Chinese to leave the country for business and tourism. Partly as a result, Chinese migration, often on overstayed short-term visas, is transforming the demographic makeup of northern mainland Southeast Asia, from northern Burma to northern Vietnam. Because of outmigration from Yunnan and other border provinces, ethnic Chinese now dominate entire towns in places like Luang Namtha, in northern Laos. The recent migrants are much more attuned to trends in China than older generations of ethnic Chinese, and they also have created a kind of renminbi zone in northern mainland Southeast Asia, where the Chinese currency serves as a de facto second currency.

Beijing's Fresh Toolbox

As China's engagement with the world has become more sophisticated, its tools of soft power have become more sophisticated as well. In the past decade, China has upgraded its public diplomacy, which has focused on selling the idea that China will not be a threat to other nations. China's public diplomacy efforts reinforce the idea of peaceful development. They include museum exhibits in Malaysia and Singapore to celebrate the 600th anniversary of the voyages of Zheng He, a Chinese admiral who sailed across Asia, encountering but never conquering other nations. Part of this new public diplomacy has been increasing cultural exchanges with Southeast Asia. China has begun hosting overseas scholars, the kind of programming the US State Department has long done. Beijing also has created a Chinese version of the Peace Corps, run by the China Association of Youth Volunteers, to send idealistic young Chinese on long-term volunteer service projects to developing nations like Laos and Burma. China has expanded the international reach of its media as well. It has upgraded the Chinese newswire Xinhua and expanded Xinhua's output in languages other than English and Chinese, and it has expanded and professionalized the international broadcasting of CCTV, Chinese state television.

The new Chinese public diplomacy includes setting up networks of informal business and cultural summits in China designed to bring together Asian opinion leaders. These meetings allow China to subtly emphasize its role as a potential partner for investment and trade and its position as a regional leader. The most prominent include the Boao Forum for Asia, which brings together Asian businesspeople for a Davos-style World Economic Forum-like event; and the ASEAN-China Eminent Persons Group, which unites former statesmen.

As China has upgraded its public diplomacy, it also has invested in improving its diplomatic corps. Over the past 15 years, the Chinese Ministry of Foreign Affairs has begun to retire older, more ideological diplomats, replacing them with a young generation of envoys who speak better English and local languages: one 2005 study suggested that one-half of the country's 4,000 diplomats are under 35. China can keep these diplomats in the region because unlike the United States, which gives its Foreign Service officers leeway to choose where they want to be posted, the Chinese foreign affairs ministry can mandate postings. Top Chinese diplomats in nations like Cambodia or Thailand now often have done three or even four rotations in those countries before rising to the rank of ambassador, building their language skills and developing extensive contacts in the local business and political communities.

Beijing supports its diplomacy through constant visits by senior Chinese officials to Southeast Asia, a short hop from Beijing in contrast with the 20-hour flight from Washington. According to a recent study of visits by top Chinese and US officials to Thailand and Cambodia in 2004 and 2005, senior Chinese officials made at least twice as many visits to Bangkok and Phnom Penh.

Promotion of Chinese culture and Chinese verbal communication studies are most important components of this public diplomacy. Beijing now funds at least the first year of what it calls Confucius Institutes, Chinese language and culture schools created at leading local universities. Beijing has tried to push instruction in Mandarin and in Chinese culture in overseas primary schools, partly by signing agreements with countries like Thailand to help integrate Chinese into public school curricula, and partly by helping students in poor nations like Cambodia attend private local Chinese-language primary schools. While promoting Chinese studies in other nations, Beijing has tried to lure more foreign students to China. The ministry of education advertises Chinese universities abroad and has boosted financial aid and loosened visa policies for foreign students. After 9-11, in contrast, the United States tightened its student visa policies, making it far harder for students from Southeast Asia to attend school in America. Even students already in the United States have had a harder time. In 2003, Washington announced that all Indonesian men residing in America would have to register with immigration authorities.

Many of them simply left. Between 1999 and 2003, the number of Indonesians studying in the United States fell by over 20 percent.

INDIA'S ENERGY DIPLOMACY: UNDER CHINA'S SHADOW

With an economy that is projected to grow at a rate of 7 to 8 per cent over the next two decades, meeting its rapidly increasing demand for energy is one of the biggest challenges facing India. Burgeoning population, coupled with rapid economic growth and industrialisation, has propelled India into becoming the sixth-largest energy consumer in the world, with the prospect of emerging as the fourth-largest consumer in the next four to five years.

Rising incomes in India, along with generating prosperity, are pushing demand for energy resources even further. India is not only rated as one of the highest energy-intensive economies in the world, energy intensity being a measure of energy required by an economy to produce one unit of GDP growth, but Indians also pay one of the highest prices for energy in purchasing power parity terms. India faces a growing imbalance between the demand for energy and its supply from indigenous sources resulting in increased import dependence.

Though it has the third-largest reserves of coal after China and the United States, dependence on imported oil is India's greatest vulnerability, because it imports about 70 per cent of its oil, and this dependence is likely to increase to around 92 per cent by the year 2020. Hydrocarbons have been viewed as better alternatives to the less efficient and more polluting coal energy. While natural gas is India's most important potential alternative to coal, the effective exploration and distribution infrastructure is yet to develop. And despite some recent attempts to think seriously about nuclear power, oil retains its primacy in India's energy matrix.

The recent fluctuations in global oil prices have been a worrying trend for India. It has been estimated that a sustained 5 per cent rise in the oil prices over a year could dampen India's GDP growth rate by 0.25 per cent and raise the inflation rate by 0.6 per cent. India can only sustain its high rates of economic growth in the long term if it is successfully able to bridge the increasing demand-supply gap. According to the Integrated Energy Policy Report of the Indian Planning Commission, India will have to quadruple its energy supply to sustain an 8 per cent rate of growth for the next twenty-five years, which calls for an energy regime that ensures supply, manages demand, and balances pricing to enable growth. The report goes on to recommend that India pursue all available fuel options and forms of energy.

The Indian government has only recently woken up to the challenge of managing the nation's energy security with the realisation that it has already fallen behind other major players, such as China. Despite this, India continues to lack an overarching energy strategy because of a lack of consensus on crucial choices that the nation needs to make in the domestic political as well as global context. In so far as India's engagement with the outside world is concerned, four schools of thought have been identified: the "self-sufficiency" school; the "cooperation with Asian states" school; the "greater integration into the global energy markets" school; and the "free-for-all" school that calls for India to pursue its interests by all necessary means.

The last school, not surprisingly, seems to have an upper hand at the moment, which is more a result of confusion in Indian policymaking circles than any attempt on the part of the government to evolve a coherent policy framework. India is now trying to work at multiple levels by opening up the domestic energy market to multiple players, thereby making it more competitive; by adopting relatively rational principles for energy pricing; by establishing credible energy pricing regulatory framework; by diversifying beyond oil to access alternative energy sources such as nuclear power and natural gas; and by focusing greater on exploration activities with its borders. India is trying to increase fuel efficiency by slashing state subsidies on all petroleum products. But this is a politically contentious policy issue, and subsidising of household necessities is viewed as essential for supporting the poor in the country. India is also trying to put its emphasis on the import of natural gas. Various proposals are in the offing to import natural gas from Central Asia, the Middle East, and even from its neighbours such as Bangladesh. India is also trying to promote investment in the exploration and production of domestic oil and gas, and it has had some successes in that regard in the last few years.

But these attempts are aimed at the long-term management of the nation's energy security. India's greatest challenge as of now is to ensure successful diversification of sources for oil procurement to minimise possibilities of disruption in supplies. It is towards this end that India has devoted its diplomatic energies in recent times as it encourages its public sector companies to acquire energy stakes in oil and gas fields abroad. India, like China, is reshaping its diplomacy to serve energy needs, because its booming economy also needs new supplies of oil to ensure its continued growth.

Not surprisingly, perhaps, the focal point of India's energy diplomacy has been the Middle East, because around 65 per cent of its energy requirements are met by this region. India's large and growing energy demand and Iran's pool of energy resources make the two nations natural economic partners. India's search for energy security in a rather volatile energy market makes Iran, with its fourthlargest reservoir of oil and second-largest reserves of natural gas, highly attractive. Iran has described India as one of its best customers and had offered to supply more crude oil to India in case of a disruption caused by an American military attack against Iraq in 2003.

This energy relationship between India and Iran is at the heart of a strong bilateral partnership between the two countries, despite the fact that Indo-Iranian relations have significantly diversified across various sectors in recent years. The proposal to build a gas pipeline between India and Iran has consumed a lot of diplomatic energy. Various options, such as offshore and overland routes, have been under consideration for quite some time now. Both these options have their problems, especially the problem of relying on Pakistan for the security of these pipelines. The United States has also been discouraging the pipeline proposal. Yet, India officially continues to insist that the 1,625-mile-long, $4.16 billion pipeline project intended to carry gas from Iran through Pakistan to energy-starved India remains firmly on track.

India has enjoyed traditional ties with Iran and Iraq for long, partly to meet its energy requirements. However, with Tehran adopting an aggressive anti-Western posture and pursuing an independent nuclear programme in defiance of its obligations under the Nuclear Non-Proliferation Treaty, and the ongoing instability in Iraq, India has been looking to expand its influence beyond the Persian Gulf to the Saudi peninsula.

As with Saudi Arabia's relations with China, energy has become the driving force in its relations with India, with India emerging as Saudi Arabia's fourth-largest destination for oil exports and Riyadh being the largest supplier of oil to India. India's crude oil imports from the Saudi kingdom are projected to double in the next twenty years. During his visit to India last year, the Saudi king emphasized his country's commitment to uninterrupted supplies to a friendly country such as India regardless of global price trends. During the state visit, King Abdullah bin Abdul-Aziz Al Saud and Indian prime minister Manmohan Singh signed an Indo-Saudi "Delhi Declaration," calling for a wide-ranging strategic partnership, putting energy and economic cooperation on overdrive, and committing to cooperate against terrorism.

Reliance, a private Indian energy firm, has decided to invest in a refinery and petrochemicals project in Saudi Arabia, and India's state-owned energy firm, Oil and Energy Gas Corporation (ONGC), is also planning to engage Saudi Arabia as its equity partner for a refinery project in the Indian state of Andhra Pradesh. The recent upheavals in India's relationship with Iran and Iran's decision to renege on some of its oil supply commitments in the aftermath of India's vote against Iran at the IAEA have also alerted India to the importance of having a diversified set of suppliers in the Middle East.

However, the Middle East remains a highly volatile region, forcing India to look beyond its regional confines in search of energy security. Following the disintegration of the Soviet empire, Central Asia has emerged as an important region, where many countries, including the United States and China, have evinced a keen interest, especially since it has emerged as a major oil-producing region. India has also actively nurtured its relations with the Central Asian states. Most notably, it has stationed troops in Tajikistan, provided it with $40 million in aid, and is refurbishing an air base near Dushanbe. The North-South International Transportation Corridor agreement signed in 2000 by India, Iran, and Russia and the Agreement on International Transit of Goods between India, Iran, and Turkmenistan, signed in 1997, are also significant, because they go a long way in cutting time and costs in the transit of goods, thereby giving a boost to India's trade with Iran and other Central Asian nations. Though India has expressed an interest in joining the proposed 1,700-kilometer Turkmenistan-Afghanistan-Pakistan gas-pipeline project as the final destination, it continues to remain non-committal to receiving the 3 billion-cubic-feet-per-day pipeline amid doubts expressed by Afghanistan and Pakistan that Turkmenistan has enough gas to make the venture viable, apart from security issues posed by the passage through Afghanistan.

It is significant that India and Iran have agreed to intensify collaboration on transport projects that could link India with the Persian Gulf, Afghanistan, Central Asia, and Europe. India will cooperate with Iran in the development of a new port complex at Chah Bahar on the coast of Iran that could become India's gateway to Afghanistan and Central Asia. There is also another project that involves linking Chah Bahar port to the Iranian rail network, which is also well connected to Central Asia and Europe. India hopes to make Pakistan marginal to its relationship with the Central Asian region so that India's relations with Central Asia can no longer be hostage to Islamabad's policies.

India's growing interest in the acquisition of energy assets in African states as diverse as Sudan, Congo, Gabon, Cameroon, Nigeria, Chad, Ghana, and Angola has also been very prominent in recent years. India has decided to offer lines of credit up to $1 billion on a government-to-government basis to a number of oil-rich but poor African countries for infrastructure projects in exchange for oil exploration rights. A $6 billion infrastructure investment deal struck in Nigeria by ONGC Mittal Energy, a joint venture between India's state-run Oil and Natural Gas Corporation and the world's largest steel maker, Mittal Steel, is seen as a major breakthrough in this strategy.

Nigeria is India's biggest supplier of oil from Africa and India hopes to source an even greater share of oil from Nigeria in the next few years. India will now look to a group of eight West African countries in a special cooperation model called the Team-9 initiative, under which India offers credit for projects set up by Indian companies through the Export Import Bank of India. Team-9 countries include Burkina Faso, Chad, Ivory Coast, Equatorial Guinea, Ghana, Guinea-Bissau, Mali, and Senegal. India is exploring the possibility of high-level cooperation and investment in oil and gas sectors across various African states with India offering assistance in developing a pipeline network and infrastructure for transportation of the LNG. India's energy diplomacy is also now forcing India to undertake a more substantive engagement with Latin America. ONGC Videsh Ltd. (OVL), the overseas arm of India's state-owned ONGC, has finalised the acquisition of 15 per cent stake in a Brazilian oil company, making its foray into the South American territory. Venezuelan president Hugo Chavez signed various energy related trade deals during his visit to India in 2005. One of these agreements is expected to result in the OVL picking up a 49 per cent stake in a major Venezuelan oil field. Chavez told the representatives of Indian big business that Venezuela had the capacity to meet India's annual requirement of 100 million barrels of crude. He emphasized that Venezuela wanted to become a permanent partner of India in the hydrocarbon sector and invited Indian oil companies to follow the example of their Russian and Chinese counterparts and become more active in Venezuela's oil sector.

India's relations with Russia are also becoming energy focused, with Russia being the world's second-largest oil producer and its leading gas producer. Both sides have expressed their keenness to expand cooperation further in this sector, which is already playing an important role in bilateral relations. India's OVL, in partnership with Exxon-Mobil, a U.S. company, runs a profitable off-shore project in Sakhalin. The public sector company, in one of the biggest oil deals signed in Russia, purchased a 20 per cent share in the Sakhalin-I project with an investment of 1.7 billion. According to the terms of the contract, 40 per cent of the production will belong to the ONGC for the first five to six years. The Sakhalin venture will tap gas that will then be piped into northern Japan. The Sakhalin group of islands lies just north of Japan. There are an estimated 340 million metric tons of oil and 420 billion cubic meters of gas in the Sakhalin oilfield.

India and Russia have also decided to cooperate in the Caspian Sea basin and have identified a few other areas for exploration. Already, OVL has signed a confidentiality agreement to evaluate the data of Sakhalin-III (Kirinsky block). This investment alone is expected to be in the range of $1.5 billion. ONGC and Russia's natural gas monopoly, Gazprom, have signed a memorandum of understanding pledging to explore possibilities for joint ventures in India, Russia, and third countries to produce oil and gas and to build trunk pipelines. The Russian company Gazprom and the Gas Authority of India Limited are also jointly developing a block in the Bay of Bengal.

While India is scouring far and wide to quench its thirst for energy, it is in its immediate neighbourhood that it has been most disappointed. It is embroiled in territorial disputes that prevent the launch of a free-for-all energy foreign policy. While its troubled relationship with Pakistan continues to create problems for its plans to import oil from Iran, its other neighbour, Bangladesh has also reneged on its earlier commitment to the tripartite agreement for transportation of gas from Myanmar to India via a pipeline running through Bangladesh. India wants to pursue this project seriously, because of all the pipeline options to bring natural gas from the Shwe fields in offshore Myanmar, the overland option via Bangladesh is possibly the most economical.

The India-Bangladesh-Myanmar pipeline idea was initially seen as a landmark in Indo-Bangladesh relations, with Bangladesh agreeing to its territory being used for transport of any commodity to the Indian market for the first time in three decades. While India seems willing to pay $125 million as transit fee to Bangladesh, Dhaka also wants transit facility through India for hydroelectric power from Nepal and Bhutan to Bangladesh, a corridor of trade between Nepal and Bhutan, and measures to reduce bilateral trade imbalance before it can conclude this agreement.

The one reality that Indian diplomacy has to confront in its search for nation's energy security is the presence of China almost everywhere and its relative success in achieving desirable outcomes, more often than not, to India's detriment.

Oil and Natural Gas Sector

The oil industry can be divided into three major components: upstream, midstream and downstream. The upstream industry includes exploration and production activities, hence is also referred as the exploration and production (E&P) sector. The midstream industry processes, stores, markets and transports commodities including crude oil, natural gas, natural gas liquids (NGLs) like ethane propane and butane and sulphur. The downstream industry includes oil refineries, petrochemical plants, petroleum products distributors, retail outlets and natural gas distribution companies. The downstream industry provides consumers thousands of products such as gasoline, diesel, jet fuel, heating oil, asphalt, lubricants, synthetic rubber, plastics, fertilizers, antifreeze, pesticides, pharmaceuticals, natural gas and propane.

Both internationally and within India the oil and gas sector is characterised by existence of "integrated" companies, which are present in all these three sectors. The Indian Oil and Gas sector is one of the six core industries in India and has very significant forward linkages with the entire economy. The oil and gas sector meets more than two third of the total primary energy needs in the country.

The sector has been instrumental in putting India on the world map. At present India is the sixth largest crude oil consumer in the world and the ninth largest crude oil importer. The country is also increasing its share in the global refining market.

At present Indian refining sector is the sixth largest in the world. At the end of 2005, India had 0.5 per cent of the Oil and Gas resources of the world and 15 per cent of the world?s population whereas the reserve to production ratio is 20.7. At the end of 1995 India had the 5.5 thousand million barrels of reserves, grown only 1 per cent till the end of 2005 whereas crude oil consumption has grown more than 10 per cent over the last 5 years.

Upstream Sector: Exploration and Production

Upstream sector, oil and gas industry, deals with exploration and production of oil and gas. Oil exploration takes place at oil wells in four stages. The first stage is drilling, act of boring a hole through which oil or gas may be produced if encountered in commercial quantities. The second stage is completion, process in which the well is enabled to produce oil or gas.

The third stage is production, production time of oil and gas and the final stage is abandonment, where the well no longer produces or produces so poorly that it is a liability to its owner and is abandoned.

An oil field is a region with an abundance of oil wells extracting petroleum (oil) from below ground.

Because the oil reservoirs typically extend over a large area, possibly several hundred kilometres across, full exploitation entails multiple wells scattered across the area.

There are more than 40,000 oil and gas fields of all sizes in the world and the largest discovered conventional oil field is the Ghawar Field (75-83 billion) is Saudi Arabia. In tandem with the stagnated reserves, the production of oil has also been sluggish over the last decade, as a matter of fact in last ten years oil production has increased by only 1.6 per cent.

Reserve to Production Ratio

Reserve to Production Ration (R/P Ratio) is the portion of the identified resource from which usable natural resources can be economically and legally extracted out of the ground.

Production can be offshore as well as onshore. An offshore system of production is defined with a platform raised above the water to support a number of producing wells whereas onshore is a platform at the sea level.

R/P ratio for the world at the end of 2005 is 40.6 implying that natural resources that has been identified subject to pull out till date is about 40 times the amount already taken out of the ground.

Downstream: Refining and Marketing

Refining, oil industry after exploration and production, is related with manufacturing petroleum products by a series of processes that separate crude oil into its major components and blend or convert these components into a wide range of finished products, such as gasoline or Aviation Turbine Fuel. Refining capacity depends on the technology used in refineries, capable of processing crude production into clean fuels.

In the recent age of decreasing oil production refining capacity have to have well supportive technology, which meet increasingly more stringent environmental Standards.

With the increase in global oil demand and stagnant reserve, refining capacity deserves new capacity addition to meet demand. But the graph shows slightly increasing trend of refining capacity till date in last decade. Refinery throuput, as opposed to designed capacity, is computed by dividing the number of refined barrels of oil processed by the actual number of days the refinery was in operation.

Onshore and Offshore Oil and Gas Fields in India

In India crude oil is produced in Onshore and Offshore. Onshore fields are in Assam/Nagaland, Arunachal Pradesh, Gujarat, and Tamil Nadu/ Andhra Pradesh. Oil India Limited (OIL) and Oil and Natural Gas Commission (ONGC) have the onshore field for crude oil production. Offshore production occurs at Bombay High run by ONGC and Private/Joint Venture companies. For the natural gas onshore fields are the same for Crude oil in addition with Rajasthan as an onshore field. For the offshore Bombay high is the one for the production.

Exploration Overseas

In keeping with the objectives of the Energy Security section of the National Common Minimum Programme, ONGC Videsh Ltd. (OVL), wholly owned subsidiary of ONGC, as well as other national oil companies such as IOC, OIL and GAIL, have been pursuing the acquisition of equity oil abroad, as well as the acquisition abroad of oil and gas exploration acreages and producing properties. These companies have participating interests in oil and gas projects located in Vietnam, Sudan, Russia, Iraq, Iran, Myanmar, Libya, Syria, Australia, Ivory Coast, Qatar and Egypt. OVL, in association with other oil sector PSUs, is aggressively scouting for E&P opportunities in countries such as Venezuela, Kazakhstan, Kuwait, Yemen, Chad, Niger, Nigeria, Angola, Cuba, Sierra Leone and Ecuador in addition to efforts to acquire more E&P assets in the countries where it is operating currently.

Production

Domestic production of crude oil has been a reason of worry for the Indian economy for some time now. For more than 16 years the total production of crude has stagnated around 32-33 MMT. This has been particularly disturbing given the crude oil consumption in the country implying an increasing dependence on imported crude. At present India?s crude dependence is around 78 per cent. According to TERI estimates, by 2030 India?s import dependency may shoot up to a disturbing 93 per cent. In the current year, the production of crude oil in the country during the first half was 16.14 MMT as against 17.00 MMT during the corresponding period of 2004-05, a shortfall of about 5 per cent.

Refining

Oil refining is a continuous process and the cost of refining of individual petroleum products is not worked out separately because all products are produced together. The cost of refining crude oil depends upon a number of factors including the type of crude oil, size of refinery, refinery configuration, age of equipment, technology used, etc.

The technology for producing the petroleum products from the crude oil differs from one refinery to another. The hydro cracker and catalytic hydro cracker technology are the two major technologies through which petroleum products are yielded. There are 18 refineries operating in the country, 17 in the Public Sector and one in the Private Sector, with a total installed capacity of 127.37 million metric tonnes per annum (MMTPA).

Natural Gas

Natural gas is a gaseous fossil fuel consisting primarily of methane. In India production of natural gas has increased over 3 times in the last two decades though the share of the production of natural gas with respect to world natural gas production wais only 0.6 per cent at the end of 2005 and reserve to production ratio of 36.2. Petroleum and Natural Gas Regulatory Board (PNGRB) Act came into force on April 03, 2006 to protect the interest of consumers and entitles engaged in specified activities to ensure uninterrupted and adequate supply of petroleum, petroleum products and natural gas in all parts of the country and promote competitive markets in Oil and Gas sector of India.

5

China's Soft Authority Diplomacy in South Asia

ASEAN has sought to restrain Chinese power by enmeshing it in regional institutions. Whereas ASEAN is attractive China to tame the aggressive realpolitik that has characterised Chinese foreign relations, Beijing views the same institutions as a way to extend its regional influence and has sought to exclude the US. In planning for the first EAC summit, which was held in Malaysia, China tried to exclude India, Australia and New Zealand, but was overruled by Japan and ASEAN members. As China's regional influence grows, most ASEAN members are working to push against or balance Chinese power. While deepening trade and diplomatic co-operation with Beijing, many members, US allies such as Thailand and the Philippines, key 'swing states' such as Singapore, and emerging regional powers such as Indonesia, have also increased security ties with Washington.

The question is why the US has changed its policy in the region from a benign power to one almost squarely focusing on hard power balance issues including terrorism as the overall obsession. For Southeast Asia, long under the United States' political and economic influence, times are rapidly moving in a new direction. A decade ago about three-quarters of US investment in East Asia went to Southeast Asia. That figure has now fallen to 10 percent. Approximately 80 percent of US investment in East Asia now goes to China.

The United States remnants the region's single biggest destination for exports, and will be for some years to come. This is probably why the White House is on the defensive in terms of coming to grasp with the regional and multilateral setting in East and Southeast Asia. As one observer remarks: ''Relations between Southeast Asia and the United States are perhaps best described as 'a policy without a strategy''. Asian leaders are organizing and building new regional institutions precisely to avoid the sort of power politics that America is practicing. Progress has been tenuous but real, and most regional leaders are cautiously optimistic about Asia's future. As long as this remains true, American emphasis on balance-of-power politics will continue to meet with only limited success. Indeed, this approach is likely to be under-mined by regional players, who are more interested in participating in economic integration and building regional communities than in divisive balancing behaviour. Most troubling for the United States, it will also cede its leadership role in Asia and limit Washington's ability to influence the future shape of regional institutions in the region.

China's ultimate strategic purpose remains a subject of debate and speculation among analysts. Southeast Asia, in this respect, is the sole region adjacent to China in which Chinese influence can most easily expand. A benign interpretation would see China as simply cultivating the sort of stable, peaceful, and prosperous regional environment that is required for its own successful modernization. A more sceptical view sees China playing a long-term game designed to curtail American influence and weave a close-knit economic and security community with China at the centre.

Beijing is in fact using nationalism and the 'glories of the Chinese civilisation' to instil a sense of unity among Chinese nationals domestically and among the Chinese Diaspora in Southeast Asia. Although Beijing may acknowledge that rampant nationalism could pose a danger to its own internal stability, it has astutely harnessed it to build a new Asian pride and identity, which it hopes might help establish a new Asian system of politics, economics, security and culture within the 'ASEAN+3' framework.

The PRC ardently hopes this could be transformed ultimately into an East Asian Community under its leadership (Teo 2005). To realize its peaceful rise, China is using a sophisticated blend of trade, confidence building measures, and development assistance to establish itself as an important regional-cum-global leader.

Of course the appeal of Confucianism offers Beijing a definite comparative advantage in its soft supremacy approach. Moreover, the relationship China enjoys with the Chinese Diaspora in the region, who dominate the economic and, in some countries like Thailand, increasingly the political scene, is another advantage. The immediate implications of such an approach are that it would be naive to believe that China is not interested in exerting a dominant influence over its regional hinterland; commercial and financial muscle will eventually be the levers of choice, perhaps spearheaded by a strong regional currency. As much as the Chinese may be more ethnically exclusive than Americans and some Europeans, they are every bit as eager to see Chinese culture and traditions adopted by others - as a mark of civilization. As more and more Chinese tourists visit the region and even begin to dominate the tourist trade, the service sector response will be to tailor to Chinese taste and custom. This will inevitably result in a revival of Chinese culture and language in local communities once believed to have assimilated. Already one of the fastest growing Chinese language media groups is based in Malaysia, where Chinese language education has an unbroken history of more than a century. Up to the present, businesses have catered to a culture that projects modernity and sophistication in a Western guise - this could change and have an impact on U.S. and European influence.

The use of culture as a tool of diplomacy highlights the sense of theatre that China skilfully deploys to exaggerate kin, ethnicity and national bonds between the Motherland and the Diaspora. It also reflects an increased appreciation by the Chinese government of the importance of norms and soft power in diplomacy. Chinese print media, television, music, food, and popular culture are spreading around the region as never before. So, too, are Chinese tourists fanning out across the region, often filling the void left by American tourists staying home after 9/11, the Bali bombing, and tsunami; 800,000 Chinese toured both Thailand and Singapore in 2004.

In this way it is safe to say that ethnic Chinese business communities scattered in Southeast Asia have facilitated 'the rearticulation of mainland China into the global economy' not least through their reciprocal involvement in more than 100,000 joint ventures in China. It is also arguable that the Chinese Diaspora has been used not 'just as a financial resource in China to fund revolutions in the past and economic reforms in the present; they have been an important symbolic resource in the construction of Chinese nationalism'.

The combination of geo-political and geo-economic strategies and cultural expansion begs an answer to the question: 'what are the implications of China's policy of soft power for US influence in the region'? Elizabeth Economy notes the important point that, China's rise to date appears to be less about the 'inevitable conflict of rising power' theory, popular in some circles, than about creeping power transition. Chinese thinkers, themselves, have recognized that the international community is concerned by the potential implications of China's rise and have taken pains to ensure that it will be perceived as non-threatening. This is well illustrated by Li Junru, Vice-President of the Central Party School at the Chinese Communist Party (CCP), who explicitly outlined the benefits to China's neighbours, stating, 'China's rise will not damage the interests of other Asian countries. That is because as China rises, it provides a huge market for its neighbours. At the same time, the achievements of China's development will allow it to support the progress of others in the region' (2005: 3-4).

In order to understand the motives and objectives of Chinese pragmatism, it is important to put both bilateral and multilateral diplomatic initiatives and foreign policy into the overall trade and security context and understand the internal and external constraints for a Chinese expansive strategy in Southeast Asia. The region as a whole maintains a trade surplus with China of US$8 billion annually, largely from its enormous exports of raw materials and precision machinery. China also agreed to an 'Early Harvest

Package' that is perceived by ASEAN as 'largely a concession' to provide benefits through tariff reductions on 573 products including agricultural and manufactured goods. Individual Chinese entrepreneurs are also now expanding China's economic reach throughout Laos and Myanmar.

In some areas, locals now use only the Yuan and speak Chinese. The forays of Chinese companies fit in with a broader strategic push by Beijing to establish closer economic cooperation with and among Asian countries. Unofficial reports by ASEAN officials claim that the foreign policy aim is part of a broader thrust by China to deploy multilateralism against what it sees as US unilateralist hegemony in the region and the world. 'This is a long-term game that China is playing,' says a senior ASEAN official. 'They want a situation in Southeast Asia that automatically takes into account China's interests. The whole objective of the policy is to avoid strategic encirclement by the U.S.' (Vatikiotis and Hiebert 2003).

Critical voices note that ASEAN's trade with Japan of $136 billion and that of the United States of more than $136 billion in 2004 exceeds trade with China. At the same time, in both Indonesia and Malaysia, people complain that jobs are being lost to China. Not least because Chinese textile exports since January 2005 have increased, thus implying down-ward competition for Cambodia and Vietnam. A growing mainland Chinese economic presence could also fuel latent resentment against the sizable ethnic Chinese economic elites in the region. In fact, almost no research has so far been done to investigate the impact of China's FDI on labour markets, environment and social issues and the question is whether China is exporting its own poor labour practices.

Factors inhibiting Chinese private investment and tourism are sensitive to the treatment of Chinese minorities in Southeast Asia and in particular in the Philippines and Indonesia. The Indonesian racial riots in the aftermath of the financial crisis in 1998 which targeted ethnic Chinese created long-term damage to the 'bamboo network'. There are also cultural impediments when it comes to expansion as noted by a senior ASEAN official: 'Unlike Americans, Chinese don't embrace foreigners - you cannot 'become Chinese''.

China's approach has been subtle, using soft power and economic diplomacy to build a benign multilateral framework in the shape of a free-trade agreement with ASEAN. 'China has shown a great deal of sensitivity,' says Singapore Prime Minister Goh Chok Tong. 'China realizes that it is a huge elephant, and even if it treads softly, it can still shake the ground.' One observer notes that 'China is seen by some to be slowly filling the vacuum left behind by the United States in the political, economic and security spheres in the region. This implies that 'U.S. Influence in Asia under Bush is Waning' (Agence France Presse, August 29, 2004.) and being replaced by China.

Beijing has also enthused the dynamics of regional cooperation in many other ways. One example is China's enthusiasm for developing the ASEAN-China dialogue into a vibrant web of multilevel and multi-sector cooperation. As noted above, the 1997 financial crisis was the main catalyst for the creation of a full-fledged diplomatic mechanism spanning summit, ministerial, and senior official levels. As Cheng-Chwee notes, the mechanism has stretched into various semi-state and civil society organizations that include research departments, media outlets, youth organizations, and the business sector. Also cooperation in agriculture, transport infraarrangement, as well as energy has been included.

Over time, these ties have interwoven into a web of interdependence between China and ASEAN. The PRC has also taken the initiative in pushing for the creation of the Network of East Asia Think-Tanks (NEAT) (2005: 115). These moves are not merely tactical but part of PRCs overall goal to utilize the ASEAN-plus-three as the main vehicle of East Asian cooperation and the creation of the hybrid East Asian Community. Although there are other factors at play, China has played a decisive role in pushing in that direction. 'China's enthusiasm for East Asian cooperation is clearly driven by its aspiration to shape the direction of the existing regional institutions' (2005: 115-116).

Diplomatically, China's goals and vision in Southeast Asia are clear as it rivals the US and Japan world-wide and regionally. Moreover it may be again considering ASEAN as its own Monroe sphere, as it was during the 400 years of the Chinese tributary system under the Ming-Qing Emperors. Southeast Asian countries appear to be accepting sub-ordination as they seek to profit from the rising China.

IMPLICATIONS FOR MULTI-TRACK DIPLOMACY

These trends present a sober picture indeed of the world of the 21st century. The realm of multi-track diplomacy, as one small player in the global drama, exists within this context, yet brings a perspective, a commitment and a set of methodologies that are at humanity's leading edge for dealing with these most difficult issues. In fact, I would go so far as to suggest that the work of peace-building is at the forefront of our planet's evolutionary journey in these times.

The very dangerous conditions described in the section above arise from, and thrive in, a worldview and set of assumptions about the world as a place of separation.

Separative consciousness sees duality and difference as opportunity for superiority, dominance and control, and breeds materialism, greed and violence. For many centuries the dominant western world organized its political, social and economic systems on this basis. The general breakdown in the global (and environmental) environment we are seeing now can be understood as the natural ripening of the inherent seed of destruction in the separative worldview, for when only the parts are seen, without reference to the whole, duality will play itself out in struggle, contest and conflict indefinitely.

We live at a time when large numbers of people on the planet are discovering that there is another worldview, a holistic or unitive view, that acknowledges the parts as inherently inter-related and part of a larger innate wholeness. Beyond the duality we share a common human experience, a common spiritual source, and a common capacity for connecting through that source to ways of being that will honour both the diversity and the unity in the family of life. The world is living through a major period of transformation, as the bankruptcy of one worldview becomes apparent, while the new worldview is still in its infant stages. This produces both the potential for chaos and the potential for great creativity. The peacebuilders of the world, and the multi-track approach to peace in particular, because of its systems orientation, carries that creative potential and is, therefore, a vehicle for humanity's evolution into a new state of consciousness.

In addition to these obvious activities, multi-track diplomacy can face the unique challenges of this transformational period in seven quite specific ways:

Maintaining Flexibility in the Face of the Unknown

The state of world affairs is, as we have seen, in a period of great flux. Many events that we can reasonably anticipate may or may not occur. Others that we have not considered may happen tomorrow. A single event of biological terrorism, for instance, could easily change the face of life on this planet as we know it.

A single expansive move by China, or new confrontation in the Balkans or the Middle East, could re-configure political relations for many years to come. The truth is, peacebuilders need to be prepared to move in several directions at once, both responding to whatever opportunities present themselves for positive and effective work for peace, and also being pro-active in turning challenges into opportunities.

To maintain this flexibility as a whole field of endeavour requires greater reflexivity, discourse and coordination among theory builders and practitioners from all parts of the world.

Recognizing Healing as the Key to Transformation

Because of the profound human trauma discussed earlier, and the brokenness of many systems, healing and reconciliation are critical aspects of any multi-track diplomacy process. New and sustainable peace systems must take into account the mending process that comes with acknowledgement of the harm done, apology and forgiveness when possible, completion of mourning, and healing at the individual and group levels.

One of the greatest challenges facing peacebuilders today is not just how to engage individuals in this type of healing, but how to engage whole systems, and especially the leadership, for unless humanity learns how to heal itself, the trauma will condemn us to repeat the same cycles of violence from generation to generation.

Building the Infrastructure for Peace

The forces of war have an existing infrastructure that enables them to mobilize and actualize their aims -they have armies and arms suppliers; transportation, commerce and communication systems; banking, taxing and other funding methods; media, education and propaganda systems; and government ministries, clans, villages, political parties and other entities capable of taking action.

The forces of peace have little of this. We have come a long way in recent years toward developing organizations and networks that can serve as vehicles for carrying and coordinating peace-building activities, with an accompanying research, education and media capability as well. Much more needs to be done to create both a human and an institutional infrastructure for peace-building, in order to concretize these methods and approaches in social, political and economic systems that can both stand on their own and work together toward a shared goal.

In addition to such institutions, we need the capacity to move money, materials, people and technologies rapidly and efficiently to wherever needed on the planet. In this way the transformation of consciousness is assisted by building alternative structures so that as the old collapses, there is something in place to sustain that which is being birthed.

Taking the Holistic and Positive View

One of the hallmarks of a multi-track approach is the capacity to see the whole, and the inter-relationship of the various parts. We know that development and peace are mutually interdependent, for instance, and that democratization requires the capacity for conflict resolution and problem solving at a group level, so we see the natural interface of several disciplines.

This kind of relational awareness is critical to building peace systems, for it encourages the kind of connections, bridges, alliances and networking that are essential to the ongoing support of the change process. Stepping back and seeing the whole picture, especially that of the evolutionary moment in which we stand, allows us to hold the gate open for a new range of possibilities. It also allows us to affirm the positive view that, despite all the problems in the way, peace is indeed possible. In this way we energize the potential rather than the despair, and keep hope, that precious and fragile flame, vibrant and alive.

Making Peace From the Inside Out

People whose life is given to peace-building, whether as outside third parties or actors within conflict systems, are generally motivated to service, and as servers, may be prone to work themselves beyond the point of balance. Certainly working in war zones, with wounded people and in tense and violent circumstances can produce symptoms of secondary trauma, compassion fatigue and burn-out. Because multi-track diplomacy is a systems approach, in which even the intervenor is part of the system, and because it is a multi-level approach, in which the personal level is just as important as the inter-group level, those involved in this field have the opportunity to use our own technology with ourselves, becoming agents of peace in our being as well as in our doing.

When we are taking the time to integrate what we teach about peace in the outer domain with our deep experience of peace within, we can be much more effective, at the individual and at the institutional levels, in two ways: we are clearer and stronger channels for the outer work when we take time to reconnect with our own inner source of peace, and we are better models for others, showing by our presence as much as by our actions that peace is a viable and dynamic state.

Creating New Pathways for Shifting Consciousness

A colleague, Robert Fuller, once spoke about finding 'a better game than war.' Peacebuilders taking a multi-track approach are engaged in this endeavour. We know that the 'war option' is a lose-lose game; we come offering a better way, a way that goes even beyond win-win toward the transformation of the consciousness that would allow us to build truly just and peace-able societies.

Because the methods and pathways for this shift are inherent in the principles and practices of peace-building with a holistic view, we occupy a position in the world analogous to the early road or railway builders. We are opening the paths, setting the tracks in place, laying down the rails, making clear the direction that will shape the future of our planet.

Our tools-methods for cooperation, creative joint problem solving, reconciliation, prevention, dialogue, mediation, negotiation, and communication, among others-are the tracks that we are setting down, so people will be able to transport themselves across old territory in new and better ways. As with all road building, once we open a path, more and more travellers will use it, especially if it carries them to where they want to go.

The ways of thinking and acting we are inviting people into is a different, and a better game than war, and our work makes it possible for people in large numbers to make that shift. Knowing this, we can be more intentional about it.

Empowering Peacebuilders for Local Action

Multi-track diplomacy invites everyone into the game of peace-building. It says that there is a place and way that people from any sector of society can make a contribution to peace.

Those of us engaged in travelling to places of conflict to make interventions there realize that building peace is primarily a local task. What we can offer is to give people a view and a direct experience of what is possible, help them do what they want to do faster and better, and perhaps strengthen their capacity to use appropriate tools and skills. We can motivate, catalyze, inspire, instruct, facilitate, encourage, support, assist, demonstrate, and convene. We can present possibilities, open minds to new ways of thinking, and cheer people on as they take charge of changing the systems they live in. We can articulate theories and best practices, provide a safe space where people can meet 'the other', or elicit inner individual and cultural wisdom about peace and conflict resolution. What we can never do impose our solutions on others, or build their new systems for them. Our power to empower is perhaps the most important role we can play in the 21st century.

The more individuals who feel empowered to work in their own systems for peace and conflict transformation, the closer the world comes to that critical mass that will allow for a massive leap in consciousness, allowing new processes for peace that were previously unimaginable to become normative, and easy.

Exercising our power to empower means generating more stories like those shared elsewhere in this book, building a base of success from which we can all learn and draw. It means enabling people to have that critical understanding of what true power is, the very opposite of the power of domination and control that characterizes war systems.

INDIA FALLING BEHIND CHINA IN SOUTH ASIAN DIPLOMACY

India has always been a local superpower, being by far the largest country within South Asia, and is, in fact, the only one in the group that borders every other South Asian country except Afghanistan, which shares a border with Pakistan. But India's economic performance was stunted by years of state control of the kind now prevalent in Iran. Over the past 15 years, however, economic growth has been strong, enabling the country to have a much greater diplomatic reach than at any time since the 1950s when India briefly emerged as the leader of those countries that were being de-colonized by the European powers. Given this situation, it ought to have been the case that New Delhi would be preeminent in its own backyard. Instead, over the past two decades, India has lost the status of being the lead player in any South Asian country barring Bhutan, a country with which it still has a treaty relationship. In almost the entire region, China has overtaken India in that intangible quality - influence - especially in Nepal and Sri Lanka, while Beijing's existing alliances with Pakistan and Bangladesh are growing stronger.

This is not due to a lack of quality within India's diplomatic service. Instead, the Indian Foreign Service (IFS) has produced a modern corps of skilled diplomats, many experts in different regions of the world, and eager to do more to advance their country's interests. The wall they face is the ambivalence that has become second nature to the country's top policy makers, both within the political crust as well as the administrative backup. Phrases such as "going all the way" and "going for the kill" are inelegant. Yet they represent a reality that is that sometimes a country has to formulate and then determinedly implement a clear policy to be carried out till success is achieved.

In South Asia, such a quality was recently displayed by President Percy Mahinda Rajapaksa of Sri Lanka. He succeeded in wiping out the terrorist group known as the Liberation Tigers of Tamil Eelam (LTTE) where, over the past three decades, all his predecessors had failed. Unlike them, President Rajapaksa did not heed (well-meaning but disastrous) advice to slow down his offensive or agree to a cease-fire, the latter being a device that the LTTE used since 1987 to gain time to recover after having lost the initiative in the field. Once the LTTE recovered its strength, the ceasefire would be abandoned. This point was repeatedly made by Rajapaksa to the peacemakers who clustered around him, especially in the final months of the brief, brutal war against the LTTE that began with his coming to office in 2005.

Once India, because of political considerations such as the need to avoid alienating the country's sizable Tamil population, refused to give the Sri Lankan army equipment, Rajapaksa turned to Pakistan and China. Both countries opened their warehouses to him, and so built up immense capital both within Sri Lanka's Sinhala most importantity as well as the country's policy establishment. Rajapaksa showed none of the half-heartedness that has characterized so much of Indian policy and, as a result, emerged a winner. In the case of India, the desire to win brownie points with key international players (by heeding their sometimes incorrect advice) as well as an aversion to risk ensured that much of Indian diplomacy was too watered down to be effective. This is especially the case in its immediate neighbourhood.

This on-again, off-again excellence can be seen in Indian diplomatic policy towards Pakistan especially in regard to the long-term pattern of instituting confidence building measures (CBM) being followed - usually after a mass terror attack - with strong rhetoric and a withdrawal of contact. The reality is that in the case of Pakistan, conventional war may have ceased to be an option. This is because the Pakistan army has itself lost control of many of the jihadis that it has trained, equipped and funded for so long.

Instead of reducing the risk of a terror attack, going after the Pakistan military would inflame a large segment of the Pakistani population thus making them susceptible to recruitment in the ongoing jihad against India. Given that situation, it may have been preferable for Indian policymakers to publicly resort to a conventional war except in the case of a conflict started by Pakistan, an unlikely possibility. The military option would work only if (a) the Pakistan army controls the jihadi networks and (b) is comprehensively defeated in battle. Neither condition exists.

A "No War" declaration by India would remove the Pakistani military establishment's most frequently used excuse to station more than 60 percent of its army along the India border, even as the force is engaged in a life-and-death struggle with the Pakistan Taliban. Instead, even though New Delhi has no intention of going to war, the prospect of one is deliberately kept open especially after terror strikes such as Mumbai 11/26-28. Thus, the benefits of India's "No War" declaration are denied, while the other side is aware that the mock-aggressive posture is a bluff and hence will not change its behaviour as a result of the threat.

A glaring example of how promoting the idea that India would go to war over Pakistani provocations has hurt New Delhi can be seen in the 2002 standoff with Pakistan in the mountains separating the two. Ostensibly to scare the international community into putting pressure on Pakistan to call off its Kashmir jihad, the then-Vajpayee government mobilized two Indian army strike corps on the border, keeping them and their support units on a hair-trigger alert for the greater part of the year. Aware that the Indians were bluffing, the Pakistan government refused to budge from its policy of helping jihadists active in Kashmir. The long Indian army mobilization created a perception of regional instability that affected India's status as a safe investment destination even as it exhausted the elite army units on the front line. Given the information that India would not attack, the 2002 mobilization came at a horrendous cost and no benefit. In a system where posturing comes easily to the higher levels of the Indian policy establishment, Prime Minister Manmohan Singh has thus far resisted jingoism and has made it evident that India would not be stampeded into military action. In the case of Sri Lanka, the policy was to intensify conflict until victory. What is needed is a clear policy that is carried out effectively, not a zig-zag routine that confuses the international community and results in a loss of credibility for India.

Military sales can become an effective instrument of diplomacy, were they deployed by India. Within the region, including in Sri Lanka and Nepal, the military is a significant component of the policy process, often the crucial player. Because of New Delhi's longstanding policy of not permitting foreign military sales save for exceptional situations, China has been provided an opportunity to fill the gap. Had Bangladesh, Nepal and Sri Lanka been more reliant on Indian equipment and training for their armed forces, New Delhi would have been in a much stronger position to influence policy in those places than it is today. Instead, the "weapons gap" isincreasingly being filled by China.

The mantra of "non-alignment" has in most instances become a cover for lack of action. Even during the period of the Cold War, when India suffered many of the consequences of being seen as a Soviet ally, not a single Soviet soldier was ever stationed in India or trained here, nor did any Indian soldier undertake any sort of mission in the USSR. In contrast, there are regular exchanges of U.S. and Indian soldiers and joint training exercises have become routine. The warming of ties is because there is a natural fit between the two sides. India has a significant pool of trained (and trainable) manpower, while the United States has abundant stocks of equipment that could be transferred to New Delhi rather than mothballed or left under-utilized. This is especially the case with naval vessels, where India is now being made to pay $3 billion for a secondhand Russian aircraft carrier that it is finding it difficult to float and move at the same time.

Progress in U.S.-India military to military relatives has been slow and is still far below its potential in substantial part because of the wariness of the Indian establishment over China's reaction. Compare this with Pakistan which has built up close military ties with both China and the United States, its friendship with one not affecting the other.

In the military field, the choice is between going with the United States or going alone, because a military alliance with China is not an option. Beijing sees New Delhi as a potential competitor and has repeatedly shown through its actions its commitment to a strategic policy that inhibits the growth of Indian power. Unfortunately, in this case, Indian ambivalence is now being matched by the United States under the Obama administration, which has downgraded ties with India to a level much below that set under President George W. Bush. It seems inevitable, however, that both countries will, hopefully within the present presidential term, awaken to the need for a partnership that can ensure that Asia does not fall under the sway of any single power.

The persistent Indian ambivalence in policy was visible in Sri Lanka, where India simultaneously called for a cease-fire while backing the unity of the island nation. As a consequence of simultaneously conveying two contradictory messages, neither the Tamil nor the Sinhala zealots have anything other than distaste for India, while the abundant provision of military supplies has led the Sri Lankan military towards becoming as close to Beijing as are their counterparts in Pakistan.

In Nepal, after first helping to get King Gyanendra to abdicate, New Delhi threw its support behind the Maoists, who promptly reacted by threatening to scrap the India-Nepal agreement and replace it with a similar deal with China. After its embrace of the Maoists, which ended only after their tilt to Beijing became manifest (by the end of 2008), no other Nepali party is willing to trust New Delhi and see it as a reliable partner, even the once-friendly Nepali Congress. Meanwhile, in a show of deft footwork, Chinese diplomats have been active in Kathmandu renewing ties with the non-Maoist parties that today run the government (after the departure of the Maoists), so as to accelerate the growth of PRC influence in Nepal.

Today, there are almost as many radical training camps located within Bangladesh as there in Pakistan, camps whose specific purpose is to replenish the stream of jihadis into India. Yet, unlike in the case of Pakistan, the Indian government is not posturing as if was is likely. A hostile Pakistan, an unfriendly Bangladesh, and Nepal and Sri Lanka heading towards the PRC. These are the wages of a diplomacy that refuses to go for the jugular in the pursuit of objectives, but almost invariably crafts a compromise that gives much less geopolitical benefit. India presents an example of how a most important power that avoids a clear policy line or a better deployment of its assets gives way to the other who is ruthless and willing to complete the marathon rather than slow down and stop before the finish line. Such a policy is the delight of politicians and anathema to statesmen, who understand the need for not just vision, but for will and perseverance.

A DIPLOMATIC GIMMICK OR STRATEGIC SURRENDER?

The year 2014 marks the 60th anniversary of the Panchsheel Agreement between India and China and the Governments declared year 2014 as 'India—China Year of Friendly Exchanges'. For the Tibetans, each such 'celebration' or the reiteration of the so-called Panchsheel principles in every Sino-Indian Joint communiqué is a haunting reminder of their national tragedy. With the signing on April 29, 1954, the much trumpeted Panchsheel Agreement, which Acharya J B Kriplani referred as 'born in sin', Tibet's political fate was sealed off as the 'Tibet Region of China'.

The treaty was the first ever International treaty that recognizes China's Sovereignty over Tibet. Much to everyone's chagrin, the Government of Tibet in Lhasa and the Tibetan people whose fate was decided through this contentious treaty were not even consulted or informed. Indeed, this was an additional injustice to the Tibetans who were passing through the most critical phase of their history.

No wonder, Indian Intelligence Chief B.N. Mullick found the Tibetan Diaspora in Kalimpong shocked and anguished. In his book, "My years with Nehru", Mr. Mullick stated, "The Sino-

Indian Treaty of 1954 caused a terrible shock to the Tibetans. They had already been upset by the unilateral Indian acceptance of the Chinese suzerainty over Tibet which, according to them, allowed China to commit aggression against that country."

Many political analysts wonder, if Prime Minister Nehru was against inheriting the British imperialist's extraterritorial rights and colonial legacy in Tibet, why then accept the British imperialist concept of Chinese suzerainty over Tibet?

Meanwhile, the Independent India's continuous diplomatic vacillations finally culminated into the recognition of Tibet as a part of China in a bid to secure peace and security across Himalayas, thus sealing the fate of Tibet for eternity.

Consequently, as India forfeit all its rights and properties in Tibet; downgrading the Indian Mission in Lhasa to a Consulate General and its gradual closure along with its Trade Agents in Yatung, Gyantse and Gartok etc., surrendering of its 12 Rest Houses and the Postal, Telegraph, Public telephone services, hospitals and withdrawal of the military escorts etc, India failed to obtain any quid pro quo in the clear demarcation of the Indo-Tibetan border. And as if that were not enough, the Indian Government agreed upon opening a Chinese Consulate General in Bombay.

It's another story that barely a month after signing of the Panchsheel treaty, Indian officials and traders in Tibet were unscrupulously harassed and intimidated and eventually coaxed to leave Tibet unceremoniously. This ludicrous harassment campaign involves diverting flashflood and damaging Indian Trade Agent etc, practice of shooting near the Site in order to threaten the lives of the officials and the border incursions in Bara Hoti and other border areas besides the occupation of Aksai Chin.

In July 1954, following the destruction of the Indian Trade Agency buildings in an unprecedented flash flood in Gyantse, Tibet (eyewitnesses suspect Chinese forces of destroying the embankment to let the flash floods into the Agency premises), the Chinese Government had created incessant obstacles in the smooth and timely renovation of the Trade Agent. Later the laborers working on the site of renovation were harassed. Further inconveniences from the Chinese officials included denying accommodation for the official, restriction on the hiring of private trucks or import of India's own trucks during the renovation. Provisions of transport and other support from the local Chinese authorities are a far cry.

To add to the Agency's woe, Chinese Government launched military firing practice over the Agency site. The shooting practice is believed to be a strategy of harassing the Indian officials. Eventually, China even restricted the movements of the Trade Agent officials and their families inside Tibet. And the mail services of the Agency too were suspended. Furthermore, in the pretext of registration of arms, the Chinese even confiscated the arms possessed by the Agency and the Indian nationals.

The harassment of the Indian traders in Tibet included locking of their shops and confiscation of goods without valid causes. And many others were prosecuted and detained on sheer unfounded suspicion. Indian pilgrims to Mt Kailash were also detained for many weeks and their movements restricted. Subsequently, the Chinese Government also prevented the Indian Government from evacuating the Indian nationals from Tibet. The Chinese Government refused to accept Indian Government's evacuation of Ladakhi Lamas and the Kashmiri Muslims to India stating that they are Tibetan citizens from times immemorial.

The Indian Government lodged constant protest over the unhelpful and unfriendly attitude of the local Chinese authorities towards Indian officials and national but to no avail. Such ghastly actions by China are hardly in conformity with principles of non-aggression and friendly co-existence enshrined in the Panchsheel treaty.

Meanwhile Chinese Government launched series of hostile propaganda against India in its official 'Lhasa Daily' newspaper accusing the Indian troops based in Gyantse of harassing local Tibetans. The Indian troops were alleged to be seizing food grains and fodders and forcing the local Tibetans to supply transport, firewood, servants, etc in return for nothing. They were also accused of forcing locals to do corvee work, and also destroying crops and colluding with the Tibetan traitor Phala etc. The Indian doctors were also alleged to be charging exorbitant fee from the local Tibetans and the Indian traders purportedly exploiting the Tibetans.

Indian Government denied the allegations as sheer fabrication. Yet, amid all these developments, curiously enough, unlike India, a small Himalayan nation of Nepal continue to retain its Consulate General in Lhasa to this day.

It was even more appalling to find that the Indian Government was supplying rice and other commodities to the occupying Chinese PLA soldiers in Tibet during the critical period. And in the Indian parliament many lawmakers were alarmed to find the Government "Feeding the enemy?" In his recent article titled, "60 years on: Unforgiving Legacy of the Panchsheel Agreement", former Special Director of The Intelligence Bureau, Mr. R N Ravi aptly asked, "Why did India go for the Panchsheel Agreement giving away all its geopolitical and geostrategic interests and assets in Tibet accrued over centuries and so crucial to its national security, even without settling the border?"

Later, Prime Minister Nehru was vehemently criticized for naively assuming that the signing of the agreement indirectly symbolizes China's acceptance of the Sino-India frontiers and that he had secured peace in the Himalayas.

Studies show that many Indian foreign ministry officials including Secretary General Girja Sharkar Bajpai did stress on the quid pro quo and in his notes to Ambassador Panikkar on 21st November 1951, Mr. Bajpai emphasized that the recognition of the Sino-India border should be a part of general settlement and that there was no question of surrendering the advantages accrued from the Simla Convention without getting a firm assurance from the Chinese on the McMahon Line and the other sectors. Mr. Bajpai further warned that there was also no question of withdrawing the garrisons in Gyantse and Yatung without securing such an assurance. Nonetheless, many geo-strategists deemed those as the best period for India to resolve Sino-Indo border crisis with China conclusively.

The First Foreign Secretary of India, Mr. K.P.S. Menon (Senior) justifying Indian Government's stand, clarified in his book, 'Twilight in China' that "Critics of the Government of India have often denounced its alleged inaction on that occasion (Chinese invasion of Tibet). They even say that India gave away Tibet to China. As if Tibet had been India's to be given away!" In that case, it could also be argued that India had no business to define the status of Tibet and that too against the wishes of the Tibetan people. Especially when Prime Minister Nehru had already asserted in the Indian Parliament on 1st November 1950 that 'according to any principles they (China) proclaim and the principles I uphold, the last voice in regard to Tibet should be the voice of the people of Tibet and of nobody else'.

Perhaps, such cold political response to the Tibetan tragedy by Nehru could not have been out of his displeasure over Lhasa Government's cynical demand of the return of 'lost' territories of Darjeeling, Kalimpong, Arunachal Pradesh and certain parts of Ladakh instead of responding promptly to the Independent India's call for ratifying the Simla Convention.

Mr. Claude Arpi, Strategic Analyst and Tibet expert, in his study titled, "The Evolution of Nehru's Policy on Tibet: 1947-1954" published in year 2000, argued that this historical blunder of claiming 'lost' territory would have incalculable consequences for Tibet and for India. Mr. Arpi stressed, "This was in fact one of the most preposterous actions of the Tibetan Government. It was not without reason that Jawaharlal Nehru and other Indian officials were very displeased with the Tibetans. This certainly marks a decisive turn in Nehru's view on Tibet." Mr. B.N. Mullick, the IB Chief, summed up Nehru's feeling when he wrote "this ill-advised claim [to lost Tibetan territories], made by the Tibetan Government resulted in the temporary loss of a certain amount of Indian sympathy for Tibet."

Strategist Mr. Mohan Guruswamy, in his article titled, "Sino-Indian Ties: 20th Century Borders for Stable 21st Century Relations" and many other articles, charged Dalai Lama of staking claim to 'Tibetan territory' in the Indian Himalayas, and wrote, "In 1947 the Dalai Lama (the same gentleman who is now in Dharamshala) sent the newly independent India a note laying claim to some districts in NEFA/Arunachal). It must be clarified that Dalai Lama did not sent the note of territorial claims to the Indian Government. Mr. Guruswamy fails to notice that Dalai Lama was just 12 years old in 1947 and that Tibet was ruled by the Regent Tagra Rinpoche in 1947. All the decisions were made by the Regent in consultation with the Kashag and the Assembly then.

Dalai Lama was called upon to assume the full political power of Tibet only on 17th November 1950 when he was barely 15 years old (16, according to Tibetan tradition). In fact when the Kashag (The Cabinet) approached Dalai Lama with a request to assume the responsibility of the leader of Tibet, Dalai Lama, in his Autobiography 'My Land and My People' wrote, "This filled me with anxiety. I was only sixteen. I was far from having finished my religious education. I knew nothing about the world and had no experience of politics, and yet I was old enough to know how ignorant I was and how much I had still to learn. I protested at first that I was too young, for eighteen was the accepted age for a Dalai Lama to take over active control from his Regent."

Later, however during an interview with Mr. Claude Arpi in March 1997, when Mr. Arpi asked Dalai Lama if the Kashag had committed a great mistake by refusing to ratify the Simla Convention and bargaining instead for the return of some 'lost territories'? Dalai Lama did acknowledge the blunder and said, "Yes, it is my strong feeling. At that time the Tibetan Government should have sent a strong delegation to celebrate the Independence of India. Of course that was a big mistake". He further clarified that although in 1914 at the Simla Convention the border was already demarcated and the [Convention] was signed, the Tibetan officials did not know the Government's decision.

However, Tibetan Government was among the many nations that had sent the message of Congratulations to the new Independent India. Mr. Huge E Richardson, British India's last and Independent India's first Representative in Lhasa, who was witness to the unfolding events, in his book, "Tibet and its History" referred to this unpleasant Tibetan request explaining, "The request to India was that counterpart of the message conveyed to the Chinese Government by the goodwill mission in 1946, in which they (Tibetan Government) asked in equally wide terms, for the return of all

Tibetan territories still in Chinese hands". Mr. Richardson however, revealed that Tibetan Government did contemplate signing a new treaty with the Indian Government but "they were dissuaded by the consideration that negotiations of that sort would have given an opportunity for renewed Chinese pressure on Tibet at a time when the Indian Government was not yet securely in the saddle."

When we realize the backdrop of unfolding political complexities of the time, we would comprehend Lhasa's lackluster reaction to the Indian overture. Tibet in the 1940s was passing through one of the most volatile phase of its history when its Government is bogged down in various political quagmire; Regent Reting conspiracy, Panchen Lama imbroglio, The neutrality during the World War-II pitting Tibet against British, American and China on the issue of allowing passage for the weapons through Tibet, indifference to the Tibetan Goodwill Mission by Britain and United States, Chiang Kaishek's Nationalist Party's political hijacking and maneuvering of the Tibetan Goodwill Mission in Nanjing Assembly, Ma Pufang's threat of further invasion of Tibet from the east and Chinese Communist Party's alarming rise in the east etc.

Eventually, after few months of initial dithering, formal agreement was signed and direct diplomatic and trade relations established between Tibet and India in accordance with its extraterritorial rights derived from the Simla Convention; maintaining an Indian Mission in Lhasa, Trade Agencies, maintaining Military escorts, Rest Houses, Postal, Telegraph, Public telephone services and Hospitals etc.

The signing of the fresh agreement and establishing a diplomatic relation between the two nations however did not clear the initial trepidations. Mr. Richardson stated that the Tibetans continued to be anxious over Indian Government's attitude towards the status of Tibet. He elaborated, "Although the new Government of India continued, as its predecessor has done, to deal with Tibet on the basis of its de facto independence, by supplying arms and ammunition and maintaining direct diplomatic contacts, the nature of their relations seemed to be misinterpreted in certain pronouncements by Nehru. On more than one occasion he referred publicly to a general recognition of Chinese suzerainty over Tibet.

He qualified that statement by describing the suzerainty as 'vague and shadowy'. Nevertheless, the Tibetans were concerned at his disregard for the obligation, which he had inherited under Simla declaration of 1914, not to accord recognition of Chinese suzerainty over Tibet, of any sort whatsoever." "By gratuitously stressing Chinese suzerainty the Indian Prime Minister appeared to serve notice on the Communists that in their designs on Tibet they need not fear any serious opposition from India", he added.

Meanwhile China's incessant deception and subsequent 1962 attack shocked and shattered Prime Minister Nehru so much that in a broadcast to the nation on October 20, 1962, he confessed, "Perhaps there are not many instances in history where one country (referring to India) has gone out of her way to be friendly and cooperative with the government and people of another country (referring to China) and to plead their cause in the councils of the world, and then that country returns evil for good."

And the Indian Parliament on November 14 1962 adopted a unanimously Resolution affirming, "The firm resolve of the Indian people to drive out the aggressor from the sacred soil of India, however long and hard the struggle may be"

Despite all the brouhaha over the Chinese betrayal and vengeance and all, the subsequent Indian Governments, even after Nehru's tragic death, continue to follow Nehru's India policy on Tibet which he announced in the Indian Parliament on 27th April 1959. Mr. Nehru affirmed, "I stated some time ago that our broad policy (on Tibet) was governed by three factors: (1) the preservation of the security and integrity of India; (2) our desire to maintain friendly relations with China; and (3) our deep sympathy for the people of Tibet. We shall continue to follow that policy because we think that is a correct policy not only for the present but even more so for the future." The policies also entail that the Tibetans in India will be restricted from carrying out anti-Chinese political activities. And that Tibet will be regarded as an internal matter of China.

Over the years, another strange justification over India's restrained political approach to the Tibetan issue is that "if India does anything more to help Tibet, it will upset the Chinese and the fate of Tibet would only worsen". Like many other weird arguments, this too would be repeated ritualistically for many decades to the great dismay of the Tibetans.

Consequently, the challenge for the Government of India's policy on Tibet and the Tibetans is to maintain a balance between the three core principles of 1) the preservation of the security and integrity of India; (2) to maintain friendly relations with China; and (3) to accord deep sympathy for the people of Tibet. But many believe that the balance has been severely tilted in favour of China to the detriment of India and Tibet's national interest. Compromising principles for the sake of cordial bilateral relation and economic gains is one thing, but compromising national security and long-term interest is anything but Realpolitik.

Indeed, India's humanitarian support to the exiled Tibetans is overwhelming and unparallel in the history of a national struggle and the Tibetan people are highly indebted for the same. But the Tibetan people will be most contented the day India intensify its political support to the Tibetans in tune with its own national and strategic interest. After all, Tibetan struggle is a political and a national struggle and not merely Humanitarian.

Furthermore, Tibet is a lever that India can utilize to further its national interest vis-à-vis China. And on every occasion, Tibetans in India have never failed to demonstrate their utmost loyalty, dedication and love for this country. However it would be morally wrong and practically inconceivable if it employs the leverage against the Tibetan people and their Interest. Thus far, such strategy had always boomeranged in the diplomatic sphere.

While it is indisputable that a policy of a country is driven more by a national interest and pragmatism than principles and emotions, it is imperative that those policies be primarily based on reality and facts rather than false expectations and gimmicks. And many strategists believe that it is in the national interest; territorial integrity, security, strategic, democratic and in the long term interest of India to adopt more assertive and pragmatic policy vis-à-vis China and effectively neutralize its half a century-long containment policies and campaign.

Thus far, Panchsheel and other appeasements have seriously failed to build a genuine friendly neighborhood with China. Therefore, stakes are definitely high and the task daunting but it's inevitable that the coming Government should revamp its policy on China as a key priority.

CHINA'S DIPLOMACY FOR THE 21ST CENTURY

"Doing our own business well first" – this is one of the admonitions left to the Chinese people by Deng Xiaoping, the designer of the improvement and opening up of the contemporary China. It is also the most direct and the simplest expression of "development demand". The half a century history since the founding of New China has proved that if the domestic economic construction and the improvement of the living of the people do not receive enough attention, the foreign policy of peace and independence would often than not remain empty and powerless, without the social base to last. Only when the domestic economy has developed and the political situation and the relations among all nationalities are kept stable, is it possible for diplomatic work to acquire a solid base. The main threat to China's state security comes not from foreign invasion or other wars, but from within, that is, whether or not China itself can maintain a stable, orderly and healthy development.

The "internal weakness" exhibit by Russia in the Kosovo subject has fully testified to this point. The most profound lesson taught by Russia is: first, a country must first of all manage its own affairs well so as to make it hard for potential or realistic enemy or rival to "penetrate" by exploiting the weakness. It is a common sense that flies hover over only rotten eggs. The fundamental destructive factor to the death of a big country lies not in external sources but the inner problems in the deep layers of the society. It is impossible to wipe out a big country. Its decline often starts from within, from the roots, say national separatism or economic stagnation or political turmoil or social disorder, for if a country were thrown into confusion, it would fall apart without being attacked. The Russian arena over the recent decade has exactly been experiencing every process of "national split—economic stagnation—political upheaval—social disorder". The serious "internal weakness" displayed before the nibbling by NATO is due, essentially, to the "internal war" without the smoke of gunpowder. If asked what we should learn from Russians, it is very simple to answer: it should not be soft toward separatists and, even more important, there should be no internal political strife or social disorder; economic development must not stop and the improvement and institutional improvement should not be interrupted. Stability of a country and growing national strength constitute the corner stone for the security of the country and a major source for having a say externally and exert international influence. "The easiest way to capture a fortress is from within". Without internal security, there would be no defending the state security to speak about, let alone safeguarding it.

It should be stressed here that in spite of the grave negative developments like Kosovo crisis, the relations among big powers have become more dependent upon each other while their relations are growing more complicated and delicate. The globalization process of the economy and science and technology has not been slowing down and the global scientific and technological creation is becoming more active than ever before. The economic growth of most countries is still strong. The world's economic aggregates are still growing. What is the most important is that the comprehensive judgment from all features shows that a worldwide nuclear war or a world war with the involvement of all major countries in confrontation could be prevented for a considerably long period of time to come. All countries will seize the time to develop their own economies, science and technology and boost their national strength and make great efforts to improve the living of the people and infrastructure facilities. Recall that during the recent 200 years, China has in most part been in a state of being bullied and humiliated or in an intense period of mobilization for "war and revolution". It did not make any real development and construction until only in the recent 20 years. But the short span of 20 years has brought about a tremendous leap forward: the country walked out of the shadow of exhaustion in the motive forces for economic development; the GDP has ranked among the first ten in the world if calculated according to the exchange rate; till today, the Chinese people are continuing to realize the most massive economic growth in human history (a country with a population of 1.2 billion has expanded its economy at an annual rate of 8% within 20 years). To look forward, even in another 20 years, not to say in another 100 years, if China should maintain the speed of the last 20 years and "concentrate its efforts on economic construction", the Chinese people have every reason to expect that the country will reach the level of a middle-developed country in per capita average and secure a place among the top three in the world in total aggregates. By then, China would have a significant say in the international affairs and the new international political and economic order will be most likely to develop toward the direction we expect.

Before talking about a methodical change in the current international relations or about making greater contributions to the external world, the Chinese people must have a sober estimation of themselves. It should be admitted that, after half a century construction, especially the rapid development over the recent 20 years through improvement and opening up, our comprehensive national strength has ascended a new stair and our international status and influence have grown greatly, China remains a developing country, still trailing behind other countries in many areas and still a far cry as compared with developed countries. This manifests itself not only in the "hardware", such as the per capita GNP, the living standards, development of roads, the modernization of educational facilities and means of information, labour productivity and product quality, and the proportion in the global trade and investment, but also in "software", such as institutional creation, comprehensive quality of services, understanding of the external world by the average people, the attractiveness of the whole country to foreign resources (including materials and intelligence), the general level of theoretical studies and the capability of keeping track with the advanced world levels. The strength of software includes the strength in political and social development and in theory and also the following factors: (1) the domestic political, social and economic system arrangements that are open, stable, lasting, and absorbing; (2) powerful culture, political and ethical appeal and rallying power; (3) theoretical guidance; (4) strategic insight and diplomatic skills; (5) effective domestic and international management, including the effective mobilization of domestic and international resources (especially non-military resources; (6) the populace of high educational level and strong cultural awareness; (7) high level of living standards. It is a long way to go for China to acquire such strength. Economic and military strength cannot substitute for the powerful political and social base". Historically, the contemporary China has not and will not possibly have what it used to experience in the heydays of Han and Tang dynasties. Ever since the modern times, it has been in "tight operation" economically, socially and politically. As the changes in the economic structure advance simultaneously with the changes of the whole social and political system, the awareness of opening up grows together with the growth of the awareness of nationalism. The whole country has grown rapidly, but with problems cropping up one after another and a large number of troubles put on the agenda before the problems left from the old system had not be rooted out, such as bankruptcy of enterprises and workers thrown out of jobs, the regional economic and educational disparities, corruption and the so-called "crises in belief, credit and confidence". The problems in themselves have already restricted its power of influencing the world. If no steps are taken to deepen improvement and opening up, no efforts are made to continue the great development, stopping there, rest contented, the prospects of China and the world would not develop toward the direction in our favour. In this sense, the focus of China's diplomacy for a quite a long period of time to come still remains to be on the creation of a neighbouring environment favourable to China's improvement, development and stability and on meeting the major demands of economic construction. Unless major wars break out not to our liking, there would be no reason to change the priority of this demand.

The above essentials show that what is referred to as "development demand" is much richer and much more extensive in content than what we used to construe or disseminate in the past. For instance, economically speaking, the Chinese people have basically realized a "comfortable living". But when measured by fairly comprehensive standards, China needs more profound political democracy and legal construction and needs the synchronization of the development of spiritual civilization (belief, ethics and values) and material civilization, needs more rational and smooth run-in between the stratification of the society and the various interest groups, needs more Chinese people who have broader and more lenient insight on the world, and needs greater development of the strategic thinking and theoretical nature about China's international relations. The term "Development" covers political development, the development of civilization, social development and development of values. Under the precondition of making economic development the central task, the development in all features mentioned above will greatly help China to raise its status and power of influence internationally in the new millennium and that will naturally provide more solid base for China's diplomacy to display its prowess.

CHINA'S SOUTH ASIAN DIPLOMACY

Long pitted next to neighbouring India as a natural adversary and one with whom territorial disputes among other subjects have eclipsed relations to date, China seems willing to move away from past acrimony. Embarking on a two-nation South Asian visit, Prime Minister Wen Jiabo's recent foray into the region struck the right balance in both India and Pakistan. Not an easy task especially when you have been to war with one whose economic standing as a regional heavyweight requires a strengthening of relations. Not to forget that it might also be a possible future challenger.

The fact that Indo-Sino ties have been noticeable by suspicion and distrust also because of Beijing's strategic ties with Pakistan in the military and nuclear fields makes for a complex brew. On top of it, the tension between Islamabad and New Delhi that resurged after the 2008 Mumbai attacks has made it trickier to walk the tightrope. What China did right was not to take sides nor make pathetic attempts to please either of the two by making unwarranted comments. For instance, Premier Jiabo pointedly refrained from castigating Pakistan in New Delhi unlike Nicholas Sarkozy and David Cameron who gave the Indian media a field day by doing exactly that.

China's increasingly practical diplomacy now includes a renewal of ties with adversaries. Cognisant of India's economic growth and potential, China has astutely set the tone for the next few decades. By earmarking a staggering $100 billion target in trade by 2015, China and India can only move forward together. The good thing is that such an economic waltz will make it challenging to indulge in arm-twisting on other fronts. It also sets a good precedent for neighbouring Pakistan and India to move beyond the downtrodden path and not allow instigating elements to sabotage the laboriously achieved peace. While Pakistani officials may deny harbouring apprehensions about the Chinese premier's visit to New Delhi, it is only natural that every detail was followed anxiously. Much to their relief, China maintained the status quo in its relations with Pakistan. Even more important than the $25-35 billion worth of trade deals and MoU's signed in Islamabad was China's defence of Pakistan's counter-terrorism policy, likely to prove a bigger boost.

It is not that Beijing is not concerned about the go up of militancy and the threat it poses region-wide, but the Chinese being master players in astuteness, know when to strike the right note. The presence of separatists from China's restive southern Muslim province of Xinjiang in Pakistan's tribal areas is a major concern.

While both states are said to be sharing intelligence on this front, Beijing expects Islamabad to do more to ensure the non-collusion of Chinese anti-state elements with terror groups in the area. Realistically speaking, this is a tall order since it is difficult to monitor the coming and goings from across the border in Afghanistan or even from the northern areas. Despite difficulties, intelligence cooperation was increased manifold as witnessed at the time of the 2008 Beijing Olympics and the recent Shanghai Expo to ward off possible threats.

Pakistan has rightfully reminded Washington that the government in keeping with environmental dynamics will decide the timing of future military operations in North Waziristan. The preposterous increase in US drone strikes besides the consequent build up of pressure on Pakistan with the planned withdrawal of US troops from Afghanistan next year has revealed deeper fissures in the US-Pakistan relationship.

Furthermore, the latest allegations pertaining the leak of identity of the CIA station chief by the ISI—(allegedly) in retaliation for the naming of ISI Chief, General Ahmed Shuja Pasha in a criminal case in New York by Mumbai terror victims' families—thereby necessitating his removal from duty is likely to create bigger ripples.

Already the US Afghan Review has shift the focus on Pakistan blaming it for ineptitude and an ambivalent and half-hearted attitude in dealing with home grown and foreign insurgents. China for one was quick to contradict this.

Wen Jibao while addressing the Parliament in Islamabad praised Pakistan's role in halting the proliferation of terror and for the sacrifices it has made so far. Instead of lashing out at Pakistan for not doing enough, the Chinese leader urged the (international community to do more to help Pakistan cope with the situation. It maybe that China may have relayed its concerns on the situation to Pakistan's leadership in private differently but it did well not to embarrass its long time ally and friend. Maybe the Americans and its NATO allies could learn a lesson or two from China in diplomacy and dealing with critical allies.

It maybe also be occasion for Pakistan to realise that some of its behaviour patterns are beginning to resemble that of a servile and shackled state, negating the whole purpose of its existence. The US is a friend and ally, not a master. Sadly, over the decades, Pakistan's leadership may have given a contrary impression but that does not translate for the state or the people. It is imperative that the state puts its own house in order and takes a firm stand as far as external diktat is concerned. No sincere leader will find it a problem to unify the masses to jointly take arms against any threat to the state—external and internal. The problem lies in who will don the mantle.

CHINESE DIPLOMACY - GOOD INTENTIONS

The current discuss in India over whether to engage with an emerging China is, in many ways, a debate over how to think about China's future intentions. India is concerned about the expansion of Chinese influence and construction of transport links to South Asia (roads, railways and ports). However, the perception of Chinese intimidation that pervades the Indian policy community's psyche is not shared by the country's border populations.

They think that if the Indian government is serious about developing roads in the region (and thus helping to develop the region itself), this could be done faster by inviting global tenders and by using advanced technologies. Instead, the government is relying on the Border Roads Organisation, which seems incapable of delivering timely projects, particularly in Arunachal Pradesh. Indeed, when Indian policy makers perceived Chinese access diplomacy as a potential threat to Indian interests, they started talking about making the border "irrelevant". Thus, a sense of insecurity in border areas worked as a catalyst in India's policy thinking in bringing attention to the socio-economic development of its peripheral regions.

In contrast, China has second-hand border trade as its main instrument to realise the goal of local economic integration. It is estimated that border trade through its 120 inland towns and ports constitutes about half of China's total foreign trade amounting to $1.3 trillion. The central government has given a high degree of autonomy to provincial governments. China looks at Nathu La Pass in Sikkim as a vital physical economic entry into the 1.3 billion person South Asian market. This is arguably the shortest route (roughly 590 km between Tibet and Sikkim) to the heartland of India, Bangladesh, Bhutan and Nepal. Furthermore, Tibet has huge mineral resources with a potential value of more than $125 billion. Due to the high cost of transportation, raw materials in Tibet cannot be easily transported out of the province. Hence, the Chinese government is significantly improving infrastructure there. Unquestionably, increasing Chinese connectivity has created new opportunities for people of the region.

People in the border areas feel that China is looking for markets and resources on an ever-increasing scale in order to sustain its developmental needs. China's access diplomacy to South Asia has very abiding and powerful objectives, including expansion of its strategic access; economic and commercial penetration into the huge South Asian market; and tackling its own potential internal instabilities. In the last 30 years, China has transformed itself from an astute proponent of ideological influence and covert supporter of insurgency, to a builder of cross-border modern infrastructures and a market grabber.

China has a aware policy of engaging South Asian countries at a local level, giving traders a literally free hand to go and negotiate. For example, China has given rights to Tibetan traders to go to Sikkim and negotiate, despite all their other concerns. This grant of autonomy is a distinct instrument of foreign policy.

Even Indian government officials (civilian and military) post in border regions feel that China's South Asia ties are dictated by geography, the need for security and stability, mutual economic advantage, shared cultural traditions, common approaches to the management of natural disasters and climate change, and developmental priorities. According to one Indian military official posted in Tawang, "China may be almost a superpower now, but it is not an irrational power. It has as big a stake in stability as India. Its economy, finance and exports are all much more globalized than ours, so do not expect China to take any risks by way of entering into military conflict with India." The talk of 'strategic encirclement' (involving naval installations on India's periphery) is viewed by many as an overreaction to facts on the ground. China, like India but in keeping with its greater resources, is investing in its military capability and doubtless seeks to extend its strategic reach.

Though there may well be a military component in Chinese behaviour in countries on India's borders, it is not the primary one. China's priorities are to protect its sovereignty and territorial integrity, promote economic development, and generate international respect. Local people see Chinese roads and railways as an opportunity for India. Are Indians much different?

It was long held that an undeveloped border area in the northeast enhanced the security of the heartland as roads and bridges might provide easy connectivity for inimical forces — not necessarily armies but a variety of subversive elements, arms and drug-runners, smugglers and even legitimate traders who might overwhelm the national economy by dumping cheap consumer goods.

But for the local population, whose development has lagged painfully, roads and bridges mean fresh possibilities for trade, quick supply of goods, closer linkages with the rest of India and a great expansion of inter-village amity in the interior. Their needs should be recognised and respected by India's strategic community, while local populations must accept that borders more open to economic intercourse with China will offer some risks to the country as a whole beyond the obvious opportunities involved.

6

China's Security Environment Strategy in South Asia

CHINA'S SECURITY ENVIRONMENT

China and India, the two largest developing countries in the world, have a commonality of history, culture, economy and social characteristics, and profiles of development. Each applies itself to internal economic development, carries out an independent foreign policy and strives for a peaceful international environment. China and India are among what Brzezinski described as "five geo-strategic players", what Henry Kissinger listed as the "six big powers", and what Samuel Huntington pointed out are "core states of seven civilizations." China is a big power in East Asia while India is a big power in South Asia. Each has advantages and influence in their respective regions.

However, they are not world powers that have global influence. In terms of institution and comprehensive strength, they cannot even be ranked as strong powers. For America, China and India, at one end, are two emerging markets offering economic benefits and developing opportunities. At the other end, China and India are also two transitional countries demonstrating uncertainty, from the United States' strategic point of view. What Washington fears most is the possibility of China and India, with Russia, forming an alliance based on a common understanding and interests of a new international political and economical order and a multi-polar world. The United States and India, the largest democracies in the world, share common political values and strategic interests. Their common geo-political, economic and socio-political interests are advancing a co-operative agenda (which their differences over nuclear proliferation may not be able to halt). With the US–India relationship moving forward over the past two years, the two countries have developed a comprehensive co-operative framework covering democracy, economy and security.

The United States now pays more attention to India's role as the largest democracy than it did before. India's continuous and fast-growing economy, especially its information technology industry, attracts great investment from transnational corporations based in America.

In the security arena, the U.S. leadership has gradually begun to 'forget' India's nuclear tests and has come to recognize India as a *de facto* nuclear power, as also its preponderant position in South Asia. With India's support for America's unilateral action in missile defence, the US and India moved from divergence to co-operation in the field of non-proliferation. After 9/11, counter-terrorism has been a new field of strategic co-operation for U.S. and India. In a related development, Pakistan turns out to be less of an 'obstacle' for the US–India framework of relationships.

China and the United States, the largest developing and developed countries respectively, also have comprehensive common strategic interests. Besides large potential economic cooperation, they also share broad interests in other fields such as regional stability and the role and reform of the United Nations.

What is more likely is the emergence of a "soft balance of power" system among the three countries. Alternately, at one end, a vicious competitive relationship among the three countries may emerge, and the "soft balance of power" may be changed into a "hard balance of power" similar to that in the Cold War era, if one of them regards the development of relations between the two other countries as a challenge to its national interests, or if any two in this triad forge a relationship as a means to contain the third country. At the other end, it is possible for China, the US and India to establish a relatively harmonious relationship if they can seek out common views and interests, and push their differences aside to deal with bilateral and trilateral relations within a strategic perspective.

SOUTH ASIA AND HORIZONTAL PROLIFERATION

As a starting point, it is helpful to focus on cases of horizontal proliferation elsewhere that are connected to South Asia. This includes potential WMD supply routes as well as entities that might be involved, some of whom may be operating outside state control. In particular, the focus is on connections between entities in Pakistan and proliferation dynamics in other regions. Three major issues need to be addressed-(i) the North Korean nuclear program, and in particular the impact of the October 2006 nuclear test on South Asia; (ii) the current state of the A.Q. Khan network and its implications for WMD supply trends; and (iii) proliferation links between South Asia and the Middle East.

The North Korean Nuclear Test and South Asia

As expected, North Korea's nuclear test put renewed focus on the dangers of nuclear proliferation, and policymakers in India assumed it would lead to more stringent criticism of its nuclear agreement with the United States. Indian experts expected the North Korean test to impact especially on any nuclear test-related provisions of the nuclear agreement with the United States. Consequently, New Delhi swiftly condemned the test and indirectly highlighted Islamabad's contribution to Pyongyang's nuclear test. Some Indian officials even stated that Pyongyang's illegal acquisition of nuclear technology would actually spur reluctant supplier countries (such as Australia) to legitimately sell nuclear fuel to India, especially since it would be used for civilian purposes.

On the other hand, Islamabad refuted any suggestion that the activities of the A.Q. Khan network had contributed to Pyongyang's test, stating that North Korea's nuclear program is based on plutonium while Pakistan relies on uranium. In this manner, both India and Pakistan tried to ensure that proliferation in South Asia was not equated with proliferation in Northeast Asia. To a certain extent, the Bush administration obliged the subcontinental nuclear powers, as senior officials dismissed any parallels between North

Korea's path to nuclear weapons to those of India and Pakistan. However, while Pakistan denied any links to the test, it did not help Islamabad's case when Japanese sources stated that days before Pyongyang's test, several Pakistani nuclear technicians arrived in North Korea through China. This augmented the suspicions that Pakistani agencies may have had some role in the test, perhaps through data sharing before or after the explosion.

The A.Q. Khan Network and Proliferation Dynamics

The A.Q. Khan network, which provided nuclear assistance to North Korea and Iran, has represented the most serious proliferation problem in recent years. Since Khan's public confession in February 2004, the Musharraf regime has consistently asserted that this network was the work of a rogue scientist and that the Pakistani government and its military leaders were not involved in these activities. However, it is not clear to what extent this assertion is accurate. Analysts and officials in Pakistan as well as in the United States have expressed skepticism over Khan's confession as well as the implicit professed innocence of the Pakistani political and military establishment. A highly publicized report released in April 2007 by the London-based International Institute for Strategic Studies, also stated that individuals and entities involved in the network could still be dormant and can conceivably be reactivated in the future.

So far, Islamabad has refused to allow foreign interrogators to question Khan even though the U.S. government has regularly expressed dissatisfaction over information released by Pakistan. > Furthermore, most individuals connected to the network are still at large, including important figures such as B.S.A. Tahir, while others, such as Henk Slebos, have been given light sentences. Moreover, the Khan claimed in a signed statement that successive army chiefs in the 1990s (Generals Mirza Aslam Beg and Jehangir Karamat) had authorized the sales of nuclear technology. While this could be taken as Khan's attempts to remove the burden of guilt, it is true that the military was closely associated with the nuclear and missile programs. In fact, in 1990, Gen. Beg warned U.S. government officials that Pakistan would be forced to provide nuclear technology to Tehran if Washington did not offer support to Pakistan.

Other circumstantial evidence, such as visits by the Pakistani military leadership to North Korea throughout the nineties, suggests that there was a barter deal between Pyongyang and Islamabad (uranium enrichment technology in exchange for missiles). Additionally, in August 2005, Gen. Musharraf conceded that Khan had transferred centrifuge machines to North Korea through which uranium hexafluoride (which was also transferred) can be enriched for eventual processing into civilian reactors fuel or for military purposes. Shipping out such large centrifuge machines without the military's knowledge would have been impossible. Therefore, it would have been highly unlikely that these activities were carried out without the military's acquiescence. On a side note, it is possible that Washington's attitude was colored by the need to retain Islamabad's support in the anti-Taliban/Al Qaeda campaign in Afghanistan. Additionally, for a country to acquire a nuclear delivery system (such as the No Dong missiles transferred to Pakistan), the decision-making process incorporates several factors, as well as the opinions of numerous government agencies to ensure compatibility among the various systems. It is therefore not very plausible that a nuclear-missile barter deal with such serious and risky international consequences could have been approved without cooperation from senior levels of the political-military establishment in Pakistan. The issue of the Pakistani military-scientific establishment's involvement (or endorsement) in the Khan's network activities is crucial due to its implications for contemporary proliferation routes and processes. If these elements within and outside Pakistan (including non-Pakistani nationals) and their methods and routes remain undiscovered, it has two broad consequences for proliferation in South Asia.

First, it allows Islamabad to potentially procure missile and nuclear technology in the future, in an attempt to catch up with India. In this regard, a Pakistani national, Mohammed Aslam, working at the Tabani Corporation's Moscow office, was named by the Russian government in 2006 as having attempted to acquire dual-use technology and other materials for Pakistan's nuclear and missile development programs. This example demonstrates that elements of the network are still active, though it is unclear if they are directly connected to Pakistani nuclear and missile development programs. Given Islamabad's need to construct a secure deterrent against India (especially long-range missiles that can reach southern and eastern India), it is possible that the above case is an instance of continuing efforts to exploit non-state networks to procure prohibited equipment. As one analyst noted, due to Pakistan's apparent inability to acquire nuclear weapons components legally, it is encouraged to look toward illegal sources. Furthermore, according to some experts, apart from Pakistan, other countries can easily utilize the same supply networks. The Iranian government has made use of these networks for its nuclear and missile programs. As the previously mentioned IISS report states, Tehran controls a clandestine nuclear materials network comparable to the one run by Khan, and in the past has procured technology from some of the same suppliers used by Khan. In context of nuclear proliferation networks, a further concern is that if North Korea dismantles its nuclear weapons program, it will create a potential source of unwanted nuclear materials in the process. Such discarded, but nevertheless lethal technology, could be bought by illegal nuclear supply entities that may or may not have had any connection to the Khan network.

Second, the continued existence of the kind of middlemen that the network generated increases the possibility of nuclear technology leakage out of Pakistan in the event of a coup or widespread instability from radical groups. Since 9/11, there have been periodic fears of internal upheavals in Pakistan, especially from groups linked to the Taliban. Recent reports have also stated that two nuclear scientists from the Pakistan Atomic Energy Commission (PAEC) were kidnapped by the Taliban in late 2006, and as of March 2007 remained in captivity in the Waziristan area. > Soon after that kidnapping, there was an aborted attempt to capture six more PAEC officials in the North West Frontier Province of Pakistan in January 2007. While it is not clear if the officials and scientists were targeted specifically because of their links to

Pakistan's nuclear program, these incidents demonstrate the potential danger of non-state actors' participation in the illegal market in nuclear technology. In order to demonstrate to the international community that it is a responsible nuclear power, Islamabad has decided to set up a "Strategic Export Control Division" in its foreign ministry that will ostensibly prevent prohibited WMD-related technology from being exported. However, this does not necessarily address the problem of possible involvement of government entities and officials that have remained under the radar even after the network was uncovered. In general, the proliferation-related fear for U.S. policymakers is twofold-first, that nuclear technology could be transferred to a terrorist organization; and second, that the Musharraf regime could be overthrown, resulting in uncertainty for the counter-terrorism as well as nonproliferation campaigns.

The case of Pakistan demonstrates the difficulty that arises when nonproliferation goals collide with other strategic imperatives such as counter-terrorism. While the Khan network problem is one of the reasons why Washington has refused to offer a nuclear cooperation agreement to Pakistan, the perceived tilt toward India (through the Indo-U.S. nuclear agreement) can also be a reason why Washington has not pressured Islamabad any further on the A.Q. Khan issue. Nevertheless, in January 2007, in a proactive step, the U.S. Congress under the Democratic leadership passed the Nuclear Black Market Counter Terrorism Act, which authorizes the administration to implement "punitive actions" against states condoning or cooperating with entities actively engaged in nuclear proliferation.

BUILDING SECURITY AND CONFIDENCE WITH CHINA

Except for the brief period of confrontation between 19591992 and the diplomatic freeze that followed for next few years the relations between China and India had never been conflictual in nature. But because of the complicated colonial legacies - which were further compounded by the Cold War dynamics and by the border war of 1962 - mutual distrust and threat perceptions have continued to undermine all efforts towards building confidence. One may ask why confidence and security building measures (CSBMs) between India and China are so critical to the evolution of their multifaceted and multilayered *rapprochement*? The one line answer would be that these CSBMs present a perfect barometer for any crystal gazing into the future of these two Asian giants. However, this answer remains far too simplistic to explain the complexity of Go-Indian ties. And it is in this context of complications that this essay tries to examine and highlight Sino-Indian CSBMs in terms of their being the first significant step forward untying the knots in the bilateral relations and mutual perceptions.

Firstly, to deal with the theoretical elements of Sine-Indian CSBMs, it has been unjustifiably fashionable to view Sino-Indian CSBMs essentially in the framework of western ready-made models. If anything, the CSBMs in the Asian context have far preceded all western models and, therefore, are neither borrowed from nor identical to those leading to the Final Act of the Helsinki process of the Conference on Security and Cooperation in Europe (CSCE) that was concluded in 1975. Beginning from the Joint Defence Council of 1948 that effected the division of assets and armed forces between India and Pakistan to the Sino-Indian *Panchsheel* Agreement of 1954, and later the Indo-Pak Simla agreement of 1971, various formal and informal agreements had already effected these CSBMs like "non-use", or the "selective use" of armed force and created various other mechanisms. Therefore these CSBMs had been institutionalised in Asia far earlier. Besides, these were also far more broad based than the Western CSBMs, including those that were later incorporated the Document of the Conference on Disarmament in Europe held in 1986 at Stockholm (Sweden).

Coming to the salient features of what can be described as the Asian CSBMs that distinguish the Sino-Indian CSBMs from most of their comparable Western models, one sees the near absence of a subjective feeling in the Asian context of an imminent threat which is so central to all those Western conceptions of CSBMs. In Asia's rather lose polycentric situation, nations had never been so clearly divided as are the communist and liberal democratic traditions that characterise the bipolar division of the West. Similarly, the second basic condition of equality of the military strength between the potential parties to the conflict, again seems very much a Eurocentric feature of CSBMs and is generally missing in the Asian situation. China, India and Pakistan can themselves be cited as ideal examples of this asymmetry of power. Nevertheless, CSBMs have continued to evolve amongst these three countries. Thirdly, the inter-state boundaries which form the basic element of European CSBMs are itself a major problem and therefore the very objective towards which most Asian CSBMs seek to provide solutions, Also, Asian CSBMs are generally backed by ever widening network of measures like state sponsored people-to-people contacts which are aimed at expanding mutual trust and understanding between the entire social elite on both sides.

Nor should we regard the Asian CSBMs in general and the Sino-Indian CSBMs in particular as the byproduct of the post-Cold War peace dividend although the global factors, have surely been much more influential in moulding the European CSBMs than those between Asian countries. This is because unlike Europe, (a) the conflicts in Asia were never seen to be vital to the national interests of both the super powers: and, (b) the middle ranking powers like China and India have become increasingly independent from the regimented bipolar world order of the Cold War years. To give two most apt examples, contrary to Cold War trends, India had initiated its CSBMs during the mid-1970s and India's Foreign Minister, Atal Behari Vajpai, paid his first visit to Beijing at the lime when China was launching its war against Vietnam and the Soviet forces were about to enter Afghanistan yet, despite India's closeness to Moscow, the new Cold War of the early 1980s did not disturb the smooth evolution of Sine-Indian *rapprochement* Similarly, following the June 1989 Tiananmen Square incident, while most of world powers had imposed sanctions thus completely isolating China, the relations between China and India not only continued to be smooth but experienced a greater momentum: the period from the second half through 1989 and 1990 saw 10 high-level visits between the two countries that included visits to New Delhi by Vice Premier Wu Xueqian in October 1989 and by Foreign Minister Qian Qichen in March 1990. The credit for this goes to (a) this unique Asian way of trial and error which, therefore, lends some sort of originality of these Sino-Indian CSBMs, and (b) to the political leadership of both the countries who were able to take and stand by such bold initiatives.

If anything, it is their expanding interactions at various levels that has been the greatest single factor behind the evolution of Sino-Indian CSBMs. Starting from their exchange of Ambassadors in 1976, these expanding official and business interactions can be divided into three major phases. The first phase (1976-1988), was characterised by both *China and India looking at* each *other* simply gauging the potential for expanding mutual goodwill and trust. Second phase (1988-1996), which witnessed five formal summits interspersed by hectic initiatives and agreements towards evolving and consolidating CSBMs. Then having established this strong network of CSBMs the recent four agreements signed during President Jiang Zemin's visit to New Delhi in November 1996, Sino-Indian *rapprochement* has now entered into its third and final phase where the two are expected to take concrete decisions on more difficult issues like the boundary question.

A quick glance through this evolution from freeze to fervour shows how, though no breakthrough has yet been achieved on the crucial boundary question quite a substantial progress has been made considering the complicated and knotty ground realities. The historic f 988 visit to Beijing by Prime Minister Rajiv Gandhi had worked as a catalyst in facilitating a U-turn in Sino- Indian relations. Especially, considering Indian sensitivities vis-a-vis China, this visit itself was an extremely bold initiative. But more than this, in the Joint Communiqué at the end of this visit India agreed, for the first time, to dropping its earlier policy stance of asking for settlement of the border as a precondition for any improvement in relations in other fields. Secondly, India not only agreed to describe Tibet as an integral part of (not just an autonomous region) of China but also expressed "concern over anti-Chinese activities by some Tibetan elements in India" -a proviso which was criticised by some as a clear sell-out of the

Tibetan interests. India's over-reaction towards Tibetan protesters during the visit by Premier Li Peng in 1991 was another demonstration of India's resolve in not letting Tibet become a problem in the way of Sino-Indian *rapprochement.* All this meant that, Rajiv Gandhi's visit had finally abandoned India's discredited forwards policy and, at least during the interim, accepted China's long-standing demand for the maintenance of tranquillity on the line of actual control (LoAC).

There were also some legal hurdles to this visit. The historic November 1962 resolution of Indian Parliament had bound successive Indian leaders from making any move towards improving Sino-Indian ties until they had obtained every inch of India's sacred land claimed or taken by the Chinese. But this December 1988 visit by Rajiv Gandhi to Beijing became possible because of another major resolution that was passed by the All India Congress Working Committee on November 5, 1988 urging the government to seek a settlement through "peaceful negotiations" based on "mutual interest" and "acceptable to the peoples of both countries" even if it took time. Apart from minor objections, no main national political parties raised any hue and cry against these "concession" by Rajiv Gandhi. This was because (a) the Congress Party, at this time, had an overwhelming majority in Indian Parliament and (b) the earlier major, initiative towards building peace with China had been taken during the Janata Party government in February 1979. Moreover, eight rounds of border talks (initiated during Foreign Minister, Huang Hua's visit to New Delhi in 1981) had already created some sort of favourable backdrop.

Apart from these interactions at the political level, Rajiv Gandhi's visit also opened avenues for direct military interactions. Because of the 1962 war, any interaction between the military personnel or on defence related matters remained a taboo until the early 1990s. The first exchange in this direction was made by the senior serving officials of the National Defence College (New Delhi) and the National Defence University (Beijing) respectively visiting each other in 1990 and 1992.The two have also since been considering undertaking an arrangement for an institutional exchange wherein at least one officer could attend the others training courses. The military-to-military dialogue was taken to a higher level by India's Defence Minister, Sharad Pawar's visit to China in July 1992. This opened the way and was followed by Vice Chief of China's People's Liberation Army, Lt. General Xu Huizi, visiting India in December 1993 followed by a visit by their Defence Minister, Chi Haotian's visit to India during September 7-13, 1994. From the Indian side, Chief of Army Staff, General B.C. Joshi and Chief of Naval Staff, Admiral V.S. Shekhawat paid reciprocal visits to various defence facilities in China during July 1994 and March 1996 respectively. This increasing interaction and transparency between the two military establishments has surely contributed to the building up of mutual confidence.

Once again, just like the lack of interactions and other historical legacies had coloured their visions during the earlier years, increasing information and confidence has led to revision and rectification of various policies on both sides. One good example of this spectrum of biases in perceptions can be seen in the way various China watchers interpreted the incident when in May 1992 China detonated a 150 megaton nuclear device just hours after President R. Venkatraman arrived in Beijing. While some called it an act of intimidation, others described it as an expression of China's solidarity with India in their strategic defiance of Washington. However, with persistent efforts from both sides, a relatively more objective understanding of each other has started to emerge during the 1990s. Observing the tenor of policy pronouncements from both sides there appears to be an obvious shift of emphasis away from the assertion of huge territorial claims or high moral principles increasingly towards "mutual concessions" and "accommodation "from the Chinese side and on historical, legal, geographical realities from the Indian side with both now calling for a "fair, reasonable, and mutually acceptable" compromise solution to their boundary question.

Also both sides today have far greater mutual understanding on various issues ranging from global problematic like the US nuclear non-proliferation to regional and bilateral contentions like Kashmir, Tibet, and border. As a result, while owing to their ideological systems and methods of operation the two had appeared to be dramatical opposites during the 1950s over the years the two sides have begun to appreciate and emphasise on their similarities and evolved common approach on certain issues like nuclear disarmament, trade and human rights. On the nuclear question, for example, while China has sought to keep its own nuclear build-up completely insulated from the ongoing disarmament debates between Moscow and Washington: yet, Beijing has also generally kept a low profile on India's nuclear and missile programme and, in fact, assisted India by supplying heavy water at a crucial stage in January 1995. Nevertheless, there still exist differences of approach on various issues and inspite of substaintial improvement, India has continued to be deeply concerned about China's supplies of nuclear components, materials and knowhow to other countries in India's neighbourhood. This is especially true of China's indulgence with Pakistan. Yet, in the end, all this has never discouraged India from making efforts at improving ties with both Beijing and Islamabad.

From the Indian side, these efforts for *rapprochement* had all started as early as late 1960s. Later, starting from Sardar Swaran Singh's (then Foreign Minister) offer in August 1970 "to settle all matters...peacefully through bilateral negotiations," India not only became the first one to take many major initiatives but also became the first one to declare and actually resume its Ambassadorial level diplomatic relations with Beijing. Besides, India also made many other goodwill gestures towards China like installing telex links in each others embassies, supporting China's candidacy for the Manila-based Asian Development Bank, inviting China to a regional UNESCO conference in New Delhi, and Prime Minister Mrs. Indira Gandhi herself making a personal gesture by visiting and signing the book of condolences in the Chinese embassy in New Delhi as mark of respect for the late Premier Zhou Enlai. The first feelers from the Chinese side came in May 1960 and April 1961 from then Vice Premier Deng

Xiaoping who revived Zhou Enlai's 1960 proposal for a package deal on the boundary question. Here, Deng proposed Chinese recognition of the McMahon Line in the eastern sector in return for Indian acceptance of the status quo along the LoAC in the western sector. In fact, according to Mrs. Gandhi's foreign policy Advisor, G. Parthasarthy, Mrs. Gandhi had even agreed to accept the Chinese package deal only that, with the Chinese assent, the formal announcement had been postponed until after December 1985 general elections. Soon the assassination of Mrs. Gandhi in October 1984 and later the Sumdorong Chu valley incident in July 1966 completely rocked this spirit of accommodation and delayed major initiatives by f9w more years.

A clear shift in China's South Asia policy, however, began to occur from late 1960s when Beijing gradually gave up its earlier post-1962 tactics of providing moral and material support to India's smaller neighbours which was aimed at: (a) tying New Delhi down to the South Asian region and, (b) trying to offset India's preeminence even in this smaller region. In 1969, for example, China not only refused to supply weapons to Nepal and gave only muted response to India's peacekeeping in Sri Lanka, it even told General Ershad of Bangladesh to expect no more Chinese support on their river water dispute with New Delhi. This has since resulted in improving India's relations with both Bangladesh and Nepal. Putting an end to its dilly-dallying of late 1980s, the Rao-Li joint statement of December 1991 clearly told China's closest ally Pakistan that Beijing now regards Kashmir as a bilateral issue between India and Pakistan. Since then China's position on Kashmir has also undergone a marked change on at least two basic counts: (a) by describing it as a bilateral issue between India and Pakistan that should be dealt not under UN resolutions of 1954 but the 1972 Simla Agreement, and (b) by broadly agreeing to underline the fear from "Islamic fundamentalism". In the second case, the Joint Statement did not directly mention either India's Kashmir or China's Xinjiang yet, as both these provinces share common borders with Pakistan, the statement has clear implications for Islamabad. But nothing perhaps stands comparison to the first Magna Carta on Sine-Indian CSBMs that came two years later and was a part of the next Rat-Li Joint Statement from Beijing.

By any standards, this nine-point "Agreement on Maintenance of Peace and Tranquillity along the Line of Actual Control (henceforth MPTA), signed between two Prime Ministers Narasimha Rao and Li Peng at Beijing's Great Hall of the People on September 7, 1993 has been the corner-stone of Sine-Indian CSBMs. Though already in vogue since the Rajiv Gandhi visit to Beijing in 1988, it was this agreement that formally institutionalised the process of Sine-Indian CSBMs.19 Picking up strings from India's first CSBM agreement of April 1954, the MPTA reiterates its faith in *Panchsheel* and asserts that these Five Principles of Peaceful Coexistence should form the basis of all inter-state relations. But unlike in the earlier Sino-Indian *Panchsheel* agreement where India unilaterally made major concessions, the MPTA clearly represents equality of two nations and lays out various CSBMs that should further buttress Sino-Indian rapprcchement. This business-like spirit is crystal clear throughout its concise text that details on number of specific points. The second CSBMs agreement was signed during President Jiang Zemin's visit to New Delhi in November 1998. This is a 12 Article document that partly fulfils the agenda of their first CSBM agreement of 1993 and it further seeks to extend the CBMs to more specific and sensitive areas in the military field. Going by its first Article that reads "Neither side shall use its military capability against the other side", it virtually stands out as a No War Pact and both sides have also projected it in that light. The agreement begins with (Article II) recognising that both have "different perceptions" on certain segments of border for which the two have agreed "to speed up the process of clarification" and under Article X both sides agree 40 exchange maps indicating their respective perceptions... as soon as possible." It is this businesslike approach to these sensitive questions that gives hope for the future as it depicts !heir growing mutual confidence on the current pace of their *rapprochement.*

As regards evolving CBMs in the military field, the agreement makes a serious attempt at effecting reductions in their military manpower and equipment deployed in the border areas. There had been major confusion as China does not consider their deployments in Tibet as being open for mutual reductions where India believes that Chinese forces on the Tibetan plateau have clear one-to-ten advantage against Indian forces. Accordingly,

Article III provides that keeping with "the principle of mutual and equal security" all future ceilings are expected to be based on "perimeters such as the nature of terrain, road communications and other infrastructure and time taken to induct/deinduct troops and armaments." Article IV clearly categonses certain type of offensive weapons withdrawal of which will be given priority These include combat tanks, infantry combat vehicles, guns (including howitzers) with 75 mm or bigger calibre, mortars with 120 mm or bigger calibre, surface-to-surface missiles, surface-to-air missiles and to start with the two sides will "exchange data on the military forces and armament" that are to be reduced. It also exhorts the two sides to 'avoid holding large scale military exercises involving more than one Division (15,000 troops) in close proximity to the LoAc" and to inform the other side on "type, level, planned duration and areas of exercise" in case it involves more than a Brigade (5,000 troops) and about deinduction "within five days of completion." The other side is free to seek any number of clarifications as it deems necessary. Taking a major step forward, the two agree that no combat aircraft which "include fighter, bomber, reconnaissance, military trainer, armed helicopter and other armed aircraft" shall be allowed to fly "within ten kilometers" of the LoAC "except by prior permission" from the other side (Article V).

Similarly, Article VI prohibits any use of "hazardous chemicals, conduct blast operations or hunt with guns or explosives within two kilometers" of the LoAC unless it is "part of developmental activities" in which case the other side shall be informed "through diplomatic channels or by convening a border personnel meeting, preferably five days in advance." Then to "strengthen exchanges and cooperation between their military personnel and establishments" Article VII provides that the two sides shall (a) increase "meetings between their border representatives at designated places, (b) expand "telecommunication links" between these border points, and (c) establish "step-by-step medium and high-level contacts between the border authorities" of the two sides. Should any land or air intrusions take place "because of unavoidable circumstances like natural disasters" the other side is expected under Article VIII to "extend all possible assistance to them" and the two shall exchange information and have consultations to work out "modalities of return of the concerned personnel." And finally, as won as the Sino-Indian Joint Working Group on Boundary Question starts "mutual consultations" (Article Xl) for "detailed implementation measures", each side shall have (Article IX) "the right to seek clarification" regarding the "manner in which the other side is observing the agreement" or on any "doubtful situation" in the border region. Finally, under Article XII though all Hindi, Chinese and English versions are "equally authentic", but "in case of divergence, the English text shall prevail." This agreement has since been ratified by both sides and instrument of ratification were exchanged at the JWG's tenth meeting in New Delhi in August 1997.

These two agreements apart from being a major take-off point for many fresh initiatives, have also provided a major boost to existing "mechanisms" for their border related CSBMs. The Joint Working Group on Boundary Question has been one most effective and generic forum for implementing Sino-Indian CSBMs. To begin with, the JWG has institutionalised regular meetings of military commanders from both sides at the following four points: Bumla and Dichu in the eastern sector, Lipulekh near Pithoragarh (U.P.) in the middle sector and Spanggur near Chushul in the western sector. These meetings are organised and conducted by these area commanders from the two sides to establish facts on the ground and can also be held more than once in case of any exigencies. Besides, commanders on both sides are now provided with "hotline" links to ensure consultations in case of any intrusions or other emergencies. Advance notices of proposed military manoeuvres on one side is provided to the other and mechanisms for handling possible intrusions on either side are put in place. The high point of these JWG meetings occurred during its eighth meeting during August 1995 at New Delhi where the two sides agreed to actually dismantle four border posts in the Wangdong tract where troops had been deployed at an alarming proximity to each other. Apart from their land-based troops, the two air forces have also been building ties and officers of the People's

Liberation Army-Air Force (PLAAF) have already visited India's Air Force bases in 1995. Similarly, the two navies have also been working together allaying each others doubts about Chinese naval presence in Myanmar or India's maritime capabilities at its Fortress Andaman. India has offered to China's envoy to visit Indian naval base at Port Blair in Andaman and Nicobar. At a certain stage there were even reports of China and India preparing for joint military and naval exercises which, however, was denied by the Chinese side.

Then there are various other bold initiatives that come about from outside the framework of JWG. Within less than two months of the MPTA, for example, a Chinese ship "Zheng He" made a port visit to Bombay, which was the first of its kind in last 35 years. Before this only INS Mysore had visited Shanghai in 1958. Also, working on the basis of Chiunese *guanxi* (personal contacts) principle, exchanges between other opinion makers and members of strategic research institutions (like Institute for Defence Studies & Analyses, United Services Institution of India, Centre for Policy Research, and Rajiv Gandhi Foundation from India and China institute for Contemporary International Relations, China Association for Friendly International Contact, Fudan University etc. from China) have also been increasingly formalised. Similarly, *Xinhua, People's Dai and Beijing Review* have their accredited correspondents in India and India's *Press Trust of India* has a resident reporter in Beijing. The agreements on exchange of scholars (between the Indian Council for Social Science Research and Chinese Academy of Social Sciences signed at New Delhi in January 1992) and their Agreement on Radio and Television Cooperation (signed in Beijing on September 7, 1993) have broadly contributed to expanding mutual awareness. The Festival of China was staged in India in 1992 and Festival of India was held in China in April 1994. In fact, the Communist Party of China now has direct links with the Indian National Congress, the Bharatiya Janata Party and the Communist Party of India (Marxists). The two had also tried opening up direct flights between New Delhi and Beijing and now have telecom lines between various cities of the two countries. Contact have also evolved between various NGOs like trade unions and woman organisations, stimulating a great deal of interest and confidence.

In the de-ideologised post-Cold War world, trade has come to be perhaps the most durable CSBM which raises stakes in mutual security and peace amongst states, Though compared to their size and total foreign trade, the volume of Sino-Indian bilateral trade remains still very small yet, more than what is visible in terms of statistics, their border trade has substantially increased the traffic of goods and people in their border regions thus consolidating their border related CSBMs.

Garbyang (in Uttar Pradesh) was the first border port to be opened in February 1991 followed by Gunji (in Uttar Pradesh) in 1992 and later Shipki La (in Himachal Pradesh) in 1994. A fourth border point agreed upon in principle is yet to be opened. India has suggested an eastern route originating in Sikkim on which China has been evasive as it means recognising Sikkim's accession to India.

As an alternative, a route from Kalimpong in Dajeeling District in West Bengal, passing through Sikkim to Yatung in Chumbi Valley, is likely to be agreed upon. Amongst its other intangibles, in 1994, India became China's largest trading partner in South Asia overtaking China's long-standing close friend and ally Pakistan, This obtains for India a greater leverage and psychological advantage vis-a-vis Sine-Pakistan ties. And finally, talking of statistics, according to a recent study by US based Centre for Global Trade Development that monitors trade patterns of 220 countries, has predicted that trade between China and India may cross $ 25 billion by the year 2000. According to the study, this is possible because at their current rate of growth India's total annual exports are expected to reach $ 90 billion and that of China (plus Hong Kong $225 billion after 1997) to $425 billion per annum. The Sino-Indian Joint Business Council has, however, put the figure at a much moderate level of $ 5 billion by 2000.

CHINA'S CURRENT SECURITY POLICY

In response to the attacks in Africa during the last five years, China has confronted the problem of nontraditional security threats in several ways. The PRC's initial reaction is to work with local governments. "China will cooperate closely with immigration departments of African countries in tackling the problem of illegal migration, improve exchange of immigration control information, and set up an unimpeded and efficient channel for intelligence and information exchange," China's 2006 *Africa Policy* stated.

"In order to enhance the ability of both sides to address nontraditional security threats, it is necessary to increase intelligence exchange, explore more effective ways and means for closer cooperation in combating terrorism, small-arms smuggling, drug trafficking, transnational economic crimes, etc." Beijing has instructed its embassies in Africa to keep a close watch on local security. The swift and successful evacuation of Chinese citizens from Chad also demonstrated that China has developed operational scenarios to deal with these emergencies. The Chinese government has also started issuing travel advisories.

In Sudan and Kenya, state-owned companies receive protection from local armed forces against attacks by rebels. Beijing has signed an agreement with South Africa to prevent the Chinese diaspora from turning into a target for armed gangs. Such measures are designed to help Chinese citizens and companies avoid some of the risks related to operating in Africa, but they do not provide any guarantee for safeguarding China's economic activities if the situation keeps deteriorating. In the case of Sudan, China learned the hard way that prodding instable governments can have drastic consequences. If problems start to occur at the regional level, supporting these emerging states might prove even riskier.

Nor does this narrow security response address China's uncertainty about the military capability of African nations. The dilemma reverts back to the realistic supposition of self-help. Is the PRC trying to safeguard its interests by building up its own military presence in Africa?

Bilateral military exchanges are a first indicator to test whether this assumption holds true. According to the Chinese government, interaction with other armed forces expanded significantly, with 174 high-level visits in 2001 and more than 210 in 2006. This upward trend was not maintained in Africa, however, where such bilateral exchanges have remained stable at an annual average of 26. Beijing has established a permanent military dialogue only with South Africa. Interviews with European diplomats in ten randomly chosen African countries also reveal that the number of accredited military officers in Chinese embassies, i.e., military attachés and their support staff, has barely or not expanded at all in the last few years. In fact, only in 15 countries are Chinese military attachés assigned on a permanent basis. China's military diplomacy in Africa remains modest, and it has not kept up with the impressive number of Chinese trade officials posted in African nations to strengthen economic ties in the last few years. Military aid is another indicator. Providing military hardware to partner nations can serve various objectives. In a context of competition, it helps to thwart defence cooperation with other states or to prevent other powers' attempts to alter the regional military balance. Defence aid might help a privileged political partner to safeguard economic interests. Whereas these three objectives are motivated by security issues and long-term economic interests, defence aid may well be the result of more short-sighted aspirations. There is no evidence that China's military aid successfully counterbalances other powers, such as the United States.

Apart from Sudan and Zimbabwe, most countries that have received Chinese military aid in the last few years are also supplied by Washington. In 2007, Beijing temporarily froze the supply of heavy arms to Khartoum after pressure from the West. When Nigeria's Vice President, Atiku Abubakar, announced that his nation would turn to China instead of the United States for arms, Beijing's response was reluctant, and no major supply operations materialized. China's military aid programs should not be considered as support for its forays into the mining industry. For instance, between 2004 and 2008, resource-rich Nigeria received only half as much military aid as Ghana or Uganda. During this period, China provided more military assistance to Angola than to Sudan, even though the security challenges in the latter were much greater.

Although violence in Somalia has threatened China's oil exploration activities in both Ethiopia and Kenya, China only made a commitment to Kenya to help in protecting its border. China has, at times, provided military aid, but such assistance does not seem to be part of any coherent strategy related to protecting its security interests.

Finally, self-help would imply the deployment of military forces whenever China's interests are threatened, possibly in an attempt to train friendly armed forces and dissuade any challengers. Yet, such a Chinese military presence is negligible. China has no bases in Africa, as does the United States and France, nor has it trained African soldiers to counter threats to its national interests.

In Sudan, Zimbabwe, Cameroon, and Gabon, China has employed teams of three to ten instructors, but they are assisting in the maintenance of equipment, rather than providing training for combat missions. In Zambia and Algeria, similar examples of cooperation exist but are limited to medical activities. Other major powers deployed naval vessels in an effort to combat piracy and to maintain the maritime supply lines surrounding Africa. During such operations, the Chinese Navy has rarely shown its flag.

In 2000, China sent its newest *Luhai*-class guided missile destroyer and a supply ship to Tanzania and South Africa. A 2002 fleet composed of a guided missile destroyer, the *Qingdao*, and a supply ship, the *Taicang*, visited Egypt. These voyages were gestures of courtesy rather than a reaction to security challenges. They were limited in duration, and no actions were attempted against pirates or poachers. In December 2008, however, the Chinese government did deploy two destroyers and a replenishment ship in the Gulf of Aden to participate in the United Nations-backed mission against piracy. A mission that was only undertaken after receiving a positive signal from US Pacific Command chief Admiral Timothy Keating.

Instead of dealing with security threats unilaterally, China has resorted to bandwagoning. Although in the 1980s and early 1990s, Beijing opposed attempts by the international community to intervene in African security issues, nowadays it tends to join them. Beijing is increasingly recognizing the United Nations' role in resolving the numerous conflicts and safeguarding the sovereignty of developing nations. In the 1990s, China began supporting United Nations (UN) missions designed to implement peace agreements between rivalling parties, on the condition that a well-defined and restricted mandate was included. Traditional peacekeeping operations such as those in Somalia (UNSOM I), Mozambique, Rwanda, and Sierra Leone all were supported. When the UN Security Council decided to dispatch forces to Liberia in 2003, China offered to support the mission and gradually increased the number of its peacekeepers to 1,300 in 2007.

At the same time, however, failed states and national governments that had actively participated in atrocities challenged the efficacy of many of the traditional UN operations. China's focus on the primacy of sovereignty, requiring at a minimum the state's consent, collided with the willingness of other nations to intervene aggressively under the UN Charter's Chapter VII mandate.

Beijing loudly opposed the move by European countries to push for Operation Turquoise in Rwanda, Washington's call to broaden the UNSOM mandate, or France's demand for a troop increase in the 2004 UN operation in Ivory Coast. Despite its strong concerns, China did not veto these interventions at the UN Security Council, but rather abstained and remained aloof from implementation. Sudan was the first instance where China actively lobbied an African government to permit a UN mission on its soil. Via active brokering and indirect pressure, China succeeded in neutralizing the incompatibility between its economic interests and the principle of noninterference on the one hand, and western appeals for intervening in Darfur and the need for long-term stability on the other.

That Beijing recognizes the importance of collective security became apparent in 2006, when China was the first nation to ask the UN Security Council for a peacekeeping mission in Somalia. In June that year, at a Security Council meeting in Addis Ababa, China's Permanent Representative to the UN, Wang Guangya, scolded other diplomats for neglecting Somalia and urged them to support the deployment of peacekeepers. "I was reluctant to take on this role," said Wang, explaining that African governments had been pushing China to raise the issue in the Council, "but there was a lack of interest by the other major powers." Initially, the proposal was tentatively received by Great Britain and the United States, but after various talks in New York, Beijing and Washington jointly sponsored a resolution for the deployment of a UN mission. In 2007, in early consultations with France, China supported a French draft resolution on Chad calling for the dispatch of mainly European peacekeepers under the auspices of Chapter VII. It was significant that China approved the "close liaising" with the Hybrid Operation in Darfur (UNAMID), where earlier it had objected to the development of links between UNAMID and UN missions. "Our support for the resolution on Chad shows that we are prepared to cooperate to tackle security issues at a regional level and that our awareness on the increasing complexity of violent conflicts in Africa grows," a Chinese diplomat explained.

China is also turning to African regional organizations to collaborate on security issues. In the China-Africa Action Plan, approved in November 2006, Beijing vowed "to support Africa in the areas of logistics" as well as "to continue its active participation in the peacekeeping operations and demining process in Africa and provide, within the limits of its capabilities, financial and material assistance as well as relevant training to the Peace and Security Council of the African Union." In June 2006, the Chinese government granted the African Union's Mission in Sudan $3.5 million in budgetary support and humanitarian aid. Earlier, it provided financial and technical support to the Association for West African States.

Slowly but surely, China is showing itself ready to participate in international efforts to prevent conflicts, fueled by the easy availability of small arms and illegally exported natural resources. In 2002, for instance, Beijing revised its regulation on the control of military products for export and published the "Military Products Export Control List" supplying guidelines for the export of military-related products. In the same year, it signed the "Protocol Against the Illicit Manufacturing of and Trafficking in Firearms," which committed the People's Republic to control the manufacturing, marking, import, and export of firearms, and to confiscate and destroy all illicit firearms. In 2005, the government launched a national information management system for the production, possession, and trade of light arms, and it introduced a system to monitor end-users of Chinese-made weapons to prevent the arms from finding their way to "sensitive regions" around the world via third parties. In 2006, China supported a draft UN resolution on the illicit trade of small arms and light weapons, in contrast to the United States. In 2002, China joined the Kimberley Process, a joint government, international diamond industry, and civil initiative designed to stem the flow of conflict diamonds originating from Africa. In 2005, China allowed a voluntary peer review of its support for the Kimberly Process. Although these actions still have many flaws, they seem to prove that China wishes to do more than just put "boots on the ground" in response to Africa's internal conflicts.

Despite the strategic importance of Africa, China does not try to safeguard its foothold in the region by unilaterally projecting military power. In Africa, its military diplomacy remains limited when compared with defence initiatives in other regions. If the PRC does pursue bilateral cooperation programs, these are more likely to be a part of its diplomatic charm offensive, rather than addressing threats to China's economic and security interests. Instead of relying on a military presence to counterbalance other powers, the PRC tends to join collective security efforts within the framework of the United Nations and African regional organizations. Over the past few years, this strategy of joint ventures has evolved from passive support to active cooperation. Beijing has softened its devotion to noninterference. While maintaining the primacy of sovereignty, it has become willing to support interventions whenever regional stability is at stake.

Although China has become a revisionist power in terms of its economic aspirations on the continent, it is acting as a status-quo power in terms of security objectives. There are several explanations for this stance. First, China only recently began its economic focus on the African continent. For the past two decades, China concentrated on curbing the military and diplomatic influence of Taiwan; the focus on "economization" of its Africa policy only began in the late 1990s.

Hence, the security challenges it is facing now are a recent phenomena, and solutions to these challenges are just starting to be explored. The PRC is going through the early stage of resecuritization of its Africa strategy, and joining with other nations in an allied strategy can be considered the easiest immediate response. Second, and related to this point, China has not developed sufficient means to back up its security policy with military power. This is a matter of budgetary constraints. Building an independent and sustained military presence is a costly affair and would, at present, overstretch the PLA's capabilities, while Asia remains its primary focus. The PLA does not possess the logistical capacity to support sustained region wide deployment in Africa. Its long-range airlift and sealift, as well as its intelligence and command capabilities, are not up to the task. Third, the Chinese government wants to avoid the People's Republic being perceived as a hegemonic power.

In the initial stage of its economic charm offensive, the PRC tried to pursue a business-as-usual approach, maintaining a low profile and steering clear of political entanglements. That approach is no longer possible now that China stands at the forefront of Africa's political scene, actively altering the economic balance of power. Beijing is well aware of the dichotomy between its weak and strong identities and is reluctant to demonstrate any independent military capacity. Such a show of strength might reduce its diplomatic maneuverability, increase resistance from African nations-just as Washington is now experiencing-and raise suspicions elsewhere regarding Chinese intentions. Yet, as interests, perceptions, and capacities are susceptible to change, the question remains whether China will stay on this track of cooperative security.

China's interests in Africa have changed over the past decades and will undoubtedly continue to evolve. The concept for its security policy in the region will depend on the role that Africa plays as a supplier of natural resources. Africa currently supplies approximately 30 percent of China's oil imports. Beijing and its African partners announced that they are preparing to increase bilateral trade to $100 billion by the year 2010. Most of this increase will come from the import of raw commodities. In recent years, Chinese companies have laid the foundation for a substantial increase in the production of resource industries. Exploration in the Gulf of Guinea, Angola, and the Horn of Africa have the potential for an increase in oil exports to China of more than 80 percent in the next ten years. Chinese companies are just starting to tap the large mines that were recently acquired in Gabon, the Democratic Republic of Congo, Namibia, and elsewhere on the continent. Given the fact that other emerging markets such as India and Brazil are shifting the use of their raw materials from export to domestic consumption, the economic relevance of Africa to China cannot be overstated.

How necessary it is to back up these Chinese economic ventures with more overt security measures is yet to be seen. The incidents described in the first section of this article, the persistent instability in nations, as well as the weak position of amicable political leaders will undoubtedly position Africa higher on Beijing's foreign security agenda and require a more complete approach. The question again arises whether it is in China's best interest to apply its African policy independently or in synergy with other nations. The short-term costs of any unilateral action would certainly exceed those of collective action, but long-term uncertainty about the intentions of other major players might influence any concerns related to cost-effectiveness. If Washington or Delhi decides to change course and contain China's expanding influence in Africa by pursing a strategy of counterbalancing and sea denial, the repercussions for the People's Republic will be dramatic. The concerns of the national security establishments in India and the United States and their expanding military presence in Africa are not unnoticed in China, and they highlight the necessity for the PRC to build a legitimate capacity to deal with crises unilaterally. China's diplomatic identity will help shape policy decisions in support of a more active and autonomous security strategy. Beijing is realizing that the comfortable cloak of frailty it previously presented to the world no longer fits. African partners do not attach much value to China's diplomatic schizophrenia and the complex image of an economic giant, political dwarf, and minor military player it projects. When mayhem erupts, China automatically ends up on the frontline, finding itself hounded by African governments asking it to exercise its leverage. The cases of Chad and Somalia are not the only examples of this. South Africa has accosted China regarding illegal immigrants from Zimbabwe. Central Africa has carefully examined the violent incursions from Sudan. The African Union has called upon China several times to play a more active role in promoting security. The possibility exists that individual countries may be compelled to form a closer alliance with China in order to reduce their current reliance on the European Union and United States for security. Nigeria's announcement that it would rely on China instead of the United States for military support hints at this direction. The ability of the PRC to keep a low military profile is diminishing.

On the other hand, China's self-perception is also in transition. The "Century of Humiliation" is far behind and is being replaced by a national attitude of confidence and assertiveness. Chinese leaders have built on the success of their policy of good neighbour diplomacy that resulted in fewer frictions and more influence in Asia. The People's Republic has drawn confidence from the successful launch of a number of new defence systems. As China sees its diplomatic leverage expanding geographically from the Strait of Formosa, via Asia to the rest of the developing world, its ability to deal with emerging security issues is likely to follow suit.

Finally, there is the factor of capacity. China is gearing its military for a greater deployment capability. Its large immobile army is gradually being converted into a highly specialized and flexible organization. Simultaneously, the PLA is launching new military systems that will enhance its capacity to transport these forces. In 2007, the Chinese government approved the development of large passenger jets, including military transport variants similar to the American C-17 Globemaster III. Beijing has also ordered several new ships in an effort to enhance its naval transport capacity. In 2006, the hull of the first T-071 vessel was laid. This landing-platform dock has a range that goes far beyond Taiwan, with the aim of providing sea-based support to operations on land, humanitarian aid, and assisting in evacuations and disaster management. These vessels will be supported by a new generation of large replenishment ships and could be escorted by advanced frigates and destroyers. The Chinese flotilla that was sent to Somalia demonstrates China's new blue-water capacity. The type 052C *Lanzhou*, for instance, is a showcase of the advanced detection capacity for China's Navy. Its multifunction, active phased-array radar has a detection range of 450 kilometers and is complemented with a long-range, two-dimensional air search radar that has a 350-kilometer range and three additional systems to detect incoming missiles and aircraft. China is advancing its ability to pursue a more confident and independent security policy in Africa.

Will all this newfound military activity be sufficient to offset the antagonistic response it is likely to provoke? Probably not. If China decides to go solo and to pursue a more aggressive security policy in Africa, it is improbable that it will be able to overcome countermoves by India and the United States. It will be difficult for China to safeguard maritime trade with Africa if India exercises its naval dominance in the Indian Ocean. The sheer geographical divide between the PRC and the African continent makes it extremely difficult to support military activities if the United States or India opposes them. Contrary to China's revolutionary phase of the 1950s and 1960s when trade and economic interests only played a small part, China's increasing reliance on Africa renders it highly vulnerable to sea denial operations or a *guerre de course*. The fragile Cold War balance between the United States and the Soviet Union that allowed Mao to meddle with America's interests in Africa without having to fear political or economic reprisals can no longer be counted on. These days China has much to lose if it provokes Washington or Delhi.

INDIA'S SECURITY CONCEPT ON ITS CHINA POLICY

Earlier sections of this book explain changes in India's post-Cold War security concept and adjustments to its China policy. In the process of this discussion, we have distinguished two phases of adjustment to both the post-Cold War India security concept and China policy, and established that these changes were more or less simultaneous. We have also found that India's China policy reflects its security concept; in other words that adjustments to the content of India's China policy correspond to continuities and discontinuities in India's security concept. It may be said that this consistency demonstrates the important influence India's security concept has had on its China policy.

Policy-making, in any event, is the linking of concepts and policy; in other words, concepts, through government policy-making, crystallize into policy. Exploring the evolution of the Indian policy-making class and mechanisms, therefore, also benefits understanding of the manner in which security concepts of different eras and phases have influenced India's China policy.

India's foreign policy behaviour during the Cold War was largely determined by a few predominant personalities, both its foreign and security policies having long been dominated by Nehru and Indira Gandhi. The two leader's views on China had decisive influence on India's China policy. When considering India's defeat in the 1962 Sino–Indian Border Conflict and the open wound it represented to both the Nehru family and the INC, their adoption of an unyielding tack toward China was the sole political means of saving face. Sino–Indian relations consequently remained in stalemate for nearly 30 years. When Rajiv Gandhi replaced his mother in 1985, he seemed at first to follow her line on foreign policy. The rapidly changing international situation, however, forced him to veer from it, and specific improvements in Sino–Soviet relations compelled his adjustments to India's China policy. Soviet leader Mikhail Gorbachev urged Rajiv Gandhi during a visit to India in 1986 to improve relations with China, saying it would suit Soviet interests, and hinting at a press conference that the USSR would no longer be willing to provide support to India in the event of Sino–Indian conflict. In this situation, Rajiv Gandhi considered that India on its own would be powerless against a threat on two fronts. He was hence forced to change his preparations for a two-front war, as it was apparent that dispelling tensions along the eastern front through reconciliation with China would allow him to concentrate India's energies on the western front with Pakistan.

The Nehru family's stately bearing was absent after the Cold War, and the INC's power had declined. The insularity that had characterized India's foreign policy-making process since independence, however, did not change. The nation's foreign and security policy stayed in the hands of the prime minister and cabinet from 1991 to 1996, during which time the views of Prime Minister Rao and leaders of the INC government on security and foreign policy matters were decisive, and the influence of parliament, think tanks and academic institutions was negligible. It is notable, however, that Rao's background as home minister, defence minister and external affairs minister throughout the 1980s, as well as his status as the Congress Party's elder statesman, signified that he was a loyal adherent of Nehruvianism, and unrepresentative of any new type of thinking. The transformation of India's security concept during the Rao administration, therefore, can be understood as entirely the result of external forces.

As earlier mentioned, changes in the international and domestic situation compelled Rao to change his understanding of national strength. He began emphasizing the strategic influence of economic strength and promoting restoration of the economy as a matter of urgency in withstanding security threats in the aftermath of the Cold War. This passive reaction to a complex situation gave the impression of India's overall foreign policy as passive and defensive. India adopted a focused approach to diplomacy during this period, directing its energies towards restoring the economy but maintaining a low profile in international affairs, as expressed in its China policy. Rao continued and furthered Rajiv Gandhi's adjustments by focusing on stabilization of Sino–Indian political relations and establishing tranquil borders as means to ensuring the recovery of India's domestic economy. Two major changes occurred in India's foreign policy-making process during 1998.

The first was the BJP's assumption of office that ended the long-standing INC power monopoly, and established foundations for a clean break with the traditional security concept. Although the BJP's domestic policies had a relatively ideological slant and promoted a Hinduist revival, the party was pragmatic as regards foreign policy. In contrast to the Congress Party, it dared to confront history, criticise India's previous foreign policy and introduce new thinking. Jaswant Singh, successively the Vajpayee government's External Affairs Minister and Finance Minister, published early in 1999 a book entitled *Defending India* in which he systematically describes his new security concept. Various views were thereafter expressed in government-issued articles. The BJP was obviously preparing to move on from the passive security concept of the Rao era. The second major change was India's refinement of its foreign policy-making mechanism. The November 1998 establishment of the National Security Council symbolized India's casting off of the influence and control of personality-based policy-making in favour of scientific research, inquiry and decision-making, and comprehensive long-term planning. The introduction by National Security Advisory Board subordinated to the National Security Council of scholarly authorities, reporters and former government and military officials demonstrated how much more open India's foreign policy-making process had become.

The BJP differed in its approach to China policy from both that of the Cold War era Nehru family, with its 1962 complex, and the early 1990s Rao government, which had been wearied and bound hand and foot by domestic and international pressure. The BJP's seizing of this historic opportunity confirmed India's rise as the nation's long-term strategic goal and placed its relationship with China on the strategic level. In other words, the BJP saw the Sino–Indian relationship as an important influence on India's rise. Although the two nations would be dealing with historically significant problems, they could be seen as a starting point.

The gradual opening of India's foreign policy-making process, moreover, made way for a vibrant exchange of ideas regarding China policy, which fell roughly into three groups: the first held that Sino–Indian cooperation suits both sides' interests and that post-Cold War China has no intention of making an enemy of India, desiring instead friendly relations and strategic partnership; the second that China is a long-term strategic threat to India because China's strategic objectives lie in establishing hegemony over Asia, which necessitates India's containment and, therefore, limitation of Indian influence. India, therefore, should adopt diametrically opposed policies; and the third group, situated between the two, held that the two nations could simultaneously rise to become main Asian powers and that competition and cooperation could coexist. Discussions on how to evaluate and understand China by Indian scholars and strategic circles are ongoing. After frequent debates among Indian National Security Council groups, the third, middle-ground viewpoint seems to be gaining acceptance.

When the INC regained power in 2004, a variety of factors led the new government to carry on with the previous administration's security concept. The new INC government's China policy was its predecessor's legacy, because the rise of India's international status during the BJP coalition government left the INC powerless to dispute the success of the previous government's foreign policy. The INC's democratized and more youthful leadership team was also willing to jettison historical baggage and look to the future. Although the Nehru family's leadership role within the Congress Party remained uncontested, the influence of Prime Minister Manmohan Singh and Foreign Minister Mukherjee on foreign and security policy could not be disregarded. Moreover, the liberalization of India's foreign policy-making process was superimposed against a long-standing civil service system which ensured continuity of policy. In other words, many masterminds of BJP foreign policy still active in the external affairs ministry, defence ministry and other relevant functional departments under the INC, as well as in consultative committees, the media, think tanks and other non-functional departments, continued to exert influence.

Substantial changes occurred in India's China policy after the end of the Cold War whereby the nation's long-standing (1962–1988) antagonistic approach became one of reconciliation and engagement. These adjustments originated to a great extent in changes in the sub-continent's post-Cold War security concept, manifest in two major shifts which effected two major phases of adjustment in India's China policy. The new post-Cold War China policy nonetheless retained traces of the former, programme, imbuing it with a duality that reflected the overlap of India's old and new security concepts. A change in India's security concept first became apparent during the period from the end of the Cold War to 1998.

The first phase of adjustments this change triggered in India's China policy was evident in the sub-continent's extended concept of military might as national strength to one encompassing economic factors, and acknowledgement of the strategic value of economic strength in countering what it perceived as the looming threat of marginalization within the international community. Restoration of the domestic economy hence became a main measure through which to resist security threats in the post-Cold War era. Having made this shift in foreign policy objectives towards economic recovery, India set about creating a favourable environment within which to achieve this goal. Overall implementation of a China policy of preserving stable Sino–Indian relations by guaranteeing border tranquillity was vital to achieving this strategic objective. India consequently focused on the feasibility of reconciliation and, in view of China's reflective, inward-looking mood, no longer viewed China as an enemy. As regards India's specific policies, while focusing on the establishment of a progressive means to guaranteeing tranquil borders, thereby stabilizing Sino–Indian relations, India at the same time sought communication and cooperation in other areas. To avoid provoking China, the Indian government made tactical adjustments to its approach to Tibet from that of exploiting the issue and causing uproar to handling the matter in a low-key manner.

The new developments apparent in India's security concept in 1999 brought with it the second phase of adjustments to India's China policy. Indian leaders considered that the nation's security environment had improved to the extent that it constituted a strategic opportunity for India to rise to global-power status. This change in thinking and understanding caused the second shift of objective in India's foreign policy from that of improving the economy to the grand goal of global-power status. It corresponded to India's acknowledgement of the crucial nature of the Sino–Indian relationship and change of focus from border tranquillity and stable political relations to comprehensive considerations of how the two nations' relationship would strategically affect India's; rise. These insights compelled a shift of objective in India's China policy towards making China a positive factor in the sub-continent's rise; also recognition that this objective could be accomplished only by maintaining a stable basis for Sino–Indian relations. Official introduction during this phase of a comprehensive security concept signalled India's adoption of a more pragmatic, comprehensive handling of its relations with China.

The specific steps it adopted were: increasing economic cooperation with China, thus benefiting India's economic development and stabilizing bilateral political relations; strengthening military communication and security dialogue, thus deepening understanding of China's strategic intentions towards India, increasing mutual trust, minimizing misunderstandings and avoiding conflict; and seeking Chinese support in its quest for a permanent seat on the UN Security Council, which would expand India's political power and international prestige. In the course of research, however, it became apparent to the author that India's security concept did not undergo a thoroughgoing change after the Cold War ended, as elements of the Cold War approach remained in place.

Although India's security concept extended after 1988 to include both military and economic security, the ultimate purpose of national defence as regards a fundamental guarantee of security nonetheless remained that of increased military strength to safeguard national unity and territorial integrity. India abandoned its strategy of pursuing security through alliances, yet still viewed parity and the principle of checks and balances as hallmarks of its national defence. Influenced as it was by traditional concepts, post-Cold War India's China policy was imbued with vigilance. Even though India did not perceive China as a threat in the short term, it was nevertheless concerned that the swing in balance of power between the two was not in its favour, and that China constituted a potential obstacle to India's rise. Indian leaders consequently embarked on a race against China to expand comprehensive national strength, particularly military force, including India's nuclear capability, as the means to a balance of power. India at the same time sought to offset Chinese influence both regionally and globally through development of strategic relationships with the United States, Japan and other nations. The sub-continent also remained vigilant in the long-standing issues of border disputes and Sino–Pakistani relations, and maintained pressure on China in this regard.

Changes in post-Cold War India's security concept were thus the result of both domestic and foreign factors. The first change during the early post-Cold War period was triggered by passive reactions to transformations in the nation's domestic and international situation that, in turn, prompted a passive transformation of thinking and understanding, manifest in passive defensiveness of India's foreign policy, specifically its China policy. The security concept that appeared during the late 1990s was comparatively proactive. The expanded strength of India's domestic economy and improvement of its external environment compelled a new understanding of security issues, as expressed in the proactive change in its security concept. This assertiveness was manifest in strategy and in an active, enterprising foreign policy. Seizing the historic opportunity to realize India's rise had become the common security objective of both major Indian political parties. Decentralization of political power and expanded openness of the foreign policy-making process, however, caused India's old and new security concepts to bind into one, and the resultant duality of India's hybrid security concept since the Cold War's end is reflected in its China policy. As India's dual security concept will continue into the foreseeable future, the duality of its China policy will be difficult to change.

NON-STATE ACTORS AND SECURITY IN SOUTH ASIA

As aforementioned, nuclear weapons development and enhancement in South Asia are intricately related to long-standing rivalries between the concerned states. However, instability does not just stem from the risk of nuclear warfare between states in the region. Non-state actors also play a significant role in the nuclear security framework, aside from their role in facilitating nuclear proliferation. First, terrorist groups (such as Jaish-e-Mohammed and Lashkar-e-Toiba) that are connected to the Pakistani religious-political establishment can provoke tensions between India and Pakistan through mass casualty attacks. This was amply demonstrated following the December 2001 attack on the Indian Parliament by Jaish-e-Mohammed militants, which led to a ten-month stand-off between the two armies.

A second danger is through a Kargil-style episode in which militants, in cooperation with official Pakistani agencies and the military, occupy territory in Kashmir. As the July 2007 siege of the Lal Masjid (Red Mosque) complex in the heart of Islamabad showed, militant groups are steadily expanding their geographical area of influence, adversely affecting the stability of Pakistan. Although the nuclear weapon complex is under military control, there might be pockets within the military that are sympathetic to fundamentalist groups. At the very least, political and religious instability in Pakistan creates uncertainty in the minds of policymakers within and outside the region.

Finally, fears have been heightened since 9/11 over the possibility of nuclear weapons technology transfers from Pakistan to terrorist networks, especially after it was revealed that some senior Pakistani nuclear scientists met with the Al Qaeda leadership prior to 9/11. A related concern in the aftermath of 9/11 is that a fundamentalist Islamic group with Taliban/Al Qaeda links could take over Pakistan and with it, possession of the country's nuclear arsenal. Thus, Indian (as well as U.S.) threat perceptions include not just bilateral nuclear stability issues between India and Pakistan, but also the consequences of nuclear technology and materials falling into the hands of militant groups.

In general, the complex nuclear weapons scenario in South Asia is shaped by two main factors. First, the intense nature of the dispute between India and Pakistan strikes at the very core of their nationhood. It involves territorial disputes and terrorist violence, and is further complicated by the desire of some terrorist groups to acquire non-conventional technology. Second, South Asia is part of a broader nuclear weapons context that includes China and the United States. Military developments by either Washington or

Beijing, which are perceived as a direct threat, also impact military policies (both conventional and non-conventional) in South Asia. At the same time, the continued strategic military collaboration between China and Pakistan (such as the joint development of the JF-17 fighter plane) is a factor that motivates India to continue nuclear and conventional modernization. Furthermore, while the territorial disputes between India and China are relatively dormant, there is no final resolution. As developments in 2006-2007 demonstrated, there is still a considerable gap between the two sides on the territorial issue. Due to this combination of factors, there are no clear incentives for either party to drastically reorient its nuclear policy.

Nuclear Policies in South Asia

Keeping the various security disputes and attitudes in mind, the next step is to consider the nuclear doctrines and policies of protagonists in the region. Both India and Pakistan strive for a minimum deterrent. The objective of India's nuclear strategy is credible minimum deterrence (CMD), meaning a secure and reliable second-strike capability after absorbing an adversary's first strike. The main potential targets of this projected deterrence capability are Pakistan and China. Pakistan's nuclear doctrine also seeks a credible deterrent, against India, and according to one senior nuclear weapons planner, its weapons are "aimed solely at India." In particular it seeks to deter New Delhi from launching a conventional military attack such as an offensive for limited war objectives, including destruction of terrorist training camps, as well as attacks on nuclear facilities.

For both India and Pakistan, key components of their attitudes in nuclear defence demonstrate the incompatibility between their mutual nuclear postures. India's offer of a no-first use pact has been rejected by Pakistan as nuclear weapons are an integral element of its (Islamabad's) defence doctrine. On the other hand, Islamabad has offered New Delhi a no-war pact, which ostensibly would reduce the prospect of full-scale conventional war and the risk of nuclear crises. However, such a proposal does not touch upon the proxy war waged by the Kashmiri militants and therefore has been rejected by New Delhi.

Thus, both India and Pakistan strive for a secure second-strike capability as an integral element of their credible minimum deterrent doctrines. Since neither side has constructed systems that are deemed completely satisfactory and reliable, nuclear modernization continues. For India, this means a survivable delivery mechanism that can conceivably strike major cities in China. At present the longest range deployed missile is believed to be the Agni-II with a range of 2,000-2,500 km, and can reach parts of western China. To have an increased range capability, the Indian Defence Research and Development Organization (DRDO) is developing the Agni III intermediate range ballistic missile, which was successfully tested for the first time in April 2007 and has a range of about 3,500 km. Nevertheless, reports have stated that the Indian military is not altogether satisfied with the nuclear capable missiles that are in its arsenal-Prithvi I (short range ballistic missiles) and the Agni I & II. Thus, India's nuclear delivery systems are deemed far from adequate and for the time being. In the opinion of the Indian Air Force, there will be considerable reliance on fighter bombers such as the Mig 27, Jaguar, and Mirage-2000 for a nuclear delivery role.

This implies that for the foreseeable future, the Indian scientific-military establishment will reinforce their commitment to adequate delivery systems, especially the Agni III and the nuclear submarine project (the Advanced Technology Vessel or ATV) that could carry a sea-based deterrent in the form of a submarine-launched cruise missile (the Sagarika-currently under development). Reports in May 2007 stated that the ATV will be commissioned in 2011-2012 and that two Russian nuclear submarines might be leased before that.

As stated earlier, Pakistan's deployed missile systems can reach most parts of India. These deployed missiles include the Ghaznavi (Hatf-3, range 290 km), Shaheen-I (Hatf-4, range 600-800 km), and the Ghauri-I (Hatf-5, range 1,500 km). Development is also taking place on the Shaheen-II (Hatf-6, range 2,000-3,000 km), which was successfully tested in February 2007. These missile developments illustrate Pakistan's desire for a more secure deterrent, once the range issue had been dealt with. In addition, Pakistan is also seeking a more secure second-strike capability through the acquisition of the Agosta 90B class submarine in late 2007. This vessel, the second to be added to Pakistan's navy, can carry the nuclear capable Harpoon cruise missiles.

Both countries have also achieved considerable progress in manufacturing another delivery system-cruise missiles. India, in partnership with Russia, has developed the BrahMos, while Pakistan has the Babur. These missiles are meant to have land, sea, and air versions, and at least in the case of the BrahMos, will also have a variant for export. In the near future, Indian defence planners hope to introduce land attack cruise missiles with the capacity to carry a nuclear warhead over 1,500 km. In addition, submarine and air force versions of the BrahMos are due to be tested in 2007. The missile is also being installed on ships and IL-38D maritime reconnaissance aircraft to give "strategic relevance" to the Indian Navy. Similarly, Pakistan has successfully tested its nuclear capable Babur (Hatf VII) cruise missile (range 700 km), most recently in March 2007.

In sum, in order to strengthen their nuclear delivery capabilities both India and Pakistan are seeking to perfect their missile arsenals, both ballistic and cruise. The dynamic nature of the pursuit of more reliable deterrence capabilities is also affected by strategic developments involving extra-regional actors, especially China and the United States.

Fissile Material Accumulation

The final factor with an impact on nuclear acquisition dynamics is fissile material production. The renewed discussion on the Fissile Material Cutoff Treaty (FMCT) in 2006 focused attention on the attitudes of India and Pakistan (among other concerned states). The argument put forward by some is that capping the production of fissile material in South Asia would be an important step toward nuclear stability in the subcontinent. However, issues arising from the South Asian security dilemma play a role in stalled FMCT negotiations.

As some analysts have stated, a key motivation for Washington's support of the FMCT is to limit China's nuclear arsenal. Beijing is unlikely to agree to the FMCT under the current circumstances without amelioration of its concerns. If Beijing does not accept the treaty, there is little chance that New Delhi would accept it either resulting in Islamabad's refusal as well. While the Chinese government considers the FMCT to be crucial, its concern also lies in progress on a framework for the Prevention of an Arms Race in Outer Space (PAROS). Beijing has effectively linked progress on the FMCT to that on PAROS. Further, while Beijing is supposed to have stopped fissile material production, there is no official confirmation of this. In addition, theoretically the Chinese government can restart production of fissile material.

The lack of progress on PAROS is said to have been one of the reasons behind China's anti-satellite test in January 2007. Certain policymakers and analysts in the United States perceived the tests as symbolic of the potential military threat from China, a view that reinforces their arguments for the need for dominance in space. In response, China needs to counter a future U.S. national missile defence (NMD), possibly by increasing its quantity of warheads through increased fissile production. China's concern is that U.S. policies under the Bush administration, such as the withdrawal from the ABM Treaty and the reinforced focus on NMD, degrade Beijing's deterrent, which relies on about two dozen intercontinental ballistic missiles (ICBMs). Also, Washington's reluctance to consider a "no first use" policy increases the threat perception of the U.S. use of nuclear weapons in a Taiwan crisis.

From the Indian perspective, Beijing's anti-satellite test refocused the attention of analysts on the considerable gap between Indian and Chinese aerospace capabilities and its consequences for the strategic balance. Indian defence scientists have stated that India would take appropriate measures to deal with this expansion of Beijing's offensive capabilities, possibly through collaboration between the Defence Research and Development Organization (DRDO) and the Indian Space Research Organization (ISRO). The test came at a time when both India and China are pushing ahead with space-based projects (especially lunar missions) and this would be the sign of a new rivalry. Thus, security perceptions in South Asia (including by extension China and the United States) contain a reinforced belief in the necessity of nuclear weapons and delivery systems development. Even if China maintains its undeclared moratorium on fissile material production, it is unclear if India would consent to capping its fissile stock at a level much lower than that of China. This also strengthens the argument of Indian analysts who advocate more than just the minimum deterrent-related warheads stockpile and propose a thermonuclear arsenal. Furthermore, the Indian government also has a problem with the lack of verification measures in the existing FMCT proposals. Pakistan for its part has opposed any FMCT that would effectively perpetuate the fissile material asymmetry in the subcontinent, and wants negotiations to cover existing stocks as well. Pakistan's contention is that since its nuclear weapons program is a product of the threat from India, Islamabad would consent to a cap on fissile material production only as part of a bilateral moratorium.

However, since New Delhi's nuclear weapon expansion is driven by the need to construct a secure deterrent against Beijing, such a proposal is a non-starter in the present circumstances. Thus, while Pakistan may have reached the fissile material capacity to suit its credible minimum deterrent needs, this is not necessarily the case for India. Nevertheless, in the context of the proposed FMCT, some Indian analysts have stated that New Delhi has to decide whether its existing stocks are adequate for "strategic purposes," and if so, the FMCT could be beneficial for international stability.

In sum, from the South Asian perspective, there are no credible proliferation disincentives that would surmount security concerns driving India and Pakistan toward strengthening their nuclear capabilities. In essence, nuclear modernization, or vertical proliferation is likely to continue in South Asia. Next, we turn to the issue of horizontal proliferation in the South Asian context.

ENTER SECURITY ISSUES FROM A GROWTH PERSPECTIVE

Security is widely considered the Number One issue for Afghanistan's reconstruction and development agenda. Dealing with the legacy of nearly a quarter-century of protracted conflict, and with the difficult security issues currently facing the country, has been and will continue to be a major challenge. The main security issues in Afghanistan from a development perspective (not necessarily in order of importance) are outlined briefly below. Needless to say, many of them are closely interrelated with each other.

Continuing conflict/insurgency/terrorism and associated insecurity. Although outright insurgency and significant military conflict are concentrated in areas in the south and east of the country (where much terrorist activity is occurs as well), this conflict has been continuing on a significant scale albeit with seasonal and other fluctuations, and is adversely affecting security in these areas with important development implications. Elsewhere, sporadic acts of terrorism have occurred from time to time, but not on a widespread scale or in a sustained manner. These have a disproportionate impact on perceptions of the security situation particularly from outside the country, and hence deter foreign investment. Another adverse implication is movement restrictions on aid agencies and higher security costs for development activities, as well as for private business. For example, highway reconstruction projects reported that their direct spending on security added 3-15% to project costs, and a recent survey of private business firms found that their reported spending on security infrastructure accounted for close to 15% of sales revenue, and that an additional 3% of sales was reportedly spent on protection payments to commanders, government officials, or organized criminals (World Bank, 2006).

Lack of rule of law and poorly functioning judicial system. This is a fundamental problem, seriously affecting Afghans in their daily lives, which is both a manifestation of underlying insecurity and itself contributes to continuing insecurity. Rule of law and the judiciary were weak during most of the past quarter-century, and restoring let alone enhancing these critical components of the security system will be a major challenge. More specifically the police, weakened and largely captured by factional forces during the conflict, has often been more a source of insecurity than of security for most Afghans. Anecdotal evidence indicates that

District officials are unable to reliably resolve local disputes in their official capacity, unless they have personal prestige through their traditional connections to do so. Few police officers in rural areas have professional training, and many are former mujahedin or militia members who became police officers when their commanders joined the Government after 2001. Police forces continue to operate largely independently from a centralized command structure under the Ministry of Interior, and many remain loyal to their former commanders. The police force is overwhelmingly male, and many districts lack detention facilities for women. The lack of women police officers to handle the arrest, detention, or transport of female detainees places any woman arrested at heightened risk of abuse.

The formal judicial system was devastated during the conflict, and its rebuilding since 2001 has been slow. In addition to the lack of recourse for Afghans and inability to effectively punish serious crimes (including those committed during the conflict), the weakness of the formal judicial system is a deterrent to business activity in the formal sector and to foreign investment. Although historically Afghanistan has relied much more on customary and traditional practices and adjudication mechanisms, these also were significantly eroded in many respects during the conflict, and/or "captured" by warlords and commanders, with adverse effects on local security as well as on business activities and livelihoods.

An important manifestation of these problems is the widespread uncertainties and disputes over land, leading to ambiguities and insecurity related to land tenure as well as theft and illegal appropriation of land. Confirming other information, recent fieldwork in Nangarhar and Laghman provinces found that conflict over agricultural land (and related water supplies) was the most common source of violence (Koehler and Zurcher, 2005). Access to land is the second most widely cited constraint on business activity in a recent survey of firms (World Bank, 2006).

Finally, there is a long tradition of the Judiciary being an exclusively male domain, and only around 3% of judges currently are women. With the exception of the heads of the juvenile and family courts in Kabul, women are not found in key positions within the judiciary. Where women do serve as judges, reports indicate that they do not perform the same functions as their male counterparts. Female judges tend to act in the capacity of judicial clerks and are rarely involved in the adjudication of cases, which severely limits the ability of Afghan women to approach the courts.

Dominant drug industry. The opium economy, which is estimated to comprise more than a third of total economic activity in Afghanistan, is a direct source of insecurity (drug-related conflict and violence, financing of armed groups and warlords and commanders who provide protection). But even more important, the drug industry is a major force working against state-building and good governance, and thereby has a major adverse effect on security indirectly as well.

The drug industry can thrive in a situation where there is a weak, corruptible state and security forces, no or ineffective rule of law, and inadequate sanctions or negative incentives to discourage the whole range of actors - from farmers to drug traders to their sponsors inside and outside of government as well as regional drug industry actors. Therefore the drug industry comprises a powerful interest group diametrically opposed to the heart of Afghanistan's reconstruction agenda and thereby promoting insecurity.

Remaining factional forces. Although as noted earlier the DDR process has been completed, there are numerous "illegal armed combatants" not included in DDR. The new program for Disbandment of Illegal Armed Groups (DIAG) is intended to address this problem; however, this is expected to take several years. Moreover, Afghanistan by tradition and even more during the conflict has had an armed population, and this is not expected to change very quickly. Widespread ownership of small arms can be a source of insecurity as long as there is not basic rule of law and a minimum adequate level of government functionality in the security sector. Popular revulsion against warlords and commanders and their armed groups potentially can be a very powerful force, but it has not yet been harnessed. The Government's MDG report makes strong reference to the urgent need for licensing of arms.

Violent and other crime, including corruption. Although it is difficult with available data to ascertain whether violent crime and other forms of ordinary crime are more pervasive than in other low-income countries, anecdotal evidence and surveys suggest that crime is an important issue for Afghans.

Criminality can thrive in a conflict or post-conflict situation where legal, law enforcement, and social checks are weakened. The same is true of corruption; rough indicators compiled by the World Bank, which have substantial margins of error, suggest that Afghanistan is perceived to be among the countries most severely affected by corruption. The recent Transparency International index of perceptions of corruption similarly indicates that Afghanistan has a serious corruption problem.

It should be noted that while corruption in government contracting, the tax regime, licenses and permits, etc. may be significant problems in Afghanistan, the enormous role of the drug industry in promoting corruption, as well as to a lesser extent the role of other parts of the informal/illicit economy, must be emphasized.

The huge sums of money involved - in 2004 gross value of opiate production in Afghanistan was roughly estimated at $2.8 billion, of which $2.2 billion went to traders and processors and only $600 million to farmers - virtually guarantee massive levels of corruption. Moreover, narcotics-related corruption most likely to a considerable extent takes the form of "grand corruption" and capture of parts of the state apparatus, which is profoundly damaging to the state-building agenda as compared with smaller "petty corruption". Corruption contributes to personal and business insecurity, as the "rules of the game" are not clear and can change depending on who is in particular government positions, and also can take coercive forms like extortion of payments.

Landmines. Afghanistan inherited from its long period of conflict one of the worst landmine problems in the world, as well as enormous amounts of unexploded ordnance. While progress has been made in clearing mines in urban areas and some other parts of the country, enormous numbers remain and continue to kill and maim people, harm livestock, and render many areas unusable.

Finally, from a developmental perspective the impact of insecurity on vulnerable groups like women continues to be very serious. In the absence of effective mechanisms to investigate gender related violence, the vast majority of such violations are not reported to the criminal justice system and almost none are subject to investigation or prosecution. The practice of detention and prosecution of women for *zina* crimes (adultery and consensual sex outside marriage) is common in major cities, while in more conservative rural areas the family might deal with such a case by killing the girl or woman involved. The predominance of customary law in traditional jirga/shura decisions by and large works to the disadvantage of women, as customary law tends to grant fewer rights to them than Islamic law or civil law in matters relating to inheritance, property, and marriage, as well as in relation to crimes like so-called "honor killings" for which the perpetrators are generally not punished. Customary law's bias against women is also illustrated when for example murder cases are resolved by the jirga ordering that the alleged perpetrator provide the family of the alleged victim with a young girl or girls, usually below the legal marriage age, to compensate for the alleged crime. The girl is then forcibly married to a male member of the victim's family. Such arrangements are also sometimes used to settle large opium-related debts. A sign of the impact of conflict, violence, and lack of access to justice on women is the reported dramatic upsurge of female suicides, often to escape unwanted arranged or forced marriages.

7

China Nuclear Strategy

China's strategic nuclear weapons were developed because of the belief that hegemonic power will continue to use nuclear threats and nuclear blackmail. From the day of establishment, the People's Republic of China faced a major economic and technology blockade from hostile powers. Further, it also faced serious nuclear threats from hegemonism. To oppose nuclear war, smash nuclear blackmail, safeguard national security and sovereignty, and keep peace throughout the world, China needed a powerful national defence and its own strategic nuclear weapons. At that time, the Central Committee of the Party, Mao Zedong and Zhou Enlai made a wise decision to make China's strategic nuclear weapons independently. This decisive and timely step paved the way for developing our strategic nuclear weapons.

As early as 1956, Mao Zedong pointed out, "We also need the atom bomb. If our nation does not want to be intimidated, we have to have this thing." In June 1958, he stated, "To make atom bombs, hydrogen bombs, and intercontinental missiles, from my point of view, is perfectly possible in ten years." Later on, he further instructed us that development of strategic nuclear weapons should "have some achievement, and be fewer but better." What Mao Zedong said gave us a clear guidance on our effort to research and manufacture our strategic nuclear weapons. It is not hard to imagine how difficult it was during those days in China to develop advanced weapons with a weak economy and a backward scientific and technological community. But under the leadership of the Central Committee of the Party and its specialized committee, all Chinese people gave strenuous support to the cadres, the experts, the technicians, and the PLA officers and men who shouldered the responsibility of developing our advanced weapons. These people exerted themselves to carry out a determined struggle for the final victory. They lived plainly, they worked hard, they devoted themselves selflessly to the projects, they relied on their own efforts in research and manufacturing, and after an extremely hard struggle they surmounted the difficulties at last.

On October 16, 1964, our first atom bomb exploded successfully; on October 27, 1966, we succeeded on our nuclear missile trial test; on June 17, 1967, our first hydrogen bomb was exploded. These tests allowed made us step into a new period, that of mastering the development of nuclear missile weapons. China's achievements within such a short period of time evoked a strong response all over the world.

The Chinese Government has declared again and again, "China is compelled to conduct nuclear tests and develop nuclear weapons in order to break the nuclear monopoly; China's nuclear weapons will be used definitely for self-defence; the Chinese Government has always advocated an all-round prohibition and a complete destruction of nuclear weapons in the world." This is the fundamental stand China maintains on possessing nuclear weapons.

In 1958 we built up the special Artillery Corps, then on July 1, 1966, the Second Artillery Corps was officially established with approval of the Central Military Committee. In the last 20 years, the Corps has gradually been developed and strengthened and equipped with different kinds of nuclear missile weapons it made by itself. The Second Artillery Corps trained in the use of weapons, coordinated training, battle simulation and tactical exercises, and successfully launched different types of missiles and improved both its ability to master strategic weaponry and fighting capability. At the same time, it strengthened its research work on the formation of weapons systems, weapons use in battle, and development of such systems, and improved weapon quality. It has also done a great amount of work on command systems, battlefield construction, weapons testing, and maintenance and repair. The

Second Artillery Corps has become a well-trained strategic missile corps with a certain level of nuclear counterattack capability.

For over 30 years, we developed our strategic nuclear weapons from short-range to medium-range to long-range and intercontinental missiles, and provided our army with a number and variety of missiles and nuclear weapons. Our armed forces are now capable of striking back with nuclear weapons, which greatly strengthens our national defence and our international status. Additionally, it helps to weaken the nuclear monopoly of the superpowers, contain nuclear war, and safeguard world peace.

Since the 1980s, the international situation has relaxed somewhat, but the role of military force in national security policy has not decreased. The number of strategic weapons owned by the big nuclear powers has already surpassed the saturation level, and weapon technology has reached a very high level, constituting a serious threat to world peace and security. At the same time, the problem of nuclear proliferation and especially the concern of nuclear weapons falling into the wrong hands have become more and more serious, and there is no end to the regional arms race. We should have a clear mind and maintain vigilance when facing such a situation, and should also follow the development of the high technology in the world, maintaining our strategic nuclear weapons in accordance with the actual conditions of our country.

The research and development of our first generation of strategic nuclear weapons were a great success, but we must understand that there is still a great distance between the world's advanced level of technology and our own. Our historical experience has shown that for the sake of our national security interests, and for world peace and stability, we must develop strategic nuclear weapons and keep pace with the advanced world level. Ours is a developing country that is engaged in economic construction. Our Party Central Committee and the Central Military Committee have, according to scientific analysis of the international situation and in consideration of the actual conditions of our country, made decisions to change the strategic thinking that guides our military development. Under the current situation, the development of our strategic nuclear weapons should focus on long-term goals. We should develop advanced weapons that suit our national defence strategy, and at the same time we should improve current weapons to raise the quality and the comprehensive fighting capability. Science and technology should be our guideposts, and we should aim for advanced levels of 21st century technology, strengthening the study of single-item high technology weapons. We should work hard on the survival, fast reaction, accuracy, and break-through and high-command technologies for weapons systems. These should be the direction for the development of our strategic nuclear weapons. We should conduct research in the following aspects:

- Improve the survivability of the strategic nuclear weapons. Survivability is an important factor in waging a nuclear counter strike. We should strengthen research on small, solid fuel and highly automated mobile missiles and on the technology of invisibility, for reinforcing defence work against nuclear or nonnuclear strike; and improve the survivability of missiles before launch and in flight.
- Improve the striking ability of strategic nuclear weapons. Accuracy and power are chief factors used to judge weapon striking power. To increase the credibility of limited nuclear deterrence, we should work to improve accuracy, and our new generation of strategic weaponry should be of higher precision.
- Improve the penetration technology of strategic weapons. Strategic weapons can be used in actual fighting only when they can penetrate enemy defences and reach and strike the target a necessary condition to protect itself and destroy a target. In an era when space technology is developing rapidly and a defence system with many methods and many layers is appearing, we should pay special attention to the study of break-through technology.

To sum up, we conclude that the development of strategic nuclear weapons is one main aspect in strengthening national defence and is an important symbol of modernization for our military. In future development, the advanced qualities of strategic weapons will rely to a large degree on the development of the high technology and reflect the comprehensive power of a country. To safeguard more effectively our national security and territorial integrity and sovereignty, plus the socialist modernization construction, we must have a modernized army and improve and develop our strategic nuclear weapons. We should, in accordance with the actual conditions of our country, develop a limited number of high quality strategic nuclear weapons that could be used effectively to strike back against an enemy using nuclear weapons to attack us. We should strive to build a small in number but effective strategic missile corps with Chinese characteristics, and make further contributions to the safeguarding of our country, world peace, and the progress of mankind.

CHINA'S STRATEGIC FORCES TODAY

China does not publish information about the size of its nuclear weapons arsenal. The United States intelligence community, however, has released considerable amounts of information. Although some of this information is contradictory—the intelligence community is certainly not a monolith—some assessments can be made by comparing quantitative assessments from the intelligence community with qualitative descriptions provided by authoritative Chinese sources.

China appears to maintain the smallest operationally deployed nuclear force (and perhaps the smallest stockpile) of any of the five nuclear weapon states party to the Treaty on the Non-Proliferation of Nuclear Weapons. According to unclassified U.S. intelligence assessments, China "has over 100 warheads deployed operationally on ballistic missiles. Additional warheads are in storage." Declassified documents from the 1990s place classified estimates of the total stockpile, including a small stockpile of aircraft-delivered gravity bombs, between 200 and 250 warheads.

The majority of these missiles were developed in the 1960s and 1970s, beginning with the 1965 *banian sidan* plan ("eight years, four missiles") to develop medium-, intermediate-, and intercontinental-range ballistic missiles by 1972. As it turns out, China did not complete deployment of its first-generation large liquid-fuelled ballistic missiles until the deployment of the first

DF-5 intercontinental ballistic missiles (ICBMs) in silos beginning in 1981.

In the 1980s, China focused on developing solid-fuelled, mobile ballistic missiles to replace its first generation of ballistic missiles. Although China deployed the first of these new missiles, the DF-21, beginning in the early 1990s, flight-testing of the DF-21 continued through the 1990s, and China did not begin large-scale deployments in earnest until around 2000. China is just now beginning deployments of the DF-31 and DF-31A, which will replace China's DF-4 and DF-5 missiles.

China is also developing a submarine-launched variant of the DF-31, called the JL-2. China has built at least two new ballistic missile submarines since 2007. The Office of Naval Intelligence believes China may build as many as five of the new submarines to replace China's lone Xia-class nuclear-powered ballistic missile submarine, which is not believed to be operational. Although the JL-2 may become operational as soon as 2010, China appears to have rather limited capabilities for communicating with submarines at sea and probably has not established operational practices for conducting deterrent patrols.

The growth in China's ballistic missile arsenal is not confined to China's nuclear forces. China has also developed new conventionally armed solid-fuel short-range ballistic missiles, the DF-11 and DF-15, which it deploys in very large numbers near Taiwan. China has also deployed a conventional variant of the DF-21, the DF-21C, and is further developing a fourth modification to serve as an anti-ship ballistic missile. Finally, China has deployed a new land-attack cruise missile—the ground-launched DH-10—as part of a broad effort to acquire ground-, air-, and sea-launched cruise missiles.

This process of replacing liquid-fuelled ballistic missiles with solid-fuelled ballistic and cruise missiles underpins China's ongoing strategic modernization. Although many observers have linked the deployment of the DF-31 and DF-31A to recent U.S. missile defence deployments, it is important to keep in mind that these programs date to the mid-1980s and were supposed to have been completed many years ago.

China is not developing new warheads for its new ballistic missiles. The warheads for the new nuclear delivery systems—the DF-31, DF-31A and JL-2—were tested during the 1990s, before China signed the CTBT in August 1996. Since that time, China has observed a moratorium on nuclear tests. Without resuming yield testing, China would have significant difficulty in designing and certifying a new design, such as those incorporating insensitive high explosives. China does appear to have a significant stockpile stewardship program that may make use of hydro-dynamic experiments at the Lop Nor Test Site.

China may also have a small stockpile of gravity bombs for delivery by aircraft, but no aircraft appear to have the primary mission of nuclear warhead delivery, and nuclear warheads do not appear to be deployed at Chinese airbases. Before permanently moving its nuclear testing underground in the 1980s, China tested numerous nuclear weapons by dropping them from aircraft; however, Chinese officials have stated that the purpose of "airdrop" tests was to reduce test debris that would assist foreign intelligence agencies in analysing the test results.

China probably does not deploy tactical nuclear weapons, although it has the capability to do so and successfully tested an enhanced radiation weapon or "neutron bomb" in 1988.

If China's modernization seems unusual, perhaps it is because China is only now completing the deployment capabilities that other countries have possessed for decades.

This is not to suggest that missile defence and other aspects of U.S. strategic modernization have no effect on Chinese decisions. China has developed and flight-tested a sophisticated suite of penetration aids for the DF-21 and DF-31 family of ballistic missiles. Some Chinese specialists have argued that China may increase the number of nuclear warheads capable of reaching the United States, rather than simply replacing the DF-4 and DF-5 on a one-to-one basis.

It remains to be seen whether China will increase its number of nuclear warheads as much as current U.S. intelligence community predictions, which anticipate very large increases in

Chinese nuclear forces to respond to U.S. missile defence efforts. In 2001, the U.S. intelligence community asserted that the number of Chinese warheads capable of reaching the United States could grow to 75–100 by 2015. In 2006, the National Air and Space Intelligence Centre warned that the number of Chinese nuclear warheads that could reach the United States "could expand to well over 100 in the next 15 years."

Although such increases are within China's economic and industrial capabilities, especially if China were to deploy as many as five new ballistic missile submarines, it is also possible that China's modernization will occur within the general parameters of its overall force posture, characterized by keeping warheads in storage and a restrictive nuclear no-first-use declaratory policy.

China's nuclear arsenal also stands out from the other nuclear powers not merely due to its small size, but also because China keeps its nuclear forces off alert and under the strictures of a no-first use pledge.

By all indications, Chinese nuclear warheads are not normally mated to their missiles. Robert Walpole, then national intelligence officer for strategic and nuclear programs at the CIA, stated in 1998 that "China keeps its missiles unfueled and without warheads mated." The warheads are stored at nearby, but separate, bases. Press reports of Chinese mobile ballistic missile exercises published by the state-run Xinhua News Agency indicate that nuclear warheads would be mated in the field to mobile ballistic missiles before launch, similar to the procedure used by Soviet Mobile Technical Rocket Bases (PRTB, in Russian) stationed in East Germany and elsewhere during the Cold War.

Anecdotal evidence from public descriptions of Chinese exercises and doctrinal materials suggest that Chinese forces expend considerable effort training to conduct retaliatory missions in the harsh environment after a nuclear strike. One Chinese textbook that is used to train cadres is forthright about the difficulty of maintaining a survivable retaliatory capability under a no-first-use doctrine. "According to our principle of no first-use of nuclear weapons," the text *Zhanyi Xue* (Operational Studies) warns future commanders, "the nuclear retaliation campaign of the Second

Artillery will be conducted under the circumstances when [the] enemy has launched a nuclear attack on us. ... The personnel, position equipment, weapons equipment, command telecommunication system and the roads and bridges in the battlefield will be seriously hurt and damaged."

Whether Chinese leaders will change these features of their nuclear posture is difficult to predict. Western analysts have long predicted, for example, that China would eventually move away from a no-first-use posture—yet China's political leaders continue to appear committed to the policy. In part, the judgment that China would dump no-first-use has been based on voluminous criticisms of no-first-use in Chinese military writings. The considerable ink spilled in Chinese military publications complaining about "no-first-use" is probably the best evidence that the policy remains in place. Dissatisfaction among some Second Artillery commanders with no-first-use might also explain the growing deployments of conventionally armed ballistic missiles, which are presumably subject to less doctrinal interference from senior leaders and Chinese nuclear weapons scientists.

Fundamental changes are more likely to result from ongoing changes in China's domestic politics, rather than as a mechanistic response to changes in U.S. strategic capabilities such as missile defence or conventional strike. China's small cadre of scientists and engineers continue to play a significant role in matters relating to nuclear policy—but today, unlike in Nie's era, they are no longer the only voices on nuclear policy. As part of an effort to ensure that military priorities are better reflected in defence science and technology investment, the General Armaments Department replaced the Commission on Science and Technology for National Defence, which was run by Nie's son-in-law as late as the mid-1990s. Although the GAD itself may be a distinct interest group, relative to the Second Artillery or the Navy, it is presumably much less independent than in Nie's day.

Moreover, the Second Artillery and the Navy are vastly more professional today than even ten years ago. In the past it would have been difficult to imagine the parochial service interests overriding a desire for central control over China's nuclear forces—

as embodied in aphorisms such as "the party must control the gun, the gun must never control the party." But today China is very different: the PLA is far more professional than ever before, and China's leaders were children when the United States subjected China to nuclear threats.

SECOND ARTILLERY'S PLACE IN CHINA'S STRATEGY

As the CMC drastically reduces personnel strength while continuously increasing the military budget, is it possible for an outsider to perceive any implications for the role of nuclear weapons in the grand strategy? The answer to this question would be found in the repository of Chinese nuclear weapons, the PLA's Second Artillery Corps (Second Artillery), also known as the Strategic Missile Force. Second Artillery operates China's land-based and tactical ballistic missiles, strategic nuclear weapons and conventionally armed SRBMs. It is composed of 100,000 officers, NCOs and conscripts and is the smallest of the various branches and services in the PLA's order of battle. Its nuclear inventory is approximately 400 warheads—280 strategic and 120 tactical.

It should be noted that being the smallest branch of the PLA, Second Artillery actually increased in numbers despite the troop reductions cited above. Second Artillery controls its own budget. Additionally, the budget for its nuclear weapons has reportedly been constantly maintained at five percent of the overall defence expenditure, which is a not a paltry sum considering that the defence spending was estimated to be between $50-80 billion this year.

What do these well-funded forces contribute to China's defence? According to the *White Paper,* "Second Artillery Force organizes and commands its own troops in case of launching nuclear counterattacks with strategic missiles and conducting operations with conventional missiles. Under it are missile and training bases, and... support troops."

Evan S. Medeiros noted in *Evolving Nuclear Doctrine*: "Indeed, the nuclear counterstrike campaign is the only nuclear contingency that the PLA leaders has identified for the Second Artillery." China's entire nuclear arsenal is estimated at approximately 400 warheads.

Presently, it is assumed that virtually all operational and deployable warheads in their nuclear arsenal are in Second Artillery's hands. Why? The airborne leg of their proto-triad is composed of 100 B6 BADGER (1965 vintage) and 30 A-5 FANTAN (1970 vintage) aircraft. It is unclear if these platforms are still assigned to strategic strike missions. Additionally, the problem-plagued, 1980s-vintage, XIA-class, (Type 092) SSBN (nuclear-powered ballistic missile submarine) never successfully performed one patrol and, therefore, still does not pose a credible threat. However, the *White Paper* stated that the "Navy aims at gradual extension of the strategic depth for offshore defensive operations and enhancing its capabilities in integrated maritime operations and nuclear counterattacks." Supporting the *White Paper*, Lt. Gen Mi Zhenyu, senior strategist at China's Academy of Military Science wrote: "China's political and economic focus lies on the coastal areas [and] for the present and a fairly long period to come, strategic focus will be in the direction of the sea." In 2006, the PLAN launched two new JIN-class (Type 094) SSBNs that are expected to be deployment-ready by the end of the decade.

"Improve the Survivability of the Strategic Nuclear Weapons"

There are other dramatic changes occurring within the Chinese nuclear forces, changes that have been on-going for decades at a modest pace. Have the Chinese told outsiders what their strategy would be regarding the upgrade of their forces? In 1989, then-deputy commander of the Second Artillery, Major General Yang Huan, published a paper on the Defence Industry of China informing the world of China's intentions:

... we should improve current weapons to raise the quality and the comprehensive fighting capability. Science and technology should be our guideposts... strengthening the study of single-item high technology weapons. We should work hard on the survival, fast reaction, accuracy, and break-through and high-command technologies for weapons systems. These should be the direction for the development of our strategic nuclear weapons.

- Improve the survivability of the strategic nuclear weapons... We should strengthen research on small, solid fuel and highly automated mobile missiles and on the technology of invisibility, for reinforcing defence work against nuclear or nonnuclear strike; and improve the survivability of missiles before launch and in flight...

- Improve the striking ability of strategic nuclear weapons...
- Improve the penetration technology of strategic weapons.

There is seemingly no deception intended in General Yang Huan's words. In fact, he actually provided a litany of items on Second Artillery's things to do list. Since his article appeared 18 years ago, China has been able to introduce road-mobile, strategic, nuclear-tipped ICBMs, the DF-31 and the extended-range DF-31A, which may target of most the world, including the continental United States. These missiles are solid-propellant—a major improvement over the previous liquid-fuelled missiles. Another significance of that upgrade is that China's ICBMs are no longer confined to silos. Additionally, launch times have been reduced from several hours to minutes, since there is no requirement to fuel the missiles immediately prior to launch with highly-corrosive, liquid rocket fuel. It is obvious that making nuclear ICBMs solid fuelled and road-mobile tremendously increased their survivability. Another open source document in the Liberation Army Daily from 30 May 2001 praised the then-new Russian road-mobile ICBM calling it an assassin's mace weapon: '"... that could ensure "the most reliable" nuclear retaliation."'

The sea-based leg of their triad has also been upgraded with the addition of the JIN-class SSBNs, which will carry the naval version of the DF-31—the JL-2 SLBM. The XIA SSBN was designed to carry 12 JL-1 SLBMs and the JIN was designed to carry 16 JL-2 missiles. The addition of the nuclear-powered JINs armed with nuclear-tipped SLBMs will provide the CMC with an additional, survivable nuclear option in its grand strategy.

A review of the items on General Yang Huan's, that many of those items have been acquired: they have improved current weapons to raise the quality and the comprehensive fighting capability, they have improved the survivability of strategic nuclear weapons, and they have obtained small, solid fuel and highly automated mobile missiles. One hears on TV commercials: Yang Huan also called for improving the striking ability of strategic nuclear weapons as well as improving the penetration technology of strategic weapons. In this case, the Chinese are waiting to see how effective the U.S. national missile defence (NMD) system will be. The Chinese will not be able to design countermeasures for the NMD system until they (and the United States as well) know if it will really work. According to Saunders:

Chinese responses to BMD could consist of three categories of programs: expansion of China's current BM forces, technical countermeasures to penetrate and defeat U.S. BMD system, and the possible use of asymmetric measures such as the development of ASAT weapons to attack key components of the U.S. system.

The Chinese have proven themselves to be capable of creating and deploying military technology without the advanced knowledge of foreign intelligence services. For example, Bill Gertz wrote about China's Yuan-class submarine that was built secretly and completely underground.

China also fired a warning shot across the bow of countries possessing space-based intelligence satellites by successfully destroying an old Chinese weather satellite with an ASAT. If the Chinese can successfully hide the construction of a submarine, successfully launch its ASAT, and deploy road-mobile ICBMs with miniaturized warheads, can they develop other assassin's mace weapons without their adversaries' knowledge? An affirmative answer would suggest that hedging will also continue on all sides, since no side can be certain of what the other side is doing and, therefore, cannot base its security on the belief that it knows everything that the other side might do to improve its relative position.

The Inferior Defeats the Superior

Chinese leaders know that they cannot defeat the United States in a face-to-face encounter. They have studied the results of the Gulf Wars. They also know that the United States, whose forces would confront theirs in a face off over Taiwan, would somehow have to be neutralized in a short-term conflict to achieve the desired results, or face defeat in a long-term conflict. The CMC knows that the U.S supply lines are long, that U.S. forces require enormous amounts of fuel and ammunition, and that they require intricate communications paths—both terrestrial and space-borne. This issue received detailed attention in *The Science of Military Strategy*:

In regard to information systems, we should firmly destroy their surface facilities, jam and cut the enemy's information feedback transmission circuits first, and then try our best to knock off his awareness platforms and damage his information flow which can form capabilities, so as to achieve the effect of "decapitation."

Chinese military planners would have to devise a means of interrupting U.S. supplies and communications for just as long as it would take for them to seize and occupy Taiwan. The Chinese do not want a protracted war, but would like a *fait accompli*. According to *Military Power*, in order to successfully accomplish their military strategy:

China's leaders have placed a near-term emphasis on asymmetric programs and systems to leverage China's advantages while exploiting the perceived vulnerabilities of potential opponents—so-called Assassin's Mace (*sha shou jian*) programs.

The Chinese have adapted Sun Tzu's ancient stratagems to today's strategic requirements. In this particular case, the doctrine is called "The Inferior Defeats the Superior." Michael Pillsbury has culled Chinese open source writings and described the process by which the Chinese will implement this assassin's mace program.

In order to be successful at the doctrine of "The Inferior Defeats the Superior," China assumes it can initially lull the opponent into complacency, or deceive him to take steps that will help China win. The premises here are quite elaborate... These concepts of how "The Inferior Defeats the Superior" are claimed to be unique to China, and to have [sic] developed by Chinese strategists over thousands of years. For this reason, PLA authors employ extensive examples from Chinese ancient military campaigns which they claim are the heart of Mao's military doctrines. Westerners are presumed to be ignorant of these Chinese "lessons learned" about Assassin's Mace employment concepts and the doctrines of "The Inferior Can Defeat the Superior."

Pillsbury further explains why the Chinese shroud assassin's mace programs in a veil of secrecy:

... some of the doctrines are considered to be highly classified in China, especially as they are taught in classified courses in military operations in the senior PLA schools. Available open sources thus only hint at the full set of concepts of the Inferior Defeats the Superior. Nor do open sources necessarily provide a full set of Assassin's Mace Weapons, either. After all, the need to surprise and even paralyze the opponent is an explicit goal of both these weapons and this doctrine. It is hardly to be expected that they would be fully described for the opponent to read and study in advance.

Having gained awareness of one of China's assassin's mace concepts and how the Chinese leadership has intentionally shrouded it in secrecy, one can better understand that Chinese military developments, as seen by Western observers, may indeed only be what the Chinese want outside observers to see. The Chinese do not try to hide the fact that they have been downsizing the PLA's end strength.

The most recent troop reductions brought the PLA down to 2.3 million personnel. That figure is almost identical to that of the U.S. Armed Forces. It is interesting to note that a country of over 1.3 billion people has the same number of soldiers as the United States with a population of only 300 million.

There are other sweeping changes occurring in China's military. The PLA, PLAN (navy) and PLAAF (air force) are undergoing a Chinese version of Goldwaters-Nicols in order to function more along the lines of U.S. joint operations. Additionally, the Chinese have coined a term: "informationalization" or what the United States calls "command, computers, control, communications, intelligence, reconnaissance and surveillance (C 4ISR)." The white paper stresses satellite and airborne sensors, unmanned aerial vehicles and information warfare. The Chinese have been funding these changes by increasing its military budget at a rate of 10 percent for the past 20 years. This year's defence budget's increase is 18 percent over last year's. There is more money for technology while there are fewer troops in the field.

CHINA'S ENERGY SECURITY AND SOUTH ASIAN

China's spiraling demand for energy, plus its growing dependence on imported petroleum, have made Beijing increasingly concerned with ensuring the uninterrupted flow of oil at reasonable prices. The Middle East plus North and East Africa provide well over half of China imported oil. Virtually all of that oil moves to China by tanker across the Indian Ocean. Beijing confronts several potential threats to its trans-Indian Ocean oil supply. A confrontation between Iran and the United States could lead — either via sanctions or by military actions — to the restriction of oil shipments through the Strait of Hormuz. An Indian-China conflict might escalate into the naval dimension. India might respond to defeats by the PLA in the Himalayas, or to Chinese support for Pakistan in the context of a "fourth round" between India and Pakistan, by using India's naval supremacy in the Indian Ocean to sever China's vital oil imports. Then there are scenarios of U.S.-PRC conflict over Taiwan that escalated into U.S. naval blockade of China. None of these contingencies is a high probability, yet military institutions everywhere devote attention to remote but potentially dire scenarios.

In any of these contingencies the ability of PLA-N warships to escort vessels carrying oil from Middle Eastern ports to China might be part of an effort to prevent hostile powers from interfering with delivery of China's oil supply. Development of robust over-land transportation systems between Yunnan and the Bay of Bengal, and between western Xinjiang and Gwadar could substantially strengthen the PLA's ability to sustain intense military operations in the eastern and western Indian Oceans. As a neutral power in a possible U.S.-Iran confrontation, China would enjoy the right under international law to continue trading with both belligerents. But historically neutral powers have often found protection by military force essential to upholding those legal rights. Were China's leaders to conclude PLA-N escort of China's oil commerce across the Indian Ocean necessary, the newly created transport lines via Myanmar and Pakistan could become quite useful. In terms of possible Sino-Indian conflict, the PLA-Navy is substantially superior to the Indian Navy in terms of overall tonnage and ship numbers, but the latter enjoys overwhelming geographical advantages when operating in the Indian Ocean. If the PLA-N could obtain bases on the Indian Ocean littoral (perhaps at Gwadar and Kyaukpyu), and link those forward bases to China by robust road and rail lines, India's geographic advantages would be substantially diminished to the PLA-N's advantage.

Multi-dimensional Collaboration

China's broad object in South Asia is to expand multi-dimensional cooperative relations with all the countries of that region.

"Multi-dimensional" signifies military ties as well as more innocuous political and economic cooperation. "All" means both India and India's smaller neighbours: Pakistan, Myanmar, Nepal, Sri Lanka, Bangladesh, Bhutan, and the Maldives.

India has sometimes objected to China's relations —especially military-security ties — with these countries. Beijing views South Asian countries as "neighbours" with whom it is especially important to have friendly, cooperative ties both to increase China's own economic and political influence and to lessen the ability of potentially hostile powers (currently the U.S.) to injure China's interests.

Economically, China seeks to draw South Asia's resources into China's development drive. India with its fast-growing, industrialized, and relatively affluent economy has become China's strongest economic partner in South Asia. Two-way Sino-Indian trade in 2003 was $7.6 billion, compared to $2.4 billion for Sino-Pakistan, $1.4 billion for Sino-Bangladesh, and $1.1 billion for Sino-Myanmar trade.

During their April 2005 meeting, Wen Jiabao and Manmohan Singh agreed to increase trade to $20 billion by 2008. While that amount is paltry compared to China's trade with countries like Japan, Germany, South Korea, or the United States, it leads China's South Asian trade by far.

The simple fact is that India produces much more that Chinese firms want to purchase than do Pakistan, Bangladesh, or Myanmar

— let alone the small countries like Nepal, Bhutan, or the Maldives. In 2003, China imported $1 billion more from India than it exported to it, while Chinese exports to Pakistan were three times the value of China's imports, exports to Bangladesh were forty times the value of China's imports, and exports to Myanmar were over five times the volume of imports.

While these figures are based on official statistics and do not reflect smuggling (which is substantial in the case of Myanmar), the broader point is that India simply has more to offer China. From India China imports a wide array of mining and industrial products: steel and iron ore, zinc, aluminum and aluminum products, copper and copper products, acids and alkalines, dyes, coloring, alcohol and other chemical products, rubber, plastics, cotton, wool, thread and yarn, leather, and machinery and machine parts. From Pakistan, in contrast, China buys largely cotton, yarn, and leather.

China also recognizes that in key economic-technological areas it has much to learn from India. Chinese analysts recognize India's world-leadership position in computer software creation and aspire to learn from India in this area, meshing these strengths with China's existing strengths in computer hardware production to help catapult China to world-class-economy status. There are no comparable inducements in the case of the other South Asian countries.

Pakistan and Bangladesh offer attractive markets for Chinese consumer goods and machine tools. But the ability of these poor countries to purchase Chinese goods, and to produce things useful to China's booming industry, is limited compared to India's. China has not been able to forge with the South Asian countries a robust foreign energy-for-Chinese-capital-goods swap such as it has engineered with Iran. The exploitation of Bangladesh's natural gas deposits could conceivably overcome this structural imbalance, with Bangladesh entering into an energy for Chinese capital goods swap similar to that characterizing the Sino-Iranian relation.

Politically, there are periodic visits between China and the larger South Asian countries at the minister and vice minister level to "exchange views" on various bilateral, regional, and international issues. Beijing seeks to engage South Asian governments in dialogue and cooperation on substantive issues of mutual concern: countering narcotics traffic, smuggling, and terrorism; stabilizing the Karzai government in Afghanistan; or dealing with Tibetan presence and activities in various South Asian countries.

Beijing also strives to line up South Asian support on the Taiwan issue: to counter Taiwan efforts to expand ties and to guarantee South Asian neutrality in the event of a U.S.-PRC clash over Taiwan.

Friendship with China is often attractive to smaller South Asian countries living in India's shadow. People in those countries often see ties with China as affirming their independence from India and as a way of gaining bargaining leverage with New Delhi.

China's voice in the U.N. Security Council is valued by South Asian governments because of Beijing's occasional willingness to say a few words on behalf of smaller South Asian countries, or even to criticize Washington on behalf of those smaller countries. China has expressed a desire for observer status in the South Asian Association for Regional Cooperation (SAARC) where its ability to offset India will be valued by the other South Asian states.

China views military links as part of the normal repertoire of international cooperation and seeks to expand military ties with South Asian countries.

Every year China exchanges with Pakistan, India, Bangladesh, and Myanmar two or three delegations at the deputy chief of staff through defence minister level, or from military regions, military academies, or defence industrial agencies. China has recently attempted to institutionalize exchange of views with the larger South Asian countries in the security / military areas. At the political level, there are periodic discussions of regional security issues of common concern.

Bangladesh, Pakistan, and Myanmar have been preferred and heavy customers for Chinese military equipment. Chinese training, maintenance, and parts have come with equipment purchases.

Exchange of intelligence between China and Pakistan and Myanmar is routine, with Yangong providing important electronic listening posts at several points in the Bay of Bengal / Strait of Malacca area. Chinese naval squadrons have made friendly port calls to Pakistani (1985, 1993, 2001), Bangladeshi (1986, 1995), Myanmar (2001), and Indian (1993, 2001) ports. In October 2003, the PLA-Navy conducted its first-ever joint exercises with the Pakistani navy in the East China Sea. The next month it conducted joint exercises in the same region with the Indian Navy. China assists Pakistan's missile development and its nuclear energy efforts. Although China's involvement in the latter is under IAEA supervision, the intrinsic fungibility of nuclear materials and know-how makes it likely there is some spill over to Pakistan's nuclear weapons capabilities.

In the history India, has objected to China's military links with South Asian nations. In 1989, for example, a Nepalese attempt to purchase Chinese weapons and initiate an intelligence exchange agreement with China precipitated severe Indian economic sanctions that forced Kathmandu to abandon the objectionable policies. Given New Dehli's opposition to Sino-South Asian military cooperation, Beijing's insistence on forging such links is testament to its determination to become a multi-dimensional power in the region, and its refusal to cede South Asia to an Indian sphere of influence.

China's response to Indian concerns over China-South Asian military cooperation has been to assert that since China does not have aggressive or malevolent intentions, China's military cooperation with India's neighbours does not threaten India. If India is concerned about China's military ties with the smaller South Asian nations, Beijing argues, the proper course is to increase mutual trust between China and India via security dialogues and other such venues. Or if New Delhi is unhappy with Chinese military cooperation with India's South Asian neighbours, China is quite willing to expand such cooperation with India itself. There is no valid reason to object to these friendly, cooperative relations, Beijing argues. In fact, such objections manifest "anti-China" sentiments and hostility toward China, which will be answer in kind by China.

The sort of punishment contained in this implied threat was demonstrated during the eighteen months after India's May 1998 nuclear tests that New Delhi had justified as a response to threat from China. After the Indian tests with their China threat justification, Beijing cancelled scheduled sessions of the Joint Working Group on the boundary.

Chinese media rhetoric became harsher, even resurrecting charges of Indian "hegemony." Beijing urged Washington and the U.N. Security Council to adopt tough measures against India, and to target mainly India, not Pakistan's "response" to India's tests. Beijing hinted it might shift to a more pro-Pakistan position on Kashmir. Beijing's carrot and stick approach seems to have been fairly successful. India has agreed to open-ended cooperation with China, even while China expands military ties with India's neighbours.

8

Chinese Power Strategy in South Asia

That China is one of the most powerful states in the world is no longer a contested claim, but cataloguing China's increasing material resources does not in itself demonstrate that China is powerful. Southeast Asia presents an apparently 'easy' case for investigating China's rising power. Given the significant asymmetry of power, if China's power has grown we would expect to see altered preferences and behaviour among these weaker neighbours in response to coercion, persuasion or inducement. Results so far are mixed. While China has been able to harness much of the region's economic energy in a favourable direction, it does not always get its way in territorial and resource conflicts.

In mainland Southeast Asia, China's participation makes feasible region-wide economic development plans for the Greater Mekong Subregion initiative of the Asian Development Bank, drawing international investment for infrastructural projects. These connect the poorer states — Cambodia, Laos and Vietnam — to the markets of China and Thailand while improving China's access to raw material supplies and ports in the Indian Ocean and East China Sea. These schemes also spur Japanese and American interest and investment in Mekong regionalism. More prominently, China's initiative for an FTA with ASEAN overcame the nagging problem of galvanising an economic integration project. When it came into effect in 2010, the China-ASEAN FTA formed the world's largest free trade area, comprising 1.9 billion consumers and US$4.3 trillion in trade. Situations in which the pre-existing preferences of other states are unclear or undecided — such as the 1990s debate about whether rising China was a threat — present opportunities for China to influence its neighbours by persuading them that its own narrative is more accurate and certainly more profitable. This campaign, from the mid-1990s, involved an alternative narrative about China's cooperative New Security Idea, and its 'peaceful rise' or 'peaceful development' as it strives for a 'harmonious world.' The message was intended to reassure neighbours that China's resurgence would not threaten their economic or security interests because of its peaceful intentions, limited national capabilities, mutually beneficial development trajectory and pluralist international mindset.

Rhetoric was accompanied by policy action. In Southeast Asia, China negotiated land (though not maritime) border disputes with Vietnam; fully participated in ASEAN institutions; and undertook highly publicised restraint and aid during the 1997 and 2009 financial crises. China's persuasive power encompassed economic inducement. Its China-ASEAN FTA Early Harvest Programmes with some ASEAN countries — the partial lifting of trade barriers on selected goods — is portrayed by Chinese analysts as China 'giving more and taking less', working towards harmony and enrichment of its neighbours.

Yet there are limits to how much policymakers in Southeast Asian states are reassured regarding the China threat. China's power to persuade is rooted in its ability to sustain benign policy action. Apart from efforts to offset some of the adverse effects of Chinese economic competition, China's neighbours are also watching its behaviour in more serious conflicts of interest.

The best way to gauge the change of power into influence is in cases where the powerful actor causes another actor to change policy on a significant subject of disagreement. In the case of China and Southeast Asia, such subjects include policies on Taiwan, defence relations with the US and policies on territorial disputes. On these potential hard cases, it is difficult to find significant changes in Southeast Asian states' policies in response to Chinese actions to date.

Of these, China has expended most effort in the disputes over atolls in the South China Sea. China and ASEAN agreed to a Declaration of Conduct in 2002, committing to peaceful negotiations. Yet the Chinese navy continued manoeuvres to assert its claims, leading to skirmishes with Vietnam and the Philippines. Two months into a Vietnamese concession to develop gas fields off the Vietnamese coast in 2007, BP suspended operations, reportedly as a result of Chinese threats to exclude it from future energy deals in China. In March this year, Chinese naval vessels tried to interrupt oil exploration by the Philippines in waters that Manila considers its own.

At a regional defence ministers' meeting in June 2010, statements suggesting that China now regards the South China Sea as part of its 'core national sovereignty interests' led US Secretary of Defence Robert Gates to warn that the US 'oppose[s] the use of force and action that hinder freedom of navigation.' One month later, Secretary of State Hillary Clinton reiterated US 'national interest' in the peaceful resolution of these multilateral disputes. In September 2010, after the Japanese Coast Guard detained a Chinese fishing trawler for allegedly intruding into Japanese waters, a Sino–Japanese standoff ensued. One direct result was the further strengthening of US interest in China's behaviour in maritime disputes. The Obama administration publicly affirmed that the US-Japan treaty umbrella extends to the Senkaku/Diaoyu Islands and reiterated the importance of peaceful dispute resolution, freedom of navigation and respect for international maritime laws in the South China Sea.

China's behaviour in these disputes constitutes a critical test of its intentions, and its hard line backfired seriously in that it led to a closing of ranks across Southeast Asia, Japan and the US. Beijing's actions lend weight to regional pessimists who are not persuaded of its peaceful rise, and sustained coercive action may prompt its neighbours towards the very containment policies that it wishes to avoid.

So far, there are few good cases of China making Southeast Asian states do what they otherwise did not want to do. Alongside Beijing's successful record of persuasion and inducement, it has shown caution in exerting pressure on its neighbours with the most challenging subjects. The recent backlash in the South China Sea is likely to make Beijing more cautious. China's still limited military capacity provides an important explanation since, particularly in the maritime access and security arena, the presence of the US still serves as a significant deterrent.

CHINA'S SHIFTING RELATIONSHIP WITH ASEAN

The history of China and its Southeast Asian neighbours during the Cold War years was one of both amity and animosity. Indonesia (April 1950) and Burma (June 1950) were among the first few countries to recognize the People's Republic of China (PRC). From the early 1950s until the mid-1960s, Beijing enjoyed an especially warm relationship with Jakarta, most prominently displayed in the 1955 Bandung Conference of Asian-African Countries and continued during much of President Sukarno's reign. Beijing also maintained a close relationship with the fellow communist regime in North Vietnam and rendered significant support to its causes against France and the United States from the 1950s to the 1970s, including sizable material and human assistance. But China's relationships with many Southeast Asia's noncommunist states were decidedly estranged. Concerns over potential threats from communism led some of them to participate in and form alliance-like regional organizations (Southeast Asian Treaty Organization or SEATO, 1954-77; the Five-Power Defence Arrangements or FPDA, 1971-) with external powers—the United States in particular—to protect their interests. There were deep suspicions over China's motives and activities, especially as they related to the large number of overseas Chinese residing in these countries. Beijing's public support of the communist insurgents in the region only reinforced their perceptions and heightened their fears. Not surprisingly, many of them did not establish diplomatic relations with Beijing until the mid-1970s (Thailand, Malaysia, and the Philippines). Others only normalized ties with China in the 1990s (Singapore and Indonesia).

The Sino-U.S. rapprochement in the early 1970s led to the establishment of diplomatic ties between China and a number of

ASEAN states. The emerging Chinese-ASEAN cooperation in the late 1970s ironically was prompted largely by their shared concerns over Vietnam's growing assertiveness and its attempt to establish hegemony in Indochina, in particular in the aftermath of its invasion of neighboring Cambodia. Thailand, being on the frontline of the Cambodian conflict, sought to develop security ties with China. China also coordinated with ASEAN in seeking a political settlement of the Cambodian issue and supported the latter's position that the Cambodian coalition government headed by Prince Sihanouk, not the Hanoi-backed Heng Samrin regime, should represent Phnom Penh in the United Nations (UN).

During the 1980s, Chinese policy toward Southeast Asia began to undergo important changes in two critical areas. Beijing started to place state-to-state relationships in precedence over ideological ties by halting its support to communist insurgence movements in the region. In 1989, it also passed laws on Chinese citizenship requiring overseas Chinese to adopt citizenship of their countries of residence. By taking these two important measures, major irritants effectively were removed from China's bilateral relationships with a number of Southeast Asian countries. Beijing now seemed more than ever eager to court better relationships with its Southern neighbours, and this has paved the way for improvement of political ties. Beijing's official contact with ASEAN as a group began in July 1991 when Chinese Foreign Minister Qian Qichen was invited to attend the opening ceremony of the 24th ASEAN Foreign Ministers' Meeting. Since then China has attended each ASEAN Foreign Ministers' Meeting consecutively. In 1994, China participated in the ASEAN Regional Forum (ARF) and became a consultative dialogue partner of ASEAN. This status was elevated in 1996, when China became a full dialogue partner with ASEAN. In December 1997, Chinese President Jiang Zemin and ASEAN leaders held their first ever summit in Malaysia and issued a joint statement announcing their decision to establish a partnership of good neighborliness and mutual trust between China and ASEAN oriented toward the 21st century. In October 2003, China and ASEAN signed the "Joint Declaration of the PRC and ASEAN State Leaders—A Strategic Partnership for Peace and Prosperity."

The emerging China-ASEAN ties were influenced by a number of developments at the time. One was Beijing's efforts, in the wake of the Tiananmen incident, in particular in response to the sanctions imposed by the West, to break the isolation. Southeast Asian countries, given their relative reticence regarding the June 4 Incident, became targets of the Chinese diplomatic good neighborly policy. Beijing and Jakarta restored, and China and Singapore established, diplomatic relations in 1990. Chinese Premier Li Peng visited Indonesia, the Philippines, Malaysia, and Laos as part of that diplomatic endeavor. A second reason was to sustain the cooperation between the two in the wake of the Cambodian settlement, in which China played a constructive role in the resolution of the dispute and had been in close consultation with ASEAN in the 1980s. But most important of all was Beijing's changing perception of its security environment and the relative place of Southeast Asia in its post-Cold War security policy. This resulted in the successful management of the territorial disputes in the South China Sea, Beijing's reassurance to ASEAN of its benign intentions and its acceptance of multilateralism and cooperative security, and China's growing economic ties with ASEAN.

ORGANIZATION TERRITORIAL DISPUTES

To ensure a conducive environment for economic development required strengthening relations and/ or mending fences with China's neighbours, including the Southeast Asian states. Disputes over the Spratly Islands began to emerge in the 1980s, especially after the signing of the United Nations Convention on the Law of the Sea (UNCLOS) in 1982. The reported rich deposits of maritime resources, including oil and natural gas, led to scrambling for atolls and islets in the South China Sea and disputes among six claimants—Brunei, China, Malaysia, Philippines, Taiwan, and Vietnam. While Beijing sought to improve relations with ASEAN, its assertiveness in sovereignty claims almost derailed such efforts. This was most evident in China's handling of the territorial disputes in the South China Sea, especially its occasional display of military might. The construction of shelters on the disputed Mischief Reef also was seen by some of the contenders as an act of aggressiveness.

In addition to strengthening its claims to the disputed territories, China's South China Sea policy also was a refection of its growing interest and ambitions in extending its influence, and as a result, greater efforts in developing a navy that could go beyond coastal defence.

Chinese assertiveness in its claims over the Spratly Islands was informed both by its strong sense of sovereignty and territorial integrity, and more pragmatic economic security considerations, including securing a peaceful external environment for economic development and protecting the country's economic interests, including protecting its land, air space, and its territorial waters. The growing attention to maritime interests and the cultivation of a "conception of sea as territory" (*haiyang guotuguan*) refected both a recognition of the potential of maritime resources for national economic development and a realization that China must enhance its ability to protect its perceived maritime territories. One Chinese analyst suggested:

To make sure that such [maritime] resources are fully tapped and utilized, China needs to ensure the security of its maritime economic activities. A strong naval defence is essential to reducing the threat posed by sea-borne smuggling and piracy to China's tariff incomes, ocean fishery, and marine transportation.

According to Chinese sources, of the more than 3 million square km of territorial waters China claims as its own, an area of more than 800,000 square km within China's traditional maritime boundaries has been illegally delineated into the domain of other nations, with 410,000 square km taken by the Philippines, 270,000 by Malaysia, 70,000 by Vietnam, 50,000 by Indonesia, and the remainder by Brunei.... With rapid economic growth, China will be in greater and greater need of energy. The 3 million square km of national marine territory is where the Chinese nation's descendants pin their hopes.

This had prompted calls for exercising one's own rights under UNCLOS that provides legitimacy for such claims. One Chinese naval offcer contended: "From a national viewpoint, the Convention allows each country to utilize the ocean according to its own needs and gain its own individual ocean rights and interests, and it supplies a legal framework." This call for more assertive sovereignty claims was understandably prompted by the fact that other claimant states reportedly already were operating 120 oil wells that could extract between 30 and 50 million tons of crude oil, which was almost one-third of China's annual extraction and surpassed China's South China Sea oil production by 40 times. The loss to China was therefore enormous.

China became a net oil importer in 1993. The need for energy to fuel economic development could create instability as countries in the region compete for energy resources, which in turn could exacerbate the already touchy territorial disputes in the South China Sea. China's ongoing naval development can be seen, apart from the Taiwan scenario, as a direct response to energy shortages and the need to be able to assert claims over territories believed to contain much needed energy reserves. For these reasons, the Chinese Navy had been given the task of broadening the traditional mission of coastal defence to that of force projection into the South China Sea and beyond. Two important factors probably explain the rising importance of maritime security to China. One is that maritime routes are becoming essential to China's growing international trade; it increasingly depends on the seaborne resources that go through the key chokepoints in Southeast Asia. With about 85 percent of its trade being transported by sea, including an estimated 50 percent of its oil imports transiting the Strait of Malacca, Beijing understandably is keen on developing its force projection capability, if for nothing else than to protect critical sea lanes. The other reason is the potential offshore oil and mineral deposits, which are crucial resources to China's economic development in the coming decades.

China claims complete sovereignty over the entire Spratly Island groups that are partly or in whole also claimed by Brunei, Malaysia, the Philippines, Taiwan, and Vietnam, and over Paracel, a claim that also is contended by Vietnam. In February 1992, China's National People's Congress (NPC), the country's putative legislature, passed the Law of Territorial Waters and Contiguous Zone that claims complete control and asserts that it will resort to the use of force to protect its territories. The controversial law, together with reported Chinese People's Liberation Army (PLA) construction of an airstrip on the Woody Island, struck the ASEAN states as showing assertive Chinese intentions toward the entire South China Sea. An internal document in China argued at the time that, given the country's increasing demands for resources and the decreasing resource bases at home, the importance of the Spratly Island groups in terms of their potential oil and mineral reserves was becoming greater and, indeed, might provide the only survival space for China.

The island groups also sit on important SLOCs and therefore are strategically significant. Chinese control over the area means that they will be able not only to enhance their power projection capabilities but also to exert tremendous leverage over countries that rely on these SLOCs for their imports of key industrial resources such as oil. In other words, the ability or the perceived ability to disrupt normal transportation can cause great uncertainty and economic fallout. China already had engaged in two military clashes with Vietnam (1974, 1988) and was slowly but steadily increasing its presence in the South China Sea. The Chinese leaders, meanwhile, were trying to assure the neighbours by expressing willingness to discuss joint exploration and development efforts with other claimant states and shelve the sovereignty issue.

However, Beijing continued to assert its exclusive sovereignty over the disputed territories in the South China Sea even as it advocated shelving the question of sovereignty. This was demonstrated by the revelation of its occupation of the Mischief Reef in February 1995, where the PLA built concrete constructs and shelters. There were competing explanations as to China's intention in occupying the reef, and the Chinese themselves explained that the structure built would be used for fishermen regardless of nationalities. Nonetheless the Philippines were alarmed.

The Mischief incident effectively raised ASEAN's concern over China's assertiveness and galvanized the organization into action. Until 1995, ASEAN had taken no public position on the South China Sea disputes. In March 1995, ASEAN for the first time publicly called for all parties to the dispute to adhere to the spirit and letter of the 1992 Manila Declaration on the South China Sea. The issue subsequently was placed on the agenda of the ARF despite Chinese objection. Member states converged on the idea of the code of conduct, refecting the principles the group had always adhered to—nonforceful settlement of disputes, norm-building, and confidence-building measures (CBMs). ASEAN itself first adopted principles of behavior among member states and then presented a united front vis-à-vis China. The approach was driven by two considerations. The first was to develop consensus among members, since not all of them lay claims to the disputed territories and as they each had a different relationship with China; secondly, it was hoped that a code of conduct, should it be accepted by Beijing, would constrain China, a stronger power in the disputes, to refrain from the use of force.

However, even as member states were contem-plating unifed approaches toward the South China Sea disputes, some also sought to strike separate deals/understandings with Beijing. Malaysia, for one, accepted China's preference for bilateral negotiation. What also was significant was Malaysian Prime Minister Mahathir's call for external powers to stay out of the disputes, effectively ruling out possible intervention by the United States, something Manila was keen on securing. Indeed, the Philippines sought U.S. support and signed a Visiting Forces Agreement with Washington in February 1998, 7 years after it had evicted American forces from its naval and air force bases. Meanwhile, the Philippines also engaged in bilateral discussion with China, resulting in a Joint Statement on PRC-RP Consultation on the South China Sea and on Other Areas of Cooperation in August 1995.

On November 4, 2002, ASEAN and China signed the Declaration on the Conduct of Parties in the South China Sea, a major milestone in China-ASEAN relations, concerning how the claimant countries to the territorial disputes would resolve them. While ASEAN was not able to get Beijing committed to a code of conduct, which would be a more stringent measure, the declaration at least obliged China to pursue a multilateral approach to the issue, a shift from the bilateralism that it had preferred. It also was symbolic in that China had appeared to be accepting ASEAN's preference for norms and regulation of the dispute. Specifcally, the Declaration commits the signatory parties: to exercise self-restraint in the conduct of activities that would complicate or escalate disputes and affect peace and stability including, among others, refraining from action of inhabiting on the presently uninhabited islands, reefs, shoals, cays, and other features and to handle their differences in a constructive manner.

What motivated Beijing to adopt a more moderate approach to the territorial disputes was a growing concern over the Taiwan independence issue, and hence the need to secure ASEAN support for its unifcation policy; the risk of pushing the small Southeast Asian countries to the United States, resulting in greater ASEAN-U.S. military cooperation that could allow U.S. access to military facilities in the region, hence posing a greater threat to Chinese security interests, especially where the Taiwan contingency was concerned; and China's own lack of power projection capability that could help enforce its claims effectively. These considerations led to changes in managing territorial disputes, moving away from more confrontational and militaristic approaches to ones that emphasize dialogue and promote joint exploration and development, without in any way giving up its claim to sovereignty over the disputed territories in the South China Sea.

The more moderate stance was meant to defate growing alarm over Chinese aggressiveness, especially in the context of the 1995-96 Chinese missile exercises in the Taiwan Strait, rather than a fundamental change of the conception of sovereignty. Indeed, if anything, western analysts suggest that Beijing may be engaged in a slow-intensity conflict where it steadily strengthens its hold on, and extends its reach to, disputed maritime territories.

Beijing also negotiated separate codes of conduct with Vietnam and the Philippines. Between 1992 and 2000, seven rounds of negotiation took place between China and Vietnam. In December 1999, Beijing and Hanoi signed a Land Border Treaty, which subsequently was ratifed by the two countries' parliaments in 2000. On December 25, 2000, China and Vietnam signed the Agreement on the Delimitation of the Territorial Seas, Exclusive Economic Zones, and Continental Shelves in the Gulf of Tonkin and the Agreement on Fishery Cooperation in the Beibu Gulf. Both agreements subsequently were ratifed by the two countries' legislatures in 2004.

In March 2005, national oil companies from China, the Philippines, and Vietnam signed a landmark agreement to conduct joint prospecting for oil and gas in the South China Sea. On the one hand, this is considered to be a major breakthrough, especially based on the idea of shelving territorial disputes and seeking joint exploitation and development. However, there also are concerns, from the ASEAN perspective, over China's "divide and rule" tactic that is establishing its dominance effectively in the region and undermining the organization's unity in dealing with the rising power.

Furthermore, the territorial disputes continue to resurface from time to time, with occasional clashes resulting in casualties and detention, or otherwise property damages. A July 1999 run-in between a Chinese fshing boat and the Philippine Navy ended in the former's sinking. Similar incidents occurred in January 2000, when Philippine naval patrol personnel boarded Chinese fishing boats, touching off protests and warnings from Beijing. Chinese media also point out that Vietnam continues to encroach on Chinese territorial integrity in the South China Sea by setting up telephone networks on atolls and islets currently under Vietnamese occupation. These activities are seen as efforts to establish *fait accompli* to strengthen Hanoi's leverage in future negotiations.

CHINA'S POWER SECURITY AND SOUTH ASIAN SEA LANES OF STATEMENT

China's spiraling demand for energy, plus its growing dependence on imported petroleum, have made Beijing increasingly concerned with ensuring the uninterrupted flow of oil at reasonable prices. The Middle East plus North and East Africa provide well over half of China imported oil. Virtually all of that oil moves to China by tanker across the Indian Ocean. Beijing confronts several potential threats to its trans-Indian Ocean oil supply. A confrontation between Iran and the United States could lead — either via sanctions or by military actions — to the restriction of oil shipments through the Strait of Hormuz. An Indian-China conflict might escalate into the naval dimension. India might respond to defeats by the PLA in the Himalayas, or to Chinese support for Pakistan in the context of a "fourth round" between India and Pakistan, by using India's naval supremacy in the Indian Ocean to sever China's vital oil imports. Then there are scenarios of U.S.-PRC conflict over Taiwan that escalated into U.S. naval blockade of China. None of these contingencies is a high probability, yet military institutions everywhere devote attention to remote but potentially dire scenarios.

In any of these contingencies the ability of PLA-N warships to escort vessels carrying oil from Middle Eastern ports to China might be part of an effort to prevent hostile powers from interfering with delivery of China's oil supply. Development of robust overland transportation systems between Yunnan and the Bay of Bengal, and between western Xinjiang and Gwadar could substantially strengthen the PLA's ability to sustain intense military operations in the eastern and western Indian Oceans. As a neutral power in a possible U.S.-Iran confrontation, China would enjoy the right under international law to continue trading with both belligerents. But historically neutral powers have often found protection by military force essential to upholding those legal rights. Were China's leaders to conclude PLA-N escort of China's oil commerce across the Indian Ocean necessary, the newly created transport lines via Myanmar and Pakistan could become quite useful. In terms of possible Sino-Indian conflict, the PLA-Navy is substantially superior to the Indian Navy in terms of overall tonnage and ship numbers, but the latter enjoys overwhelming geographical advantages when operating in the Indian Ocean. If the PLA-N could obtain bases on the Indian Ocean littoral (perhaps at Gwadar and Kyaukpyu), and link those forward bases to China by robust road and rail lines, India's geographic advantages would be substantially diminished to the PLA-N's advantage.

Termination

China's omni-directional friendship policy in South Asia is not cant, but serves Chinese interests well. Chinese relations with other South Asia nations will be more robust and stable if India views those ties as non-threatening. A friendly and cooperative relation with India will give China a stronger position in South Asia than would a conflictual Sino-Indian relationship. An economic, diplomatic, and even military partnership between China and India, surrounded by similar partnerships between China and the other South Asian countries — a sort of Asian zone of friendship and cooperation — would maximize Chinese influence in South Asia, and ensure that threats to China did not emanate from that region. China's omni-directional friendship diplomacy toward South Asia is working relatively well. China's broad strategic objective is to persuade India to look benevolently on an open-ended and expanding Chinese economic, political, and military presence in South Asia and the Indian Ocean, to eliminate suspicion in Sino-Indian relations, and to transform India into China's partner. In this way the rise of China in Asia will not lead to Indian efforts to countervail China in coalition with the United States. But the conversion of India to friendship with China is to be done without making concessions to India on the status of Tibet, the Sino-Pakistan strategic link, or by restricting China's expanding military, security, and transportation ties with other South Asian nations.

China's optimal outcome would be open-ended, growing political, economic, and military cooperation between China and all the South Asian countries, with India accepting an open-ended expansion of Chinese influence in that region and learning to live comfortably under China's benevolent protection. India would gradually evolve into a key Chinese partner in South Asia. China's intention, its objective, in South Asia is most definitely not to establish dominance over that region, or draw it into some sort of Chinese sphere of influence. That, however, might be the outcome over a period of twenty or thirty years.

China and the South Asian Equilibrium of Power

China has an interest in maintaining the existing balance of power between India and Pakistan. The existence of a strong and confident Pakistan able and willing to challenge India confers important advantages on China. Politically it hobbles India's efforts to act on the global stage as China's equal. Militarily, it forces India to confront the possibility of a two front war, thereby compelling it to divide its military forces. This is the geopolitical rationale for China's large and long-standing economic and military assistance to Pakistan. It is *possible* that one reason why Beijing is not in a hurry about resolving the boundary dispute with India is that it would fundamentally ease India's two-front problem, intensifying Indian pressure on Pakistan. China's interest in keeping Pakistan strong was one reason why Beijing endorsed Islamabad's re-engagement with the United States after 9-11. While that re-engagement diminished somewhat the potential utility of Pakistan and Gwadar as a logistics "back door" for China in the event of confrontation with the United States or India, it also brought Pakistan in from a situation of increasingly dangerous isolation. Pakistan's close ties with the Taliban in Afghanistan plus the growing Islamisization of Pakistani politics and the steady deterioration of Pakistan-Western relations since the mid-1990s, posed an increasing danger of Pakistan's isolation, perhaps even designation by the international community as a "rogue state." This would have been a serious blow to China's interests, and to the extent that U.S. re-engagement with Pakistan could move Pakistan in a different direction, it served China's strategic interest in a strong Pakistan that constrains India. U.S. engagement with Pakistan also made development of India-US strategic partnership more difficult, and diffused Indian anger over China's own strong military and nuclear links to Pakistan.

This is not to say that Beijing's interests are served by confrontation between Pakistan and India. Beijing's objective, as noted earlier, is to develop cooperative ties with all the countries of South Asia. Confrontation between Pakistan and India would put Beijing in the unfortunate position of having to choose between Islamabad and New Delhi. Failure to support Pakistan could endanger China's fundamental interest in keeping Pakistan strong and independent of Indian domination, and threaten China's strategic partnership with Pakistan. Alignment with Pakistan, on the other hand, would spoil China's ties with the most important south Asian power, India, and possibly push that power further into alignment with the United States. In this sense, peace between India and Pakistan is in China's interests.

In the event of Pakistan-Indian confrontation, China will piggy-back on the peace diplomacy of the United States and other powers, adding its voice to efforts to restore peace and the status quo ante as quickly as possible. A Chinese tilt toward Pakistan but well below the level of threatened belligerency on Pakistan's behalf, would be virtually certain, but only in the event that India roused itself and threatened to decisively subordinate Pakistan (perhaps in the aftermath of a nuclear exchange) would Beijing move toward actual co-belligerency on Pakistan's behalf.

MANIFESTATION OF EQUANIMITY OF A BIG POWER

Comparing the three most important interests and demands, "responsibility demand" is the most uncertain and the most elastic, a demand that has been revealed only in recent years. I believe that, with the growth of the comprehensive national strength and the rise of the international position, such demand will be increasingly felt in China's diplomatic strategy, economic strategy and security strategy. Such demand covers a wide range, at different levels, such as playing a more active and more constructive role in the Security Council of the United Nations, getting a fuller representation in most important international organizations, taking the initiative to safeguard the rights and interests of developing countries and playing a more positive role in peace-keeping actions, refugee relief actions, anti-drug trafficking and anti-smuggling actions and in the action of protecting the international ecological environment.

However, China's global responsibility still remains a long-term prospect. For the present, its responsibility and interests are still regional and in important countries, with the latter providing the staircases for the former. In terms of Asian-Pacific security, such demand mainly covers such contents as eliminating or easing the destabilizing factors on the Korean Peninsula, reducing frictions arising from the territorial waters on the South China Sea, preventing Central Asia from becoming a new "powder keg" due to the fight for oil and gas resources, curtailing the tense confrontation and arms race in the sub-continent of South Asia, and preventing the confrontation between the two sides of the

Taiwan Straits from escalating into an international event. It can be said that all the instable "latent troubled spots" in the Asian-Pacific region are of direct interests to us and all require China to have creative thinking diplomatically and display responsible roles. From a long-term point of view, if properly handled, they will become the "touchstone" and "paving brick" for China to become one of the first-rate big powers in the world.

China is an oriental country with a time-honoured history and exclusive cultural tradition, a rising developing country with one-fifth of the world's population, and one of the most important and most attractive of a limited number of socialist countries in the world today. It is, at the same time, a permanent Security Council member of the United Nations that possesses such "killer weapons" as atom bombs and long-range missiles. All these important attributes are factors crucial in determining the basic interests and demands of China's diplomacy. Analysis shows that there would be no fundamental changes in the above attributes in quite a long period of time to come, except that of a developing country, which is likely to change with the growth of China's economy and its comprehensive national strength. It signifies that it is likely to endow China with the composure and responsibility of a big power, likely to reduce utilitarianism characteristic of the period of drastic development and thirst for food and clothing and more systematic and more perfect medium- and long-term strategy. After developments for 30 or 50 years, or when China has turned from a developing country into a middle-income country, profound changes would take place in its field of diplomatic vision and its international point of view just like the tremendous changes that have taken place in its domestic system and economy. For instance, due to the drop in the proportion of spending on food in the whole income, there would be more money and time for travel and sightseeing and therefore showing more concern about the quality of the ecological environment and be more mindful and sensitive to the external appraisal of China's environmental protection work.

The Chinese people should be adequately ready ideologically for all kinds of new problems. For instance, what the new resource and technical demand of greater scope will be raised and what external security environment and what international institutional restrictions China will face when China's economy has further developed? What are the difficulties in coordinating the different requirements between growth in strength and soothing of neighbors? What responsibilities the international community would demand of China after China has grown in strength and what obligations we are prepared to undertake and what demands we are not going to accept? Several dozen countries in the world have come out with several dozen plans on how the UN Security Council should improve work efficiency and display greater role. What is the attitude of China? While opposing the wanton intervention in a weak and small sovereign state of Yugoslavia by NATO headed by the United States, how should China exert itself (such as taking the initiative to advocate and participate in the peace-keeping force or military supervision group under the framework of the United Nations) to make related UN mechanisms display greater and more positive roles on the Kosovo problem?

In such specific cases as WTO, international land mine ban convention, the methods of controlling missile parameters and the nuclear non-diffusion mechanism, what international organization, international conventions and international systems China is prepared to join (or refuse to join) in the short run and what change might be taking place in the medium- and long-run? Again, suppose the noted "Seven-Nation Economic Summit" extends an official invitation to China, will China prepare to become a member and attend its annual summit and how China should prevent itself being a showpiece and even being utilized after joining the club? In view of the positive results of China's participation in some official and non-official multilateral security dialogues in recent years and the "collectiveness" of the attack of Yugoslavia by NATO, is China going to make greater efforts to establish according to actual circumstances a multi-level mechanism concerning Asia-Pacific security? While criticizing the new guide to US-Japan Security Treaty, especially TMD, will China produce a substitute plan acceptable to most Asian-Pacific countries? There are many more to add to the list. We must admit that on such problems, we lack not only any ready-made plans but also careful study and exploration and our statements on many occasions look like passive and perfunctory and playing for time. I belief that, with the passing of the time, the traditional tactics and skills may not be as successful as in the past and the Chinese will consciously transcend the olden times at a still higher level. The above and many other problems that cannot be dealt with here does not only demand China to avoid its excessive pragmatist attitude and "percussion reflection" reaction but also demand that it has greater foresight, broader mind and strategy of more global in nature. With a view to construct the international relations that are oriented toward the new millennium and are more progressive, I should like to give, from the angle of a researcher, a few principled and outlined indicators about the new international order for which China undertakes responsibilities and obligations.

First of all, the world is in need of a more stable and more rational structure. This means, chiefly, to realize the constructive run-in of the multilateral relations including the global order, regional order and internal order of countries (especially the relations between the state and the society) on the basis of respecting the sovereignty principle, human rights principle, the principle of equality and progress, the principle of fairness and the market principle. The sovereignty of a national state is of course the cornerstone that cannot be dispensed with in the international system. In this regard, we must resolutely resist the "new interventionism" advocated by Britain, the United States and other countries. Meanwhile, all countries should make uninterrupted efforts to build their democratic, just and progressive social and political systems so as to avoid the misfortune of being sanctioned or even being expelled from the "the global community". Marketization is an irresistible trend and the economic globalization on this basis has more advantages than disadvantages. But the new international relations and its institutional setup should allow all countries to work out with ease their schedules of utilizing the advantages and avoiding disadvantages. And the substantial improvement in the South-North relations and the global marketization should at least be kept in step. Globalization and regional grouping should promote rather than restrict the self-integration process toward rationale in the internal structure.

Secondly, the world needs reconfirmation and support of the moral authority and capability of action of the United Nations so as to avoid the re-emergence of the situation in which regional security framework overrides the UN Security Council in disregard of the commonly recognized international norms. Opposition against hegemonism of all descriptions is of course one of the preconditions for revitalizing the United Nations. But what is more pressing is perhaps to discuss how to build a more steady and more effective institutional arrangement, such as improvementing the UN Security Council, increasing the say of the UN congress and realizing multiple legal restrictions on international conflicts. As a permanent UN Security Council member, China is heavily duty-bound to make its efforts in this regard. What we need is not only to condemn the hegemonist acts such as NATO bombing of Yugoslavia or veto some unjust motions but, and more so, to take the initiative to put forward its own plans and constructive opinions and taken a more active part in the multilateral arrangements and activities within the framework of the United Nations. The most typical of such actions include the participation in the peacekeeping action and the reorganization of the bureaucratic organs of the UN Secretariat. We can also take the initiative to properly increase the membership fees to the UN at an opportune moment in the light of the national strength. We can also propose in the negotiations on international climatic change convention that China will officially announce that will undertake the obligations of reducing the discharge of hothouse gas at a certain time in the future.

Thirdly, the world needs to review and improvement the international financial system with the IMF and the World Bank at the core so that they will reflect more accurately the current conditions of the economic development of most countries and their capability of withstanding risks. As a matter of fact, the developing world does not have the ability of "setting up its separate kitchen" and they have to get involved in the current system and obey its rules. But this should not serve as a pretext for not improvementing and improving the current international political and economic systems. In fact, many people of insight in the West admit that it is extremely necessary to adjust and transform the international financial system. Correspondingly, the international community and its rules have to pay particular attention to the problem of development. Experience of all countries has time and again proved that less economic development plus hopelessness and helpless is a factor that induces internal extreme acts of a country and conflicts in many of the regions of the present-day world and, more so, the fundamental cause of the tense situation of the South-North relations and the difficulty in easing many of the global problems (such as ecology, resources, drugs, debts, population and food problems). Stagnation is the source of catastrophe. "Development is the hard truth". The internal improvement of various countries, the modification of the current international institutions and the stability of the international system, the maintaining of world peace and the coordination of international economic relations should all make development of the countries their first objective. This is truly a "win-win interaction".

9

China's Strategy of Containing India

On the surface, relations between India and China are positive. India's economic ties with China are booming. China is set to emerge as India's leading trade partner in the near future, leaving its current number one partner, the United States, behind. Between 2000 and 2005, trade with China registered a hike of 521 percent, whereas India's trade with the U.S. increased by only 63 percent during the same period. There are regular high-level meetings between Asia's two rising powers. India and China have just concluded their second round of bilateral "strategic dialogue" and declared 2006 as a Sino-Indian friendship year. More importantly, they have agreed to cooperate, rather than compete, for global energy resources. The incipient Sino-Indian entente has prompted some to argue that it has the potential to alter Asian geopolitics radically.

Long-time observers of India-China relations, however, maintain that some improvement in the rhetoric and atmospherics notwithstanding, India-China ties remain fragile and as vulnerable as ever to a sudden deterioration. The combination of internal issues of stability and external overlapping spheres of influence forestall the chances for a genuine Sino-Indian rapprochement. Though both sides are working to expand and deepen economic cooperation, there is as yet no strategic congruence between the two giants. Indeed, the issues that bind the two countries together are also the issues that divide them and fuel their rivalry because they have different positions in the international system, contrasting strategic cultures, world views, political systems, and competing geostrategic interests.

In the power competition game, China has clearly surged far ahead of India by acquiring potent economic and military capabilities, and the existing asymmetry in power and status serves Beijing's interests; therefore, China has resisted any Indian attempts to narrow the power gap. Unlike China, India's fractious polity continues to limit its economic and military potential. Nor has New Delhi been able to lend a strategic purpose to its foreign and economic policies. Beneath the surface, frictions and tensions are simmering between the two countries over some fundamental issues: the territorial dispute, the nuclear issue, the U.N. Security Council reform issue, to name a few. Both remain locked in a classic security dilemma: one country sees its own actions as justifiably self-defensive, but these same actions appear aggressive to the other. In the past year, India has found itself ranged against China at the United Nations, the International Atomic Energy Agency over Iran's nuclear program, the East Asia Summit and the Nuclear Suppliers Group (N.S.G.) over the issue of India's membership.

Three major developments which shook the ground beneath South Block (India's External Affairs Ministry building) in New Delhi recently were the emergence of a pro-China axis comprising Pakistan, Nepal, and Bangladesh at the 13th South Asian Association for Regional Cooperation (S.A.A.R.C.) Summit in Dacca, China's opposition to the July 2005 India-U.S. nuclear energy agreement, and Beijing's moves to confine India to the periphery of a future East Asia Community at the first East Asia Summit in Kuala Lumpur in mid-December 2005. Add to this Beijing's worldwide campaign against India's (and Japan's) bids for permanent membership in the U.N. Security Council, the continuing stalemate in the India-China border negotiations, coupled with their ever-expanding economies and widening geopolitical horizons, it is clear that the bilateral relationship between the two rising Asian giants continues to be characterized more by competition and rivalry than by cooperation.

Despite the hype over India's burgeoning trade with China, it consists mostly of raw materials, iron ore, steel, and like commodities that are used to fuel China's economic growth while China exports manufactured goods, electronics and machinery to India. Even in the information technology sector, the focus of Chinese diplomacy remains on leveraging India's strengths to China's advantage without any quid pro quo in the technology hardware or manufacturing sectors.

Neither power is comfortable with the rise of the other. Each perceives the other as pursuing regional hegemony and entertaining geographical expansion. Each puts forward its own proposals for multilateral cooperation that exclude the other. Both vie for influence in Central, South and Southeast Asia, and for leadership positions in global and regional organizations. More than ever before, the state of the India-China relationship is increasingly being influenced by "the U.S. factor" as the Southern and Central Asian region becomes an arena of strategic competition in Asia.

CHINA AND INDIA : THE 'EMERGING GIANTS' AND GROWTH

The economic performance of China and India is critical. This holds the key to global progress. China and India have been relatively 'closed' economies with limited dependence on trade. But they have been opening up. This is particularly so in the case of China.

Trade as a % of GDP has been 32% in China compared to 25% in India. This should be seen against a backdrop of relatively open East and South Asian economies: Malaysia (206%), Korea (Republic) (72%), Thailand (82 %), Pakistan (36%) and Bangladesh (35%). India's import duties as a % of imports, a key measure of openness, have also been declining in China and India. But it is lower in China compared to India: 3% in the former and 24% in the latter.

Foreign Direct Investment (FDI) can enable access to resources and increase productivity. There are two types: one by the transnationals from industrialized countries and the other by overseas Chinese and Non Resident Indians. In China overseas Chinese have been primarily responsible for Chinese FDI while

India's FDI has been channeled through the Transnationals. Net flows of FDI as a % of GDP in China have been 12% in contrast to India's 0.61%.

Both countries have been growing fast over the last 25 years: China by 21 fold and India by 8 fold. The growth rate in China has been over 9% per annum making it possibly the fastest growing world economy while India's, too, has been impressive with over 8% per annum. The % living below the poverty line (1 $ a day) has also been appreciably reduced in both though it is more impressive in China compared to India: 12% in the former and 26% in the latter.

The major effect of China's and India's economic advance is evidenced by their contribution to global output: China's and India's share being 20% and 7% respectively in 2004. Both, moreover, have rising demand for energy, raw materials and commodities. This has a positive impact on increasing the exports of developing countries, improving their terms of trade, and initiating shifts in their pattern of trade and investment.

Liberalisation policies have enhanced the economic prowess of both nations. China, moreover, as a recent member of the World Trade Organization (2001), could firmly influence global trade negotiations, possibly joining forces with India, and champion the rights of poor nations. They could establish a 'level playing field' in world trade. Indeed the combined efforts of China and India could ensure that the Uruguay Round (1986-93) to accelerate trade liberalization can be successful. They could pressurize the developed nations to fulfil their promise of opening up their markets to developing country agricultural and non agricultural exports.

Liberalisation emerged much earlier in China, in 1978, while it was initiated in India in 1991 though initial steps were taken in the 1980's. Pre-reform or pre-liberalisation forces laid the basis on which such measures were evolved. China's policies unfolded in the context of bold economic policies in the East Asia region between 1960-1990 emphasizing agricultural development, primary education, macroeconomic stability, firm public policies to support markets, and regional dynamism. China's liberalization has been embodied in market based thrusts in agriculture, industry and services, state owned enterprises, and deregulation of product prices. These have been backed by measures to induce labour mobility, and formation of Special Economic Zones.

On the domestic front, in the pre reform era in China, the savings level was high with significant capital formation (30%) and investment in infrastructure, irrigation and land development. Literacy and primary health care, too, have been impressive with virtual elimination of landlessness. It has also shed surplus labour-a move which has been inhibited in India possibly due to strong trade unions to safeguard the interest of workers. On the external front China's integration with the world economy, as mentioned earlier, has been advanced through its trade and FDI policies. This has made a significant contribution to China's growth and productivity.

India's growth rates have been relatively low in the pre-liberalisation period-4%-5% per annum compared to East Asia's 7%-8% per annum. The level of savings, too, has been lower than in China and East Asia; the levels of literacy and health care, too, have been lower, coupled with the presence of significant landlessness, and marked poverty and inequality between and within regions, sectors and socio-economic groups.

Liberalisation was initiated in India in the 1980's with a shift in attitude towards the private sector. Its momentum was increased from 1991 onwards. The high growth rate (8% per annum) in the post liberalization period and the future targets (9%-10%) are necessary but not sufficient. The structure of the economy has to be transformed. In this respect, though the % contribution of agriculture to GDP has been reduced to about 25% it still absorbs over 60% of the employed, while manufacturing and services contribute 28% and 55 % respectively to GDP. Over 62% of India's growth over 1990-2003 has been in services but it has been employment inelastic. Hence, the pace of industrialization has to be reinforced.

Though poverty in India has been reduced to about 26% it is critical to widen participation by the poor in development programmes. This can ensure that high growth rates are sustained.

This calls for the use of labour intensive techniques, investment in human and physical capital, and infrastructure, enhanced flexibility in labour laws, and supporting institutions to meet socio-economic goals. The state has to play an active role to fulfil such goals though market forces may guide policies. This could enable the poor to be lifted from poverty.

No doubt China has grown faster and sharply reduced the % of people below the poverty line compared to India. However, inter regional and inter group inequalities in China have increased. China and India need to persist with their integration with the international economy to sustain growth. This should encompass incorporating the poor in the process, particularly in India, and reducing regional and inter-group disparities in China. Such goals are intertwined with maintaining peace within the respective regions. This is exemplified in India by efforts to minimize conflicts with neighbouring Pakistan, curbing terrorism from within and outside the state, resolving historical border disputes between India and China, and meeting the needs of dissatisfied groups within the state. In China it is essential to respect human rights.

China-India co-operation

Enhanced economic cooperation between India and China could bolster their economic power in spite of differing positions on politics and international affairs. Thus, it emerges that the economic relationship between China and India has taken place against a backdrop of tensions.

This is exemplified by China's past political, military and economic support for Pakistan, and China's claim to Arunachal Pradesh which has been vehemently challenged by India. Leaving aside such differences China and India are seen as contributors rather than competitors to each other's development. This is welcomed by India which has adopted a 'Look East' policy to expand trade and investment links with East Asia and forge strong ties with regional institutions (eg. Association of South East Asian Nations, Asia Pacific Economic Cooperation).

The recent visit of the Chinese President Hu Jintao to Delhi is a significant move in initiating a platform on development, peace and stability in Asia and the world. This was underscored by the Chinese President. He perceived the relationship between China and India as being between 'old and close brothers' citing the vision of Rabindranath Tagore the Nobel Indian poet. The President's visit culminated in a pledge to double trade between the two nations to $ 40 billion by 2010. This contrasts with $ 250 million in the 1990's.

China and India have been competing for resources in Asia and Africa. China has been the winner in virtually all the sectors excepting technology. However, the two nations could devise policies to complement each other's need. Thus, India could meet China's growing appetite for raw materials (iron ore, steel and plastics) fuelling its massive manufacturing sector. China in turn could furnish manufacturing expertise and investment for Indian infrastructure. Indian critics of Chinese policies have expressed concern over the lack of transparency exemplified by their high level of subsidies. They are also anxious over the sharply increasing Indian imports from China of clothes, electronic goods and even fireworks. The Chinese have responded by highlighting India's blocking of their investments in ports and telecommunications. This has been justified by India on grounds of security. Overall, though, as the Chinese President reaffirmed, the relationship between China and India was "an opportunity and not a threat." This could pave the way for cooperation between China and India and enhance the nature and pace of globalization.

INDIA'S CHINA POLICY

Certain scholars believe that India's China policy has undergone three major phases of adjustment since the end of the Cold War: the pre-1998 phase policy of reconciliation; the 1998–2000 phase policy of hostility; and the 2000 to present phase policy of engagement. The second phase around the time of the 1998 nuclear tests featured harangues from the Indian government regarding the 'China threat' and a brief deadlock in Sino–Indian relations. The author, however, believes that two, rather than three, phases of adjustment are applicable to an explanation of the state of bilateral relations between China and India in the post-Cold War era. When considering India's overall strategic aims at the time of the 1998 nuclear tests and the implications and specific actions of its subsequent China policy, it is difficult to pinpoint two 180 degree-policy shifts in the course of just two years. Facts demonstrate that India named China as a threat at the time of the 1998 tests as a matter of expedience to acquiesce in the anti-China stance of certain parties in the United States and other Western nations; it was a ploy whose purpose was to divert attention from and rationalize the nuclear tests, thereby dispelling any notion of sanctions.

It should be borne in mind, however, that India's understanding of comprehensive national strength deepened after the Cold War, as did its leaders' belief that nuclear arms and credible nuclear deterrence were hallmarks of a superpower. Entering the nuclear club was consequently a stride towards achieving one of the sub-continent's greatest national aspirations. The Rao government, which pursued a China policy of reconciliation and engagement, had made preparations for nuclear tests but stopped short of carrying them out for fear of the potential burden on the newly recovered economy of international sanctions.

Prime Minister Vajpayee and other political leaders repeatedly and publicly expressed soon after the 1998 tests that India had no wish to hold China as an enemy or a threat, stating, to the contrary, their desire for reinforced friendly relations. At no point during this period did diplomatic engagement between India and China cease. Indian External Affairs Minister Jaswant Singh's visit to China in June 1999 demonstrated that the Sino–Indian relationship had recovered in the space of a year from any damage that the nuclear tests had inflicted upon it. That becoming a nuclear power while maintaining stable relations with China were post-Cold War India's strategic goals was also implied by the sub-continent's explicit moves towards repairing its relationship with China. The 1998 nuclear tests constituted no fundamental change to India's China policy and should, within the scope of Sino–Indian relations, be regarded as a minor episode. Moreover, the shift of India's China policy in 1988 was not prompted by any change of security concept; Prime Minister Rajiv Gandhi's trip to China that year was motivated by the fact of Sino–Soviet reconciliation. Changes in security concept explicitly propelled India's; post-Cold War China policy adjustments. This book, therefore, primarily examines developments and changes in India's China policy after the Cold War. It holds that a substantive change indeed occurred; specifically from one of hostility and antagonism during the Cold War (especially 1962–1988) to reconciliation and engagement thereafter. This policy change, however, was by no means instantaneous but characterized by gradual, phased development. Two, rather than three, phases of adjustment tally with changes in India's post-Cold War security concept.

India's China Policy from the End of the Cold War to 1998

Indian leaders believed after 1962 that hostilities between China and India were inevitable, and viewed China as a major enemy. Prime Minister Indira Gandhi considered Sino–Indian antagonism as going far beyond border disputes, and that China was pursuing the more 'complex' policy of pressing India on all fronts and, moreover, displacing the sub-continent by establishing its own dominant position in the Asian power hierarchy.

The goal of India's China policy during this period, therefore, was to ensure its supremacy over China in Asia and, in the event of armed conflict, to avoid repeating mistakes that had led to its defeat in the 1962 Sino–Indian conflict. India's policy at the time can be so summarized: strengthen military capability and deployment; seek aid from major powers, respectively, the United States, United Kingdom and USSR; and support Chinese separatist forces.

After the Cold War ended, however, changes in India's domestic and international situation brought tremendous challenges, and its position as regards China and its related policy goals showed clear adjustments. India considered China as a nation going through a reflective, 'inward looking' period and, as such, had no intention of attacking the sub-continent. In the short-term, therefore, it constituted no threat. The goal of India's new China policy was to maintain stability in Sino–Indian relations, ensure peaceful borders and create conditions suitable for India to gather its resources and restore economic and military strength. The specific policy adjustments were as follows.

Achieve Simultaneous Progress in Solving Border Disputes

For almost two decades after 1962, India made resolution of border disputes a pre-condition for normalizing relations with China.

Its insistence in this regard was the main reason for the longstanding chill in Sino–Indian relations. Although the two nations restored ambassadorial-level diplomatic relations in 1976, and in 1981 agreed to begin talks on the border issue, this principled standpoint did not change.

Upon meeting with visiting then-External Affairs Minister Vajpayee early in 1979, Comrade Deng Xiaoping proposed an agreement that would provide 'a package solution' for relevant border disputes. He said that if it were not possible completely to resolve border disputes at an early date, he would consider cooperation in other areas.

But it was not until 1988 during Rajiv Gandhi's trip to China that the Indian government accepted this suggestion and formally initiated the process of normalizing bilateral relations which the successive Indian governments pursued and implemented after the Cold War ended.

It is notable that during the time the two sides promoted negotiations on border issues they also exchanged high-level visits in which the two nations signed cooperative agreements in such areas as trade, technology, education and culture, and that cooperation between them grew ever greater in depth and breadth.

Shift Strategies on Border Talks

As India needed a peaceful, stable environment in which to concentrate on economic recovery, securing Sino–Indian borders was its primary goal in the early 1990s. Because of India's; pre-1988 insistence on not normalizing Sino–Indian relations until the border issues were settled, there were suspicions that the sub-continent was 'taking improvements in bilateral relations as a bargaining chip through which to force China to yield in border disputes'. India consequently insisted in the talks that began in 1981 on its own position as regards a segmented solution to the issue.

India's objective understanding of the complexity of the Sino–Indian border dispute after the Cold War and of realistic strategic considerations and needs prompted an adjusted strategy for these talks. This was manifest in its suggestion of a gradual solution to border disputes: the first step would be to stabilize the Line of Actual Control (LAC) situation and eliminate disagreements over its demarcation; the second to reach agreement on preserving peace and tranquillity along the LAC; and the third to take measures to establish mutual trust along the LAC.

This accomplished, the two nations could then address substantive problems in their border dispute. This tentative plan enabled India and China to approach a consistent position whereby the two sides worked to achieve a solution to Sino–Indian border disputes and create an atmosphere of reasonableness and peace.

The two nations made progress, signing in 1993 the Agreement on Maintenance of Peace and Tranquillity along the Line of Actual Control in the Sino– Indian Border Areas, and in 1996 the Agreement Between the Government of the Republic of India and the Government of the People's Republic of China on Confidence-Building Measures in the Military Field Along the Line of Actual Control in the India–China Border Areas.

India saw these two agreements as on the one hand ensuring the two sides could resolve border disputes peacefully without resorting to violence, and on the other that border disputes would not inhibit the development of their bilateral relations.

Tibetan Issue and do not Provoke China

Leaders of India's independence movement had at the time of the British Raj followed the British colonialist concept of Tibet as a 'buffer region' between India and China. After winning independence, therefore, the Indian government supported from the very beginning the so-called 'Tibetan independence movement'.

At around the time of the founding of the People's Republic of China, India seized the opportunity offered by China's political upheaval to promote the international standing of the local Tibetan government and thwart China's liberation of Tibet.

New Delhi continued unremittingly in its efforts to convince China's central government, even during the 1950s heyday of Sino–Indian amity, to give Tibet substantial autonomy and to reduce to the greatest extent possible the size of its garrison there. After the insurrection of 1959 the Indian government was more overt in its support of Tibet, giving asylum to fugitive rebels and propping up the so-called 'Tibetan Government in Exile' established by the Dalai Lama in 1960 in the Indian city of Dharamsala. India further incited and encouraged Tibetan independence activities after the Sino–Indian conflict of 1962.

In truth, Indian leaders considered their support for exiled Tibetans' separatist activities as an effective containment against China. But when Prime Minister Rajiv Gandhi visited China in 1988 he issued the statement: 'The Indian side reiterates the long-standing and consistent policy of the Government of India that Tibet is an autonomous region of China and that anti-China political activities by Tibetan elements are not permitted on Indian soil,' which implied India's change of approach from that of support for Tibetan independence. Indian leaders reiterated this pledge after the Cold War ended and imposed limits on Tibetan fugitives' anti-China political activities.

For instance, Indian officials would generally contact the Dalai Lama and leaders of the so-called Tibetan government in exile before a visit by Chinese leaders to India, requesting that they refrain from Tibetan protests, demonstrations or other anti-Chinese behaviour.

Yet, differences still exist between China and India on the issue of Tibetan autonomy. Although, proceeding from the requirement of preserving stable Sino–Indian relations, the post-Cold War Indian government has been low-key in its support of the Dalai Lama and other Tibetan fugitives, this does not signify a substantial change in its strategic treatment of the Tibetan issue.

Changes in India's China Policy from 1999 to Present

Achieving recovery, contending for the status of global power had been India's ambition for decades. The growth of the sub-continent's comprehensive strength and improvements in the international environment in the late 1990s presented to it a real possibility of realizing this ambition, as well as a number of other unprecedented strategic opportunities.

Against this backdrop, reconciliation with China and the unchanged overall direction of the relationship produced several new adjustments to the positions and goals of India's China policy. At this stage, India saw China neither as enemy nor friend, believing that cooperation could coexist with competition between the two nations.

India still considered China as constituting no threat in the short term, but began focusing on long-term trends in the balance of power. The emphasis of the goals of its new China policy are on ensuring that future Sino–Indian relations are of benefit to India by making China a positive factor in the process of its rise. Maintaining the stability of Sino–Indian relations remains fundamental. The new policy adjustments are as follows.

Expand Economic Cooperation with China

Trade between the two nations ceased after the 1962 Sino–Indian Border Conflict, and did not resume until 1977. The volume of trade between the two sides in the 1980s wavered at around roughly Us." million. But after the Cold War ended, Sino–Indian trade experienced a seemingly spontaneous phase of rapid development. The trade volume between China and India increased from $264 million in 1991 to $1.988 billion in 1999—a yearly average of 31.2%—or an increase factor of 6.5 over eight years. Indian leaders' concerns about India's economic recovery nonetheless maintained at this point the China policy focus on stabilizing political relations and establishing tranquil borders. Indian leaders' understanding of economic strength and security having becoming more profound since 1999, their enthusiasm for developing bilateral trade soared.

As China and India were the world's two most rapidly developing nations, Indian leaders could see the obvious potential for trade between them and that strengthening bilateral trade would be of great mutual benefit. Also that close economic ties could have a stabilizing influence on their political relationship. Statistics show that bilateral trade since 1999 has entered into a new period of growth.

The average yearly growth to 2006 was 44.4%—a rate which exceeded that of the preceeding period and which is being achieved on an ever-stronger numerical foundation. The volume of Sino–Indian trade reached US$24.8 billion in 2006, having increased by a factor of 11.5 over 1999 and one of 93 over 1991. China became India's second largest trading partner in 2006, and India China's tenth largest. It may be said that the role of Sino–Indian trade has grown from one unworthy of mention to a decisive aspect of the overall bilateral relationship.

CHINA'S, INDIA'S AND SOUTHEAST ASIA'S TRADE-POLICY FRAMEWORKS

Trade-and-economic policy reforms

In China, since 1978, economic-policy reform has been incremental and ultra-pragmatic. The more comprehensive transformation of the Chinese economy and society belongs to the post-Tienanmen phase. A headline reform package was introduced in 1994, covering banking, finance, taxation, investment, foreign exchange and foreign trade. It included the unification of the exchange rate and a new Foreign Trade Law. Currency convertibility, privatisation, the formal recognition of private-property rights and a host of other market-based reforms have followed.

China's integration into the world economy, particularly through its trade reforms, is also more a product of the latter phase, following more gradual opening in earlier phases. Liberalisation has whittled down licensing coverage (down to 5 per cent of imports in 2000 from two-thirds of the total in 1988), and the use of plan prices (to less than 5 per cent of retail commodities by 2000). Even in agriculture, where state pricing is more important, over 80 per cent of sales are at market prices. The overall coverage of non-tariff barriers (NTBs) (licenses, quotas, tendering requirements, state trading and designated trading) had come down to 21.6 per cent of imports and less than 10 per cent of tariff lines by 2001. NTBs fell by about 80 per cent during the 1990s. At a rough estimate, the protective impact of NTBs has fallen from 9.3 per cent in the mid 1990s to 5 per cent today.

Tariffs have come down sharply in tandem with the decline in NTBs. The simple average statutory tariff was 43 per cent in 1992. Waves of tariff reform, particularly one in 1996, had brought it down to 17.5 per cent by 1998 and 16.6 per cent by 2001. Extensive duty exemptions almost completely liberalised imports of intermediate inputs and of investment goods used for export processing.

In sum, as Nicholas Lardy argues, China had undertaken enormous unilateral liberalisation of trade and FDI, and with it sweeping industrial and agricultural restructuring, in the decade *before* WTO accession. That still left significant knots of up-front protection: declining state-run industries; oil and sensitive agricultural commodities subject to monopolistic state-trading arrangements; high-tech industries targeted for industrial-policy promotion; and, most important, services sectors.

China's accession to the WTO and subsequent initiatives have taken reforms even further. That will be discussed later. But it is now clear that the main obstacles to doing business in China have less to do with formal border barriers and more with (formal and informal) non-border barriers.

These concern the unpredictability and arbitrariness that come with large regulatory discretion; the lack of a rule of law in terms of impartial judicial oversight and enforcement of property rights and contracts; and the anti-competitive drag of state-owned industrial enterprises and state-owned banks. All this gets deep into domestic economic policies and institutions. It concerns the long-term restructuring of the Chinese state, away from pervasive interference and in the direction of a smaller, more limited operation that can perform fewer functions better. This is a vast trade-related reform agenda; but it has as much to do with the liberalisation of internal trade and the integration of domestic markets as with further external liberalisation. Growth and more widely shared prosperity can only improve if there is a better interaction between external openness and the internal market, mediated by market-supporting institutions.

Indian trade-policy reforms have not been as dramatic or breathtaking, but still considerable by Indian standards. In 1991, the average unweighted tariff was 125 per cent, with peak tariffs on agricultural products going up to 300 per cent. The tariff structure was extremely complicated, with high tariff escalation (higher tariffs on processed goods compared with semi-processed and unprocessed production inputs). This was accompanied by extremely high NTBs (quotas, licensing arrangements and outright bans). Inward investment was either banned or severely restricted. Exchange controls and the internal restrictions of the licence raj (almost) completed the picture.

Much has changed almost fifteen years on. Most border NTBs have been removed, as have internal licensing restrictions. Applied tariffs have come down to an average of about 20 per cent. The maximum tariff on manufactures was lowered to 20 per cent in 2004, and then to 15 per cent in the 2005 budget.

Manufacturing tariffs will be rationalised into three bands (0-5-15 per cent); and the intention is to bring average tariffs down to ASEAN levels (around 10 per cent) soon. However, agricultural tariffs remain very high, averaging over 50 per cent. Most restrictions on manufacturing FDI have been removed. Executive orders are being used to relax FDI restrictions in services (given the difficulty of securing a parliamentary majority for such measures).

Hence Indian trade-policy reforms have come far, especially in manufactures. This leaves much to do on tariffs and NTBs in agriculture; and on FDI as well as domestic-regulatory restrictions on foreign services providers. These are much tougher nuts to crack, as are domestic labour-market regulations, privatisation of SOEs, domestic agricultural policies, and a bloated public administration.

What about southeast Asia? Overall, largely as a result of reforms in the 1980s and 90s (earlier in Singapore), the old ASEAN members have average tariffs in the 10-per-cent range or lower, with correspondingly low NTBs.

FDI restrictions have been progressively lowered. Tariffs, NTBs and FDI restrictions are particularly low in manufacturing – hence in large part the integration of the region into east-Asian and global manufacturing supply chains, especially in IT products. But agricultural protection is much higher; tariff escalation is not insignificant; and services markets are subject to high FDI and domestic-regulatory restrictions.

Dual-economy structures have resulted: relatively open and efficient manufacturing sectors driven by FDI and exposed to global competition coexist with protected, inefficient domestic sectors. The new ASEAN members, either stuck with planned economies or in transition from Plan to Market, have much higher tariff and especially non-tariff barriers.

Singapore is the regional exception. After Hong Kong, it has the world's most liberal trade policies and is the world's most globalised economy.

It is a free port with zero tariffs on all imports except four tariff lines (on alcoholic beverages). It is fully open to FDI except for a few services sectors. Unilateral liberalisation and domestic regulatory reform, especially since the Asian crisis, have reduced protectionist barriers in some services sectors.

Malaysia is one of the world's most globalised economies with relatively liberal trade policies by developing-country standards. However, there are peak tariffs, tariff escalation and assorted NTBs in politically sensitive goods sectors; and protection in services remains high. Protection must also be seen in the context of *bumiputera* policies to discriminate in favour of the Malay majority.

Thailand retains relatively high protection by the standards of other old ASEAN members, but its average tariff has come down closer to their levels. However, it still has greater tariff dispersion and escalation; NTBs are not insignificant; and protectionism in services is considerable. No meaningful liberalisation of the economy has occurred under the present Thaksin administration.

Indonesian trade policies have swung from high protection to openness in a comparatively short period. Its average tariff has come down to under 10 per cent.

The IMF Structural Adjustment Programme agreed with the Indonesian government in 1998 significantly accelerated trade-and-FDI liberalisation and domestic regulatory reform in goods and services sectors. However, there are higher tariffs and tariff escalation, particularly in agriculture. There is also recent evidence of creeping protectionism through higher NTBs, particularly on agricultural products, textiles and steel. Overall, government enthusiasm for further liberalisation has clearly waned in recent years.

The situation in the Philippines is rather similar to that in Indonesia. Trade policies have swung from high protection to openness in the past decade.

The average tariff has come down to well under 10 per cent. But this coexists with peak tariffs and tariff escalation in sensitive sectors, particularly in agriculture. There is recent evidence of creeping protection through higher NTBs, again concentrated on agricultural products.

Protectionism is much higher on FDI and trade in services than it is on trade in goods. Restrictions on foreign ownership written into the Philippine constitution remain the most visible market-access hurdle. Overall, the government has displayed little enthusiasm for further liberalisation since the Asian crisis, and domestic protectionist pressures have increased.

Vietnam's transition from Plan to Market has proceeded in stops and starts since 1986, but it has come far cumulatively – though not nearly as far as China. Liberalisation, including trade, has picked up since 2000, though domestic institutional reforms have lagged behind. Foreign trading rights have been liberalised extensively; quantitative restrictions and other NTBs have come down; and the average nominal tariff now stands at about 18 per cent, though the tariff structure contains higher tariffs on many products and high tariff dispersion. Protection in services remains very high. The government continues to discriminate heavily in favour of state-owned industrial enterprises and state-owned banks. Overall, Vietnamese protection in terms of tariffs, NTBs and FDI restrictions remains much higher than it is in the old ASEAN members. It also compares unfavourably with China, given the latter's huge external and internal liberalisation measures before and after WTO accession.

Cambodia has progressed with trade-policy reforms, crowned by its accession to the WTO in 2004. Laos and Myanmar are much further behind.

The foreign-policy dimension

Trade policy stands at the junction of domestic economic and foreign policies, with tight links to both. The imperatives of China's modern foreign policy are steady integration into the global economy and political stability in the east Asian neighbourhood. These objectives have driven fundamental change in China's relations with other major powers, and its participation in international institutions. The Beijing leadership sees China as an emerging great power, indeed part of a concert of great powers, with shared global interests and responsibilities. That is one new frame in which to view Chinese foreign policy.

"Constructive engagement" characterises China's key bilateral relationships, especially the central one with the USA, but also with the EU, India, ASEAN and others. The overriding objective is to forge stronger commercial bonds, contain protectionist pressures directed against Chinese exports, and prevent geopolitical tensions from getting out of hand.

Constructive engagement in international institutions proceeds alongside closer relations with major powers. China joined a host of international organisations through the 1980s. It has participated actively in the IMF, World Bank, WIPO and other international economic agencies, tapping into technical expertise and policy advice in addition to financial aid. It has also been active in the UN. In all these forums, China has acquired the good-citizenship credentials of a "system maintainer", not a "system wrecker". Its approach to international law is the same: it wants to join existing arrangements, make them work better, and play its part in future rule-making.

The rapid professionalisation of the leadership and higher levels of public administration reinforces these trends. Since the 1980s, a new technocratic and outward-looking generation of officials and diplomats has emerged, many with significant foreign exposure.

In sum, Chinese foreign policy has evolved a pragmatic mix of nurturing big-power relationships and active participation in international institutions. The former is a *Realpolitik* calculus; the latter an expression of multilateral credentials. The two approaches are seen as complementary. Their common denominator is much less confrontational, more flexible, sophisticated and nuanced diplomacy, low on megaphone rhetoric and high on patient, behind-the-scenes cooperation to achieve practical results. Trade diplomacy, multilaterally in the WTO and on bilateral and regional tracks, is perhaps the most visible sign of this foreign-policy transformation.

However, this foreign-policy story, on its own, would be Panglossian. Set against the very real trends mentioned above are occasional tendencies of aggressive nationalism. This seems to be directed at Taiwan and Japan, notwithstanding ever-closer commercial ties with them. Finally, the Chinese government seems happy to maintain cosy relations with some of the most repulsive regimes around the world. An optimist would argue that foreign policy will ultimately be swayed by the imperatives of global economic integration. Optimism, however, should always be tinged with realism.

India's foreign policy has undergone a parallel transformation since the end of the Cold War. It has switched from leadership of the "non-aligned" Third World and support for the Soviet Union to constructive engagement with other powers in the developed and developing worlds. Its relations with the USA are blossoming, both on the "high politics" of security and the "low politics" of commercial relations. It is trying to cement parallel alliances with China, ASEAN, Brazil and South Africa. It is playing a more forward-looking, system-maintaining rather than system-wrecking game in international institutions. However, this has not yet translated into much more pragmatic and flexible diplomacy in the WTO – one key difference with China.

Generalisations about ASEAN are difficult in that its members have different foreign policies with few common denominators, despite ASEAN rhetoric to the contrary. Hence there are substantial intra-ASEAN differences in bilateral relations with external powers; and ASEAN cooperation in international institutions, including the WTO, is lacking. However, security concerns and global economic integration have given ASEAN countries one common denominator: nearly all want to have good relations with the USA and the rising powers of China and India. But this is mostly a matter of bilateral (country-to-country) cooperation rather than cooperation involving ASEAN as a group.

Bibliography

Ajey Lele: *Strategic Technologies for the Military : Breaking New Frontiers*, Sage, Delhi, 2009.

Allen Carlson, *Unifying China, Integrating with the World: Securing Chinese Sovereignty in the Reform Era,* Stanford: Stanford University Press, 2005.

Amitabh Sikdar: *India and China : Strategic Energy Management and Security,* Manas, Delhi, 2009.

Anil, K.C.: *Military and Democracy in South Asia : Challenges, Politics and Power,* Sumit Enterprises, Delhi, 2009.

Atar Singh Jadoan: *Military Geography of South East Asia,* Anmol, Delhi, 2001.

Bhat, T.P. : *India and China : Trade Complementarities and Competitiveness,* Bookwell, Delhi, 2008.

Conway, G. 1992. *Sustainable Rural Livelihoods: Practical Concepts for 21st Century*. Sussex: Institute of Development Studies.

Deepak, B R : *India and China : 1904-2004 : A Century of Peace and Conflict,* Manak, Delhi, 2005.

Digumarti Bhaskara Rao: *Military Conversion : Impact on Science and Technology,* Discovery, Delhi, 2003.

Dixit, A.K. : *Military Wars and Rescue Techniques,* Cyber Tech Pub, Delhi, 2010.

Evelyn Goh, *Meeting the China Challenge: The U.S. in Southeast Asian Regional Security Strategies,* DC: East-West Center, 2005.

Friedman, G.: *The Future of War: Power, Technology and American World Dominance in the 21st Century,* N.Y., Random House, 1996.

Gao, Mobo: *The Battle for China's Past: Mao and the Cultural Revolution,* London, Pluto Press, 2008.

Gautam, P.K. : *Environmental Security : New Challenges and Role of Military,* Shipra, Delhi, 2010.

Huntington, S.P.: *The China Modernisation Military and the State*, N.Y., Vintage Books, 1964.

Jagannath P. Panda: *China's Path to Power : Party, Military and the Politics of State Transition*, Pentagon, Delhi, 2010.

Jones, W.H.: *The Government and Politics of Indian Military*, London, Hutchinson, 1971.

Marie Lecomte : *Hindu Kingship, Ethnic Revival, and Maoist Rebellion in Nepal*, Oxford University Press, Delhi, 2009.

Mary, W.: *Military Space Force: the Cultural Dimensions of Authority*, Cambridge, Belknap Press, 1985.

Raj Kumar: *Weapons and Military Technology*, Sumit Enterprises, Delhi, 2009.

Randall Forsberg: *The Arms Production Dilemma: Contraction and Restraint in the World Combat Aircraft Industry*, Cambridge, Massachusetts: MIT Press, 1994.

Rosen, P.: *Societies and Military Power: India and its Armies*, Ithaca, Cornell University Press, 1996.

Samuel P. Huntington: *The Soldier and the State : The Theory and Politics of Civil-Military Relations*, Natraj Pub, Delhi, 2005.

Shaun Narine, *Explaining ASEAN: Regionalism in Southeast Asia*, Boulder, CO: Lynne Rienner Publishers, 2002.

Thapa, Deepak : *Understanding the Maoist Movement of Nepal*, Centre for Social Research and Development, Delhi, 2003.

Index

T

W

❑❑❑